THE INTOXICATION OF POWER

SOVIETICA

PUBLICATIONS AND MONOGRAPHS

OF THE INSTITUTE OF EAST-EUROPEAN STUDIES AT THE

UNIVERSITY OF FRIBOURG/SWITZERLAND AND

THE CENTER FOR EAST EUROPE, RUSSIA AND ASIA

AT BOSTON COLLEGE AND THE SEMINAR

FOR POLITICAL THEORY AND PHILOSOPHY

AT THE UNIVERSITY OF MUNICH

Founded by J. M. BOCHEŃSKI (Fribourg)

Edited by T. J. BLAKELEY (Boston), GUIDO KÜNG (Fribourg), *and*
NIKOLAUS LOBKOWICZ (Munich)

VOLUME 43

MAUREEN HENRY

St. John's University, Jamaica, New York

THE ＼INTOXICATION OF POWER／

An Analysis of Civil Religion in Relation to Ideology

D. REIDEL PUBLISHING COMPANY

DORDRECHT : HOLLAND / BOSTON : U.S.A.

LONDON : ENGLAND

Library of Congress Cataloging in Publication Data

Henry, Maureen, 1947–
  The intoxication of power.

  (Sovietica ; v. 43)
  Includes bibliographical references and index.
  1.   Christianity–United States.   2.   Religion–History.
3.   Communism.   I.   Title.   II.   Series.
BR515.H45   291.1'77   79-21601
ISBN 90-277-1027-9

Published by D. Reidel Publishing Company,
P.O. Box 17, Dordrecht, Holland

Sold and distributed in the U.S.A., Canada, and Mexico
by D. Reidel Publishing Company, Inc.
Lincoln Building, 160 Old Derby Street, Hingham,
Mass. 02043, U.S.A.

Printed in The Netherlands

For my teacher,
Gerhart Niemeyer

TABLE OF CONTENTS

TABLE OF CONTENTS

PREFACE

[God] will command a blessing on us in all our ways, so that we shall see much more of His wisdom, power, goodness, and truth than we have formerly known. We shall find that the God of Israel is among us, and ten of us shall be able to resist a thousand of our enemies. The Lord will make our name a praise and glory, so that men shall say of succeeding plantations: 'The Lord make it like that of New England'. For we must consider that we shall be like a city upon a Hill; the eyes of all people are on us.

John Winthrop to early Puritan
settlers in America, 1630

When the Soviet people will enjoy the blessings of Communism, new hundreds of millions of people on earth will say: 'We are for Communism!' It is not through war with other countries, but by the example of a more perfect organization of society, by rapid progress in developing the productive force, the creation of all conditions for the happiness and well-being of man, that the ideas of Communism win the minds and hearts of the masses.

The force of social progress will inevitably grow in all countries, and this will assist the builders of Communism in the Soviet Union.

Programme of the C.P.S.U.,
22nd Congress, 1961

There is now in America, and also in the West as a whole, a much-debated crisis of confidence which is described in many ways but which can best be understood as the very simple fear that the Soviet Union's appropriation of Christianity and the Christian myth for its own purposes has proved to be more powerful, more appealing, more efficacious than the American version of the same myth. The fear is not expressed quite so explicitly, but this is nevertheless the crux of it – the tacit assumption that America has botched the job of creating the perfect society and has in the process revealed itself to be as evil and corrupt and generally as fallible as every other society. The result is not so much the feeling that the Mandate of Heaven has passed to Communism which becomes the new City Upon a Hill, as the feeling that the failure of the American experiment to achieve the ideal society has been the failure of mankind, a failure that leaves behind a vacuum, a complete lack of defense against the more resolute forces of totalitarianism. In the process two things are not sufficiently considered: one is that both the American civil theology and Communist ideology are basically a more-or-less secularized

ix

version of Christianity and are in many respects remarkably alike; the second
is that, underneath even its most extravagantly nationalistic rhetoric, America has always possessed a much more realistic understanding of the world
and the tradition from which the American society developed. This is a luxury
which the Soviet Union, in its public discourse at least, has never allowed
itself to enjoy. The difference is crucial, for the fundamental question is
whether man prefers a myth that he controls or a myth that is created to
control him.

It seems, then, an instructive exercise to examine the developments of
both the American civil religion and the Communist ideology in order not
only to arrive at a better understanding of the true philosophical meaning of
both, but also to understand the process in modern European philosophy of
which Marxism—Leninism can be seen as the culmination. The American civil
religion is studied here also for a secondary purpose — as perhaps the most
articulate example of a civil religion that developed gradually and spontaneously within a historically acting people, it can serve as a kind of standard
against which we can compare those civil religions developed in abstraction
by isolated thinkers. The last such civil religion has been forcibly imposed on
a society from without, although it now serves as its civil theology, and the
similarities between Communism and the pre-Revolution Russian civil religion
derive mainly from the ideology's susceptibility to manipulation for nationalistic purposes. In its essential emphasis on the country's salvific mission,
expressed, for example, in the symbol of Moscow as the Third Rome, the
earlier Russian civil religion was similar to the American. Nevertheless, the
inner structural articulation of this civil religion is inferior to that of America,
and so the latter has been chosen as providing a more adequate basis for
philosophical, metaphysical analysis, as well as for reasons of contemporary
international politics.

The purpose of this discussion is in no case to provide an exhaustive analysis of any of the topics or thinkers examined, nor is this intended to be a
history of civil religion. What is attempted is a thorough exegesis of the
endogenous, metaphysical structures of civil religion and what these imply for
an understanding of the meaning of civil religion in general and Communist
ideology in particular. The discussion begins with an analysis of certain aspects
of the Roman state religion to provide an introduction to the major concepts
to be used in the analysis. The treatment is cumulative and analytic, the analysis being carried on within a definite framework which is more fully articulated in chapter VIII. Throughout the focus is on the metaphysical structures
and implications of man's attempts to provide his earthly existence with a

purely earthly meaning, which is, to a great extent, his search for power to determine and satisfy his earthly desires.

A few acknowledgments are in order. The Earhart Foundation of Ann Arbor, Michigan, supported me with a grant while I did the research for the first part of this book, and during the same time the School of Philosophy of the Catholic University of America gave me a special post-doctoral research appointment.

My philosophical debt to Eric Voegelin should be fairly obvious to those familiar with his work, but my debt to Professor Gerhart Niemeyer, although less obvious, is the greater. It was his suggestion that got the second part of the book underway as my doctoral dissertation six years ago and during the course of that work he contributed many suggestions and criticisms and much general influence. My thanks also to Professors Joseph Evans, Walter Nicgorski, and Edward Goerner of the University of Notre Dame, who read the second part of this book in its dissertation form and provided many helpful suggestions.

To my parents I owe much for all their support over the years, and for the finishing of this book I owe a special debt of gratitude to Mr. and Mrs. Elias Koster of Manhasset, New York, whose gifts to me have made all the difference.

MAUREEN HENRY

ACKNOWLEDGMENTS

The author and the publishers would like to extend their thanks to the following publishers for permission to quote copyright material appearing in their publications:

Penguin Books Ltd.: *The Confessions of Saint Augustine* Tr. by R. S. Pine Coffin (Penguin Classics, 1961, pp. 21, 24, 36, 52, 146–7, 165, 171, 210, 211, 213, 223, 231).
Encyclopaedia Britannica: *Great Books of the Western World*: Aristotle, *Nichomachean Ethics*; St. Augustine, *The City of God*; Thomas Hobbes, *Leviathan*; Hegel, *The Philosophy of History*; and *The Federalist*, Vol. 43. Also, from the Series *Annals of America*, quotations from John Winthrop, Peter Bulkley, John Cotton, Joel Barlow, John L. O'Sullivan, and Abraham Lincoln.
J. M. Dent and Sons Ltd., and E. P. Dutton and Co. Inc.: J.-J. Rousseau, *Emile, The Social Contract, Discourse on the Origin of Equality*, and *Discourse on Political Economy* Tr. by Barbara Foxley (Everyman's Library).
The proprietors of the *Southern Review*: Maureen Henry, 'Tradition and Rebellion' (appeared originally in *The Southern Review*, January 1976, Vol. 12, No. 1, pp. 32–53).
McGraw-Hill Book Company: *Karl Marx Early Writings* Ed. by T. B. Bottomore, 'Economic and Philosophical Manuscripts' and 'On the Jewish Question'.

CHAPTER I

FOUNDATIONS: THE ROMAN CIVIL RELIGION

Civil religion, in some form, is probably as old as political society. Certainly among the most ancient societies of which we have records, such as Egypt and Babylon, religion was inseparable from and even identical with the political order, an intimate relationship which has been called consubstantiality; that is, religion and political order, in so far as they could be separated, were simply different aspects or manifestations of the same reality, the same truth or cosmic order.[1] What we might call a problem of the civil religion developed only under the supposition that religion and politics address themselves to different truths, or perhaps to one truth and one falsehood, or thirdly, that one was, as an articulation of truth, significantly superior to the other. This has at times produced a serious psychological dilemma and conflict of loyalties, but most seriously of all a sense of a lacuna or a rift in reality. The human psyche finds the toleration of two truths difficult, and when the consubstantiality of religion and political order dissolves there is almost always an attempt, conscious or unconscious, to restore the understanding of the world to a seamless whole by subordinating one to the other, or interpreting one in terms of the other, or simply eliminating one.

While nearly all ancient societies went through a crisis when the traditional concept of order broke down, it was in Rome that this process of dissolution and attempted restoration seems to have been most articulate; and it is Rome that most clearly illustrates the problems involved in the dissolution of civil religion and in its restoration as a kind of hypostatic union of religion and politics. In the ensuing discussion the term *civil religion* will be used as a general term for all the possible modes of a society's self-interpretation.

The origins of the Roman religion can be traced back to quite primitive roots, antedating even the establishment of cities. In its pre-Roman form this religion seems to have been a kind of animism, preoccupied with fertility and reproduction, with a strong concern with the afterlife and care for the dead. Numa Denis Fustel de Coulanges, in his classic work *The Ancient City* begins with a study of "the oldest belief of the Italians and Greeks [that] the soul did not go into a foreign world to pass its second existence; it remained near men, and continued to live underground."[2] A great emphasis was placed on performing the proper rites for the dead in order to insure their rest and

1

happiness. Eventually the dead were regarded as gods who required worship, and the practical consequence of this belief was a religion of agricultural households, each preserving the worship of its own ancestors as gods and each centered around its own sacred fire, through which offerings were made to the household gods. The entire familial and social structure seems to have been based on this private domestic worship of household divinities.

Apparently the actual founders of the city of Rome were the Etruscans who took over and combined several hilltop villages around the middle of the sixth century, B.C. and called the result *Roma*. This is significant as a qualitative rather than a quantitative change, for the difference between a city and a village is far more than a matter of size or population — it is a difference of purpose and orientation. As Aristotle several centuries later in the *Politics* described the evolution of the state from the primordial relationship between man and woman, the village exists for the supply of daily needs, but the state exists for the sake of, not just life, but the good life, the life serving the needs of the highest part of the soul and fulfilling human nature. So when the Etruscans came to found a city, whether or not Rome was the first and regardless of the precise process by which the city had evolved from the family with its sacred hearth and ancestor worship, what they created was a realm in which men could live for something beyond the biological processes of life, some purpose transcending the satisfaction of everyday needs.

The actual founding of the city was accomplished by means of an elaborate ritual which enclosed a space for human and divine habitation. The city was built first symbolically, then physically. Before the walls were built, a "magic circle" — called the *pomerium* — was ploughed around the area of the city to serve as a protective barrier against contamination or intrusion by foreign gods. Within the *pomerium* only the gods of that particular city could be worshipped, for the worship of the particular gods was the basis of that city's sense of identity. The city was closed around this worship. According to Fustel de Coulanges, once the families or tribes had agreed, by whatever process, to combine their respective private worships into one common worship, "they immediately founded the city as a sanctuary for this common worship, and thus the foundation of a city was always a religious act." [3]

In the ancient world a people was distinguished by the gods whom it worshipped and there was a strong personal bond between the citizens and their gods. Men honored and worshipped the gods and in return the gods protected and promoted the interests of the city. Moreover, the city was founded by both gods and men, their respective actions and motivations being seen as virtually identical, even consubstantial. While men may have

laid the stones, it was the gods who decreed the city and inspired and em-
powered men to found it. So the human purpose manifested and fulfilled the
divine purpose.

Later Roman accounts, perhaps largely as a result of Greek influences,
attribute the founding of Rome to a specific individual, Romulus. According
to Roman legends it was Romulus who followed established Etruscan ritual
in founding the city and who slew his twin brother Remus for the impiety
of jumping over the sacred *pomerium*. The more important figure for our
purposes was Romulus' successor, Numa Pompilius, who founded and gave
his name to the state religion as the "religion of Numa".

Numa, although a Sabine, was chosen by the Romans as most worthy to
be their king, but he was reluctant to accept the office because he feared that
his mortal birth (Romulus was reputed to be the son of a god) and peaceful
disposition rendered him unfit to rule the Romans who had been habituated
by Romulus to a rather martial existence and mentality. At length, however,
Numa was persuaded, but he refused to be invested with the robes of authority
until he had consulted with the gods of Rome and had his kingship officially
approved by them. Accordingly, with priests and augurs, he ascended the
Capitol and waited until auspicious birds appeared passing on the right, which
augured that he was "a holy king, and beloved of all the gods". He then
assumed authority and proceeded to use the sanctions of religion to soften
the character of the people, that is, he set up the official state religion of
Rome. According to Plutarch, he established "the office of Pontifex Maximus,
or chief priest, [which] was to declare and interpret the divine law, or rather,
to preside over sacred rites; he not only prescribed rules for public ceremony,
but regulated the sacrifices of private persons, not suffering them to vary
from established customs, and giving information to every one of what was
requisite for purposes of worship or supplication". The Pontifex Maximus,
in accordance with his title, was the primary means of communication between the gods and the citizens, responsible for maintaining the proper forms
and rituals of discourse between them.

In Livy's account, in his *Ab Urbe Condita* (From the Founding of the
City), Numa chose as first pontifex Numa Marcius, the son of one of the
senators, and gave to him complete written directions for the details of
worshipping the gods — when, where, with what sacrifices, and what money.
"All other public and private sacrifices he likewise made subject to the decrees
of the pontifex, that there might be someone to whom the commons could
come for advice, lest any confusion should arise in the religious law through
the neglect of ancestral rites and the adoption of strange ones." (I, xx). The

adoption of strange rites amounted to an undermining of the city's foundation and a weakening of its sense of identity. The pontifex was also responsible for teaching the proper funeral observances and propitiation of the spirits of the dead, as well as the proper procedure regarding prodigies. In short, his was the task of maintaining the religious foundation of the political order. Nevertheless, it was Numa, not the Pontifex, who discerned the minds of the gods and determined their wishes regarding religious ritual so that the Romans could live according to a divine rather than a merely human order.

But at this point in Livy's account we suddenly find ourselves confronted with a question as to the truth of the state religion, for apparently it only appears that the gods are invoked, and this for the sake of political expediency, which seems to reduce the state religion to a merely pragmatic truth. As Livy tells it, "as [Numa] could not instill [the state religion] into [the Romans'] hearts without inventing some marvellous story, he pretended to have nocturnal meetings with the goddess Egeria, and that hers was the advice which guided him in the establishment of rites most approved by the gods, and in the appointments of special priests for the service of each." (I, xix) The crucial words here are *inventing* and *pretended* – the frame of reference for the state religion, according to Livy's analysis, is the order of the society rather than the divine order, and it seems to be essential to the acceptance of the state religion that the people be deceived, that the masses be manipulated and controlled by means of myth, or superstition.

Pretended consultations with the gods gave Numa the authority to pacify and civilize the people by imbuing them with the fear of Heaven through the state religion. According to Livy the emphasis on fulfilling duties to the gods succeeded in diverting "the thoughts of the whole people from violence and arms. Not only had they something to occupy their minds, but their constant preoccupation with the gods, now that it seemed to them that concern for human affairs was felt by the heavenly powers, had so tinged the hearts of all with piety, that the nation was governed by its regard for promises and oaths, rather than by the dread of laws and penalties". (I, xxi). Therefore, by establishing the state religion Numa achieved the governing of the nation by virtue rather than by military ambitions, or the sheer coercive force of the political authority, as long, that is, as the people believed in the divine origin of the state religion.

In such matters Livy himself seems to have been a sceptic, regarding stories of divine origin, divine birth, and so forth as mere "poetic legends" to which he attached "no great importance". In the preface to his *Ab Urbe Condita* he wrote that "it is the privilege of antiquity to mingle divine things with human, and so to add dignity to the beginnings of cities". Because of their great military achievements the Romans certainly had earned the right to "profess that their Father and the Father of their Founder was none other than Mars", the god of war. Since the conquered nations submit to Rome's dominion they may as well also accept Rome's belief in its own privileged relationship with the most powerful gods.

In general Livy seems to hold that the state religion is a purely human invention, calculatingly established to control, pacify, and order the Roman people, as well as to impress and more easily control the numerous conquered peoples. For the people, temporal power provides the verification of the truth of the myth, but for sceptics such as Livy, public order provides the justification for the existence of the myth. In this opinion the historian Polybius concurs: "But the quality in which the Roman commonwealth is most distinctly superior is in my opinion the nature of their religious views. I believe that it is the very thing which among other peoples is an object of reproach, I mean superstition, which maintains the cohesion of the Roman state. . . . My own opinion, at least, is that they have adopted this for the sake of the common people. It is a course which perhaps would not have been necessary had it been possible to form a state composed of wise men, but as every multitude is fickle, full of lawless desires, unreasonable passions, and violent anger, the multitude must be held in by invisible terrors, and suchlike pageantry. For this reason I think not that the ancients acted rashly and haphazardly in introducing among the people notions concerning the gods and beliefs in the terrors of hell, but rather that the moderns are most rash and foolish in banishing such beliefs." (*Histories* VI, lvi, 6–12)

Polybius' point regarding the lack of need for a state religion in a society of wise men, a state such as Plato's *Republic*, is worth some attention. It seems that these myths are not necessary or even useful for those who live by virtue and wisdom and the order of the cosmos. The value of these civil superstitions lies in their ability to restrain those less virtuous from giving free rein to their lawless and disorderly passions. In other words, the "truth" of the state myths lies not in what they say but in what they accomplish. It is a pragmatic truth, and in this case it amounts to a fashioning of the cosmos in the image of Rome. It is not because Rome is favored by Mars that it achieves military glory, but rather its achievement of military glory is an indication that it is favored by Mars and will continue to be so favored. And so the citizen must also be intimidated with the belief that his offenses against the order of the state will be punished most unpleasantly by the gods after death, for the gods are dedicated to the order of Rome. To an objective observer this means that the gods are more or less created by the state as the most powerful guardians of the order on which the state was founded.

So, according to this view, the purpose of the state cult is simply to terrorize, manipulate, and deceive the unruly masses for the sake of maintaining the cohesion and power of the Roman state. Such a state religion is a lie, but a highly expedient lie, given the potential for disorder of the Roman mob.

Regardless of what the ordinary Roman thought of the state religion, by the latter days of the Republic there had developed a great deal of scepticism regarding the myths among the educated class, which included Cicero. In his *De Divinatione* Cicero wrote that "experience, education, and the lapse of time have wrought changes in the art of augury; but with an eye to the opinion of the masses the practices, rites, discpline, and laws of augury and the authority of the college of augurs have been maintained for their great political usefulness ... ". (II, xxxiii, 70)

Hence, by the end of the Republic the educated view seems to have been one that the eighteenth century would have regarded as 'enlightened', for the truth of the state religion has become merely political usefulness — whatever promotes the order of the society is "true". The essential difference between the believing and the sceptical views is that if myth embodies cosmic or divine truth, the center of the order of the society is outside and above the society, whereas if myth is the tool of political utility, then through such myths the society becomes the center and source of a cosmic order that can and perhaps must be seen as a merely human fabrication. However, we rarely find a society in which one view of the cosmos exists without some form of the other view.

By the latter days of the Republic the Roman state religion was in fact in decline. There are several reasons for its falling away from its former hold over the minds and hearts and patriotic sentiments of Romans, particularly but not only educated Romans. For one thing in the last two centuries of the Republic the state religion had been seriously undermined by the machinations of politicians such as the dictator Pucius Cornelius Sulla, who filled the ranks of the Roman priesthood with men whose only qualification was their personal loyalty to him. The inevitable consequence was the loss of the religious knowledge that depended on oral tradition; hence the state cult became increasingly sterile and less able to satisfy the religious, emotional needs of the people. This led to a further difficulty, since the people turned for satisfaction to an indiscriminate importation of foreign gods and the orgiastic cults of Oriental deities, gods and goddesses quite alien to the Roman state religion who turned the emotions of the people away from the traditional and patriotic cults toward foreign, alien cults.

With these two problems relatively easy remedies were possible – a restoration of the integrity of the priesthood and the establishment of Roman cults designed to provide a greater outlet for mass emotions. But the third and probably decisive problem, in relation to the possibility of manipulating the state religion, admitted of no easy solution. This was the intellectual problem created for the educated man by the introduction of Greek philosophy into Roman society. The problem was that the later Greek philosophers, such as the Stoics, had convinced educated Romans that philosophy provided a much more intellectually and spiritually satisfying view of the cosmos than did the state-approved myths of the sometimes less than edifying doings of gods and goddesses. Yet, as Jesse Carter puts it, "all the philosophy in the world could not take away from a Roman his sense of duty to the state."[4] The religion was an essential part of the foundation of the state, and so the citizens' duty to support the state included a duty to support the state religion. "Hence there arose that crass contradiction, which existed in Rome to a large degree as long as these particular systems of philosophy prevailed, between the duty which a man, as a thinking man, owed to himself, and the duty which he, as a good citizen, owed to the state."[5]

If, according to Stoic teaching, it is the individual philosopher who realizes and contemplates the truth of cosmic order, and if the society is ordered, or appears to be ordered according to its own pragmatic truth, there would seem to be a serious rift between thinking men and the public order. In other words, a tension between religion as the servant of the state and the state as the servant of religion has been created by the introduction of Greek philosophy which undermines the credibility of the ancient civil myths and rites while being itself incapable of stepping into the vacuum thereby created. The primacy of the cosmos and its truth has demoted the public order to at best an inferior level of truth and at worst complete falsehood. This obviously created intellectual problems for educated Romans, for how could a thinking man take seriously the myths of Rome, especially if for many of them the meaning of the myths had been lost?

One of the first Roman thinkers who perceived and grappled with this problem was Quintus Mucius Scaevola, who, as Pontifex Maximus at the beginning of the first century, B. C., was in an excellent position to appreciate the difficulties involved. According to Augustine's account in *The City of God*, "it is recorded that the very learned pontiff Scaevola had distinguished about three kinds of gods – one introduced by the poets, another by the philosophers, another by the statesmen. The first kind he declares to be trifling, because many unworthy things have been invented by the poets concerning the gods; the second does not suit states, because it contains some things that are superfluous, and some, too, which it would be prejudicial for the people to know." (IV, 27) The sort of thing it would be prejudicial for the people to know is the truth, or, more specifically, such facts as that Hercules, Aesculapius, Castor and Pollux are not gods, that the true God "has neither sex, nor age, nor definite corporeal members", and is indeed not anthropomorphic at all and may, in fact, not be particularly concerned about either the glory of Rome or the petty personal affairs of the Romans. By arousing the suspicion that the gods are not concerned with human things, philosophy would serve only to weaken the people's patriotism, and therefore it is better that they not be exposed to it. Augustine's comment is that Scaevola "thinks it expedient . . . that states should be deceived in matters of religion", but he misses Scaevola's dilemma. On the one hand the civil religion had been seriously eroded by a number of causes, among them philosophy, yet on the other hand the Roman society was scarcely in a position to jettison its tradition and attempt to base its order on a new, alien and universal truth. The traditional state religion was an integral part of the Roman identity, and the Roman civil religion pervaded all aspects of life. Even Livy said, "There is not a place in this city which is not impregnated with religion, and which is not occupied by some divinity. The gods inhabit it." Or as Fustel de Coulanges described the situation, the Roman state religion "regulated all the acts of man, disposed of every instant of his life, fixed all his habits. It governed a human being with an authority so absolute that there was nothing beyond its control." [6]

Scaevola perceived that the best or most adequate symbolization cannot be contained or expressed in a civil religion, which is limited in its capacity to embody truth by the limited understanding and perspective of the members of the society. The kinds of gods introduced by the statesmen are designed to express the order and to meet the needs of the society — social order then becomes the truth that is the measure or criterion of the truth of cosmic divine order. There is here perceived a kind of diremption in the symbolization of cosmos and society: the truth, the true symbolism, has been differentiated from the pragmatic, "superstitious", merely "poetic" symbolism of the society. The former represents the ideal, true cosmic order to which human existence ought to conform to be perfectly ordered. But since this is impossible, certainly within the ordinary civil society, the second, the gods of the statesmen, then symbolizes the highest level of order possible for the society, which order tends to be regarded within and by the society as the paradigm of all human order (although, to be sure, the existence of other state religions, in other states, is acknowledged). In this case the cosmos becomes macropolis, the society writ large. Scaevola then adheres to the general understanding of the civil gods as introduced by the statesmen for the sake of preserving social order. Since in the present context we can ignore the gods of the poets, we are left with two apparently conflicting symbolisms in the gods of the political and social order and the gods of the cosmos. At best the gods of the state represent an inferior level of truth, at worst an outright falsehood. The question was, of course, that of the truth and foundation of a particular society. An educated, patriotic Roman who found himself knowingly worshipping human inventions craved some union or common denominator between his intellectual and patriotic allegiances.

But the Roman civil gods and myths were not really just human fabrications designed to mold the people into submission. The civil religion was actually the Roman experience and interpretation of itself and its order and role in history, and this interpretation was governed by a mythic view of the city as the community of gods and men, and, since, at least during the Republic, there does not seem to have been any sense that the Roman gods were the only true gods of all mankind, such gods quite easily appeared inferior to the universal cosmic gods of the philosophers. Yet, while according to the Romans' own self-understanding the state religion interpreted actions and events according to the gods, from the point of view of anyone not governed by the myth the Romans were interpreting the gods in terms of events and of the actions of men.

Cicero was an educated Roman who was much concerned with this problem, and in his *De Natura Deorum* the difficulty of the educated man who yet wants to be a loyal and conscientious citizen of the Roman state is personified by Cotta, a philosophical sceptic, but also a Roman high priest. As a sceptic Cotta belongs to the followers of the New Academy who denied virtually all knowledge and relied on custom and tradition for sustaining the order of society. At the beginning of Book III Cotta picks up the discussion from Balbus, who has been discoursing upon the Stoic deities. Cotta maintains that he always has upheld and always will uphold the beliefs about the inmortal gods which have been handed down from the ancestors. In matters of religion the authorities are not philosophers but the high pontiffs. "The religion of the Roman people comprises ritual, auspices, and the third additional division consisting of all such prophetic warnings as the interpreters of the Sybil or the soothsayers have derived from the portents and prodigies. Well, I have always thought that none of these departments of religion was to be despised, and I have held the conviction that Romulus by his auspices and Numa by his establishment of our ritual laid the foundations of our state, which assuredly could never have been as great as it is had not the fullest measure of divine favor been obtained for it".

What Cotta is literally saying is, of course, that the glory of Rome is due to the favor of the gods, which is the point of view of the man who uncritically accepts the civil religion. However, according to the opinion, say, of Livy, the real meaning of Cotta's statement is that the gods are believed to be propitious because Rome is great and powerful. Insofar as a man is some kind of philosopher the civil religion seems to him purely pragmatic, but insofar as he is a loyal citizen the state religion is Truth. This inner conflict between the patriotic Roman citizen and the thinking man or philosopher is that of Scaevola, and of Cicero and his contemporary Marcus Varro as well, both of whom sought diligently to reconcile the two beliefs.

Although the text of Varro's monumental work *Roman Antiquities* has been lost, it is possible to reconstruct the essentials of the work from the praise and criticism of other writers, particularly Cicero and Augustine. In his analysis of Roman religion Varro had divided all theology into three types, much as Scaevola: the fabulous or theatrical, that is, the portrayal of the gods, usually in a somewhat less than edifying fashion, in the theater; the natural or philosophical, that is, the gods of nature and the cosmos as understood by philosophers such as the Stoics; and the civil, which, as Augustine quotes him, "is that which citizens in cities, and especially the priests, ought to know and to administer. From it is to be known what god each one may suitably worship, what sacred rites and sacrifices each one may suitably perform." (VI, 5) Varro uses *civil theology* as the technical term for the state religion with its array of divinities, myths, cults, and rites, and henceforth that term will be employed in this discussion to refer to the state cult and the gods of the statesmen with everything included therein. It is the civil theology that is designed to order the lives of the citizens by prescribing what god each citizen may "suitably" worship, what rituals each citizen may "suitably" perform — the suitable being determined by the Roman tradition and the needs of the public order.

Augustine observes that Varro said he undertook all the labor involved in producing such a comprehensive study because he was afraid that the gods of the state religion might perish, "not by assault by enemies, but by the negligence of the citizens", and essentially Varro's work was designed to accomplish three things: " ... first, by a review of the history of Rome to show how essential the state religion was; second, by an examination of Greek mythology to purify the state religion from its immoral influences;

third, to show that the state religion so purified was fully in accord with Stoic philosophy." [7]

Unlike Scaevola, Varro did not regard the state religion, or civil theology, and philosophy as being two separate truths, the real and the pragmatic; rather Varro saw them as "two forms of the same truth", that is, the civil theology was merely a presentation of Stoic philosophy in terms the uneducated people could understand. In other words, Varro sought to establish philosophy, or the symbolism of unchanging cosmic order to which human existence ought to conform, and the civil theology, or the projected symbolism of the actual order and experience and sense of identity of the society as the manifestation of divine actions and decisions, as analogous or equivalent symbols, thus resolving the tension between them.

We can infer that philosophers are included with the citizens from Cicero's praise of Varro in his *Academica*, praise which well indicates the degree of mental discomfort created by the tension between philosophy and civil theology. In the dialogue, Varro has been discussing philosophy and the Greeks as the fountainheads of philosophy, and states that his intention, in the prefaces to his *Antiquities*, was to write for philosophers. Cicero rejoins, "What you say, Varro, is true ... for we [philosophers] were wandering and straying about like visitors in our own city, and your books led us, so to speak, right home, and enabled us at last to realize who and where we were. You have revealed the age of our native city, the chronology of its history, the laws of its religion and its priesthood, ... the terminology, classification and moral and rational basis of all our religious and secular institutions ... ".

The import of Cicero's praise is that Varro has reintegrated the educated Roman, partly by restoring his pride in Roman intellectual and cultural achievements, but primarily by supplying a "moral and rational basis of all ... religious and secular institutions", that is, a philosophical foundation for the civil theology of Rome. Thanks to Varro's lucubrations, an educated man need no longer regard philosophy as true, and civil theology as, at best, traditional; now the civil theology itself can be accepted as fundamentally rational and moral. It is not necessary to regard the civil theology as merely a reflection of the baser passions of the masses or a necessary means of controlling them, or as mere superstition; it is as valid as philosophy because it is itself a form of philosophy.

Cicero himself sought quite explicitly to reconcile Stoic philosophy with the civil theology, and even to base the latter upon the former in his political works, the *De Re Publica* and the *De Legibus*. For Cicero, the ideal state, as he elaborates in the *De Re Publica*, is early Rome, and in the *De Legibus* he provides this ideal state with the laws of a civil theology (according to Varro's term) grounded upon the Stoic universal natural law of rational order. This ideal nature of Roman law and institutions is indicated in the *De Legibus* at the end of the section on religious laws, where Quintus observes, "it seems to me that this religious system of yours does not differ a great deal from the laws of Numa and our own customs", to which Cicero, speaking as Marcus, replies, "Do you not think, then, since Scipio in my former work on the Republic offered a convincing proof that our earthly State was the best in the world, that we must provide that ideal State with laws which are in harmony with its character?" (*De Leg.* II, ix, 23)

The ensuing discussion indicates the major characteristic of the civil theology founded on the universal principles of Stoic philosophy — it is a remedy for disorder that is universally applicable. In Book I Marcus states, "Our whole discourse is intended to promote the firm foundation of States, the strengthening of cities, and the curing of the ills of people", and after the religious laws have been presented he observes, "We are composing laws not for the Roman people in particular, but for all virtuous and stable nations." (II, xiv, 35)

The founding principle of the order of the ideal virtuous and stable society is reason, which implies Law, which in turn implies Justice. All nature is governed by the immortal gods, who possess and are ruled by reason, with man being the only creature that also actively participates in reason, which is better than everything else that is, and "the first common possession of man and God". Right reason being Law, men also have Law in common with the gods. "Further, those who share Law must also share Justice; and those who share these are to be regarded as members of the same commonwealth. If indeed they obey the same authorities and powers, this is true in a far greater degree; but as a matter of fact they do obey this celestial system, the divine mind, and the God of transcendent power. Hence we must now conceive of this whole universe as one commonwealth of which both gods and men are members." (I, vii, 23).

The universal principle of order is reason; men who order their society according to right reason participate in the order of the cosmos and the divine mind. The civil theology becomes the cult then not simply of the gods of Rome, but of the gods of the entire cosmos and of all men, gods which are worshipped in Rome under their anthropomorphic representations.

Justice is the pre-eminent political and social virtue of the cosmic commonwealth and therefore the necessary foundation of all states. Since all men participate in human nature they all share in the sense of Justice. And Justice cannot be a matter of mere customs and conventions, but must exist in Nature, otherwise the virtues necessary for human society will be destroyed. Cicero saw the foundation of Justice in "our natural inclination to love our fellowman", our natural generosity, patriotism, gratitude, loyalty, or desire to be of service. Without this natural inclination to Justice, "not merely consideration for men but also rites and pious observances in honour of the gods are done away with; for I think that these ought to be maintained, not through fear, but on account of the close relationship which exists between man and God." (I, xv, 42) Without Justice, a philosophical principle, there can be no civil theology to serve as a symbolization and reinforcement of man's intimacy with the divine through the proper political and social order. Cicero has thus made a necessary out of a virtue.

Here we can observe Cicero attempting to integrate philosophy and theology — the order of the society requires that Justice exist, but Justice is not a god who can be created according to a society's wishes or peculiar needs, created as almost automatically propitious toward the society's particular desires or ambitions for conquest or glory. Justice is instead a universal, cosmic, rational principle to which men and societies and civil theologies must conform if they are to be truly ordered, as is evident in Cicero's observations on the need to persuade the citizens to believe the proper notions concerning the gods. "So in the very beginning we must persuade our citizens that the gods are the lords and rulers of all things, and that what is done, is done by their will and authority; that they are likewise great benefactors of man, observing the character of every individual, what he does, of what wrong he is guilty, and with what intentions and with what piety he fulfills his religious duties; and that they take note of the pious and the impious. For surely minds which are imbued with such ideas will not fail to form true and useful opinions." (II, vi, 15–16). The gods have here become an absolute, ineluctable moral standard, more concerned with the virtue and proper inner disposition of the citizens than with the outward punctilious empty formalism of religious rituals. Cicero is thus recasting the civil theology in the mold of Stoic philosophy and on that basis advocating a renewal of Numa's avowal that what he did was by the authority of the gods. Such are the general philosophical principles on which the religion of the ideal state, that is Rome, is to be based.

Regarding the ordering of particulars, Cicero first presents a list of religious laws governing the civil theology, concerned primarily with the proper mode of and disposition for worshipping the gods in order to satisfy the requirements of good citizenship. On the whole, the laws prescribe generalities and

dispositions, rather than the formal details of worship, and their concern is
the sanction of the gods and the virtues for the order of Rome. Cicero prescribed that the citizens shall worship the gods in purity and piety, without
any concern for wealth. He who does not approach the gods with the proper
disposition shall incur punishment from "God Himself". Publicly, all citizens
may worship only those gods recognized by the State, although privately they
worship the gods worshipped by their ancestors. "They shall worship as gods
both those who have always been regarded as dwellers in heaven, and also
those whose merits have admitted them to heaven; Hercules, Liber, Aesculapius, Castor, Pollux, Quirinius; also those qualities through which an ascent to
heaven is granted to mankind: Intellect, Virtue, Piety, Good Faith. To their
praise there shall be shrines, but none for the vices." The remainder of the
laws are devoted to the general principles of the public rites, the kinds of
priests, the holidays, the gods who are to be worshipped, punishment for
sacrilege and impiety. The details of the rituals are left for the priests to
prescribe; the purpose of Cicero's laws is to refound and strengthen the civil
theology or state religion, to preserve its forces of order and suppress its
forces of disorder, and to presuade the citizens, educated and uneducated,
that this is the one true civil theology.

Cicero has, of course, attempted to resolve the tension between a Rome-
centered civil theology and a cosmos-centered philosophy by refounding the
civil theology directly on the Stoic philosophy, which henceforth must serve
as a kind of civil or public philosophy, for insofar as they accept the civil
theology, the citizens are also implicitly accepting the principles of Stoic
philosophy. Cicero has sought to establish Rome as the ideal or model society
by embodying its order in a particular civil theology based on a universal
philosophy of the cosmos. In this way there is only one truth, subject to
different manifestations.

However, despite the valiant efforts of Scaevola, Varro, and Cicero the
problems of the civil theology were not readily curable by grafting the civil
theology onto a philosophy, and the civil theology did eventually collapse,
to be replaced by the Emperor Augustus with emperor-worship as the unifying religion of the multi-cultured Roman Empire. By the time Augustus
assumed power Rome was the ruler of most of the known world, and it has
been observed that throughout Roman republican history "expression and
consolidation, differentiation and integration, conquest and assimilation went
hand in hand to produce not only one empire in fact but also a general sense
of one central and controlling power in the affairs of men." [8] As an empire of
the *ecumene*, or the world, Roman existence seemed to conform to the Stoic

belief, expressed by Cicero, that "we must now conceive of this whole universe as one commonwealth of which both gods and men are members". Even had it not been in a state of decline, the Roman republican civil theology, the religion of Numa, could not have served as the civil theology of an ecumenic and cosmic commonwealth, an empire uniting a multitude of peoples, cultures, and religions by the ordering power of Rome. This new civil theology of the empire was a new religion created in response to and as a cohesive force in a new state of affairs. The civil theology has become universal by being the expression of a universal and not simply paradigmatic society, rather than by being based on universal philosophical principles. A new world order, a universal order required a new, universal religion, or, as Lidia Storoni Mazzolani expressed it, "The vast territorial expansion of the Empire began to demand a doctrinal basis on which it could proceed . . . "[9] In other words, the expansion of a City into an Empire required a reason justifying such events in terms transcending the human and possibly arbitrary. Such an unprecedented event must mark a turning point in the history of the world, and hence the necessity of myths to anchor the empire in the absolute will of the gods and in a glorious destiny of saving the world from barbarism, ignorance, and disorder.

And therefore Augustus became the Numa Pompilius of the Roman Empire, for he sought to establish a religion of imperial Rome. In order to promote unity Augustus re-established the state religion with its temples, festivals, and cults, and he "emphasized all phases of social life that would tend to unite people in a common interest for the state". The primary purpose was not nurturing the intimacy between gods and men, but supporting and furthering the interests of the Roman state. Gradually Augustus established worship of the emperor as divine, the person of the emperor thus serving as the object of common religious devotion throughout the empire.

Augustus also encouraged writers and poets to compose myths for the past and future of Rome, myths that would endow the city with a divine origin and the empire with a glorious destiny in the unification of the world. Perhaps the preeminent mythmaker of Rome in the Augustan Age was Vergil who, particularly in the *Aeneid* and the *Eclogues*, became the poet of Roman glory, and the glory and divinity of Augustus. For example, in Book VI of the *Aeneid*, he speaks of "Caesar Augustus, a god's son, who shall / The golden age rebuild through Latin fields / Once ruled by Saturn." Rome is to be the source of order for the entire realm, and its power and glory are to reach to the very outer fringes of the cosmos. "Lo! 'neath his auspices yon glorious Rome / Shall bound, my son, her empire with the world, / Her pride with heaven . . . " And in the *Fourth Eclogue*, Vergil describes the dawning of a new era, a return to pristine perfect order with the rise of the Empire.

> Now the last age by Cumae's Sybil sung
> Has come and gone, and the majestic roll
> Of circling centuries begins anew:
> Justice returns, returns old Saturn's reign,
> With a new breed of men sent down from heaven.
> Only do thou, at the boy's birth in whom
> The iron shall cease, the golden race arise,
> Befriend him, chaste Luciana; 'tis thine own
> Apollo reigns. And in thy consulate,
> This glorious age, O Pollio, shall begin,
> And the months enter on their mighty march.

In the Augustan Age the Roman civil theology moved toward the other possible basis for universality — a universal society, encompassing the world. Unlike Cicero's civil theology, which acquired a basic universality by being grounded on universal philosophical principles, the Augustan civil theology served as the self-understanding of a society of the world, a society co-extensive with the cosmos. In other words, the cosmos is made in the image of Rome. And, according to the myth, the ascent of Rome to imperial domin-ion ushers in a new age of peace, order, and justice, a golden age for the world under the aegis of Rome. As Elwyn Wilsey explains the motives of Vergil, Horace, and other myth-making writers of the Augustan Age, their patriotism was "a demand that Rome be recognized as the steward of civiliza-tion. Her mission was to save the world from disorder and disintegration and to keep it tied to a humanizing destiny."

So, the intellectual problem as it developed in Rome was that of reconciling a perception of universal order with the requirements of a particular social order. So far as the civil theology declined through negligence, it could be restored relatively easily, but so far as the civil theology declined in impor-tance through unfavorable comparison with a less crude or anthropomorphic view of the divine as well as a perception of universal principles of order, its status became far more questionable. It could be restored to truth only by being based on some universal — either principles or society. Intellectually, or psychologically, it seems to be virtually impossible for a particular civil theology to be regarded as embodying a truth separate from but equal to the truth of philosophy. There must be some common ground between them, although this does not imply that the civil theology and the public philosophy should be identified or that one should be reduced to the other.

To summarize: In its earliest form the Roman state religion most likely consisted of ancient myths and rituals honoring ancestral deities, with the city itself being founded upon an expanded form of the religion of the household. Such a religion had no basis other than belief in the myth and endured only so long as the myth was not broken. But when, for various reasons, the myth came to be regarded as mere superstition, as not embodying any truth but serving merely as a means of maintaining the order of the city by exploiting the ignorance of the masses, it became evident that a more secure basis was required. At the time of Scaevola, Varro, and Cicero, particularly, we find the state religion being revived as a civil theology, according to Varro's use of the term, grounded upon a body of philosophical principles regarding the truth of universal order — such principles as reason, law, and justice. These philosophical principles must be accepted as an essential basis of the *res publica*, the public thing, and therefore they serve as a kind of public philosophy. However, when based upon the universal principles of the public philosophy, the civil theology lost much if not all of its particularity, becoming instead paradigmatic, for it could be applied to any society and could no longer serve to identify any one in particular. Augustus managed to restore to the civil theology uniqueness and add universality by making Rome, according to officially approved myths, the one universal society, the only society founded upon true universal principles and therefore the salvific society to which all men must belong if they wish to participate in the truth of order. Therefore the civil theology of the Augustan Age provided Rome with the myth of a special destiny in ruling mankind according to the principles of the public philosophy. Vergil's myths are clearly designed to provide a cosmic framework to explain, justify, and give meaning to Rome's rise to world dominion. Such an ecumenic civil theology is quite different from the much earlier, closed civil theology of the city, for it neither regulated all the acts of man, disposed of every moment of his life, nor fixed all his habits, nor did it provide Rome with a special identity or exclusive meaning as one society among others. To the extent to which Augustus restored the ancient, closed civil theology these functions were also restored. But the ecumenic civil theology transcends the closed civil theology by prescribing an ideal order for uniting all the world in one cosmic order, mediated through one center, one omphalos, Rome.

We find then in Rome three types of civil theology: (1) the closed civil theology of early Rome which provided the city with its own gods and identity as one particular people; (2) the paradigmatic civil theology which leaves the outward form of the old state religion intact while filling it with the substance of a universal philosophy. It seeks the greatest realization of truth and universal order in the public cult, and so provides the society with no sense of uniqueness or destiny or special divine favor, except insofar as being the paradigmatic society can be regarded as a special destiny; and (3) the ecumenic civil theology which legitimates Roman rule, actual or potential, over all other societies. This type has a certain salvific aura in the tendency to envision a golden age.

And there must also be kept in mind the distinction between civil theology, of all three types, and public philosophy, which is a distinction between a society's creation or interpretation of the gods according to its own desires, experience, and self-understanding, and a society's creation, interpretation, and measurement of its order and institutions according to the gods, or a divine, cosmic, or transcendent order. In a society based compactly on the myth, such as early Rome, these two views of order cannot be truly distinguished, for the Romans had not as yet acquired a basis for distinguishing between the affairs of gods and the affairs of men on the political level.

If, as Polybius suggested, it were possible to set up a society of wise men who perceive and live according to a universal cosmic order, no civil theology would be necessary, because the society would be completely receptive to the truth of order and so would be based entirely on a public philosophy. At the risk of oversimplification we might say that the significant difference between public philosophy and civil theology, as will be seen more clearly in the discussion on America, is that between reason and desire, the public philosophy being a rationally perceived and implemented order, an order that exists irrespective of any human goals or wishes, and the civil theology being a symbolically ordered expression of the society's desires for power and destiny, which desires normally develop out of the sense of order and meaning in the public philosophy. This distinction is not yet fully developed in Rome but it is possible to see it in adumbration.

In general, in ancient societies, including Rome, the public philosophy and civil theology are at first almost completely indistinguishable because in such societies there are no private beliefs or philosophies in tension with the public beliefs. As they do become distinguishable, however, we find that the public philosophy provides a largely intellectual basis for unity, while the civil theology becomes the medium of a largely emotional unity. It is through the civil theology that the state provides the citizens with common, expressed beliefs, in distinction from the public philosophy which often remains tacit, or largely so. The civil theology has the advantage of providing a more emotional and intense awareness of unity than the public philosophy is capable of providing.

With this in mind we can turn briefly to the critique of the Roman civil theology by the early medieval Christian philosopher and theologian, Augustine of Hippo. Augustine's point of view is important because it throws more light on the meaning of the tension between the civil theology and the public philosophy.

The first ten books of Augustine's *The City of God* are primarily devoted to a polemic against the pagans who attributed the fall of Rome to the wrath of the gods whose altars were abandoned by converts to Christianity: the neglect of the civil theology led to the downfall of Rome. Augustine was well-acquainted with Roman history and culture and much of Book VI is devoted to a discussion of Marcus Varro's *Roman Antiquities*, which Augustine recognized as an extremely competent, scholarly study of the Roman state religion.

Augustine's objections to Varro's work, and beyond that to the whole of the Roman civil theology, fall under two main points. The first is that the civil cults, rites, and deities are nothing more than superstition, human fabrications concocted by the particular states for their own purposes. This was essentially Polybius' conclusion, but whereas he approved of this policy, Augustine violently condemned it.

As Augustine recounts, first in writing his book Varro chose to deal with "human things" and only secondly with "divine things", because "as the painter is before the painted tablet, the mason before the edifice, so states are before those things which are instituted by states."[10] That Varro did not regard the gods purely and simply as creations of the state is indicated by his statement that he would have written first concerning the gods "if he had been writing concerning the whole nature of the gods", and not merely that portion of their nature which is involved with human affairs. In fact, Varro was considering the gods from the point of view of their significance for the proper order of the state. Augustine, regarding this ambiguous view of the gods as evidence of Varro's theological insincerity, takes strong exception to it on the grounds that human authority is metaphysically incapable of legislating the truth, but can strive only to be itself founded in the truth. "This very Varro testifies that he wrote first concerning human things, but afterwards concerning divine things, because the states existed first, and afterward these things were instituted by them. But the true religion was not instituted by any earthly state, but plainly it established the celestial city." Although to Varro it was self-evident that for their own preservation states had to concern themselves with a civil theology, in Augustine's eyes earthly states are competent to institute only false religions which are not worthy of acceptance. The true religion is the basis not of any earthly society but only of the celestial city, the City of God, which is Augustine's universal society, and civil theologies are therefore nothing but lies.

The second objection derives from the heart of Augustine's faith that the *summum bonum* or highest good for man is eternal life with God. Considering the multitude of Roman gods and goddesses and the often minute aspect of human life with which a particular god might be concerned, Augustine finds it incredible that any of these deities should be capable of bestowing the highest good on human beings. "Is it not the most insane impiety to believe that eternal life, which is without any doubt or comparison, to be preferred to all terrestrial kingdoms, can be given to anyone by any of these gods?" (Vi, 1). It is not only somewhat imprudent to believe in the gods of the city, it is simply insane, for it requires preferring the temporal, "the tottering and falling affairs of earth", to the eternal, which is man's goal and measure of his actions. In comparison with this the civil religion is seen as "ridiculous, contemptible, detestable", for the falseness of its symbolism, for the impiety of its beliefs, and for its power to turn men away from the true God and salvation toward an "insane" immersion in earthly existence and damnation, or loss of the highest good.

All of Augustine's objections to civil theology are conceived *sub specie aeternitatis*, and on this basis Eric Voegelin points out in his *The New Science of Politics* the root cause of Augustine's lack of sympathy for civil theology. "What St. Augustine could not understand was the compactness of Roman experience, the inseparable community of gods and men in the historically concrete *civitas*, the simultaneousness of human and divine institution of a social order. For him the order of human existence had already separated into the *civitas terrena* of profane history and the *civitas coelestis* of divine institution."[11] As far as Augustine was concerned, to live according to earthly desires and aspirations is to choose a life of sin. The heart of his objections to civil theology is that it inclines men to be preoccupied with this temporal, imperfect world and to neglect the love of God. It is not that Augustine saw any radical disjunction between transcendence and immanence — transcendence permeates immanence — but rather that he did see an irreconcilable contradiction between living for God and living for any other purpose. To worship civil gods for the attainment of earthly success, and thereby to neglect the true God and eternal life, is simply to ground one's life in falsehood. The political societies of this world had for Augustine no purely immanent meaning, but had meaning only with reference to man's attainment of eternal life. So, whereas the patriotic Roman citizen believed, as a patriotic citizen, that he was able to enjoy the privilege of worshipping his gods only within the domain of the city, of which the gods were the co-founders and protectors, Augustine, as a Christian, believed that union with the true God was possible only within the depths of the soul, and that, if anything, the city constituted a grave distraction from the truth.

In Augustine's view there cannot be any acceptable civil theology that is not Christianity, but Christianity is not so easily made a civil theology, for two major reasons: First it is a universal religion worshipping the God of all men, and therefore could at best serve only as an ecumenic civil theology of a society governed by a universal Church, although conceivably it might also function as a paradigmatic civil theology. At any rate, Christianity cannot serve to distinguish one political society from another with respect to immanent meaning and destiny. The second reason is that, certainly in Augustine's view, Christianity is so much preoccupied with eternity and transcendence that it contents itself for the most part with counselling Christians to bear patiently the ills of this life. Augustine saw earthly life as a vale of tears, a time of trial and suffering, and he did not find it possible that an earthly society could use the true religion for its own political purposes. Christianity was the religion of the City of God, and possibly of an earthly society composed of Christians, but such a society would not be an object of patriotic love, nor would it concern itself much with the customary interests of earthly states, primarily because the central concern of Christianity is with the personal relationship between the individual and God. And as a divinely founded religion it is difficult to see how Christianity could be under the control of the state as state.

Christianity as a universal truth cannot assume the role of civil theology for a particular society, as the Roman civil myths did, without distorting its form and altering the meaning of both itself and temporal society, for the society acquires a salvational character while Christianity loses its transcendent meaning, or certainly a large part of it. But, since Christianity did refuse to allow the gods of the city to exist beside it, to allow the legitimacy of earthly aspirations alongside the desire for eternal salvation, although it took some time for this attitude to crystallize during the power struggles between Church and State during the Middle Ages, it created a vacuum in the political order. During the Middle Ages the problem was mainly the states' desire to rule themselves and their own interests apart from the Papacy, but once that was achieved the deeper problem emerged, the problem, namely, of finding gods for the states.

We shall return to Augustine with a consideration of other aspects of his philosophy in a later chapter. The next subject we must consider is how a Western Christian society, the United States, grappled with this problem, and what solution it arrived at. It is necessary, before considering developments in Europe, to see how a distinctively Christian society worked out its self-understanding in the tension between reason and desire.

REFERENCES

[1] See Henri Frankfort, H. A. Frankfort, John A. Wilson, and Thorkild Jacobsen, *Before Philosophy*, Baltimore, Penguin Books, 1968, pp. 71–78.

[2] Numa Denis Fustel de Coulanges, *The Ancient City*, [1864], tr. by Willard Small [1873], New York, Doubleday Anchor Books, p. 15.

[3] *Ibid.* p. 132.

[4] Jesse B. Carter, *The Religion of Numa*, London, MacMillan and Co., Ltd., 1906, p. 139. For a history of the Roman state religion see Jesse B. Carter, *The Religious Life of Ancient Rome*, Boston, Houghton Mifflin Company, 1911.

[5] *Ibid.* p. 139.

[6] de Coulanges, p. 141.

[7] Carter, pp. 142–43.

[8] Elwyn Donald Wilsey, *Roman World Philosophy* – *The Unity of Empire, Religion, and Law in the Conception of a System of the World*, Columbia University, Doctoral Dissertation, 1930, p. 53.

[9] Lidia Storoni Mazzolani, *The Idea of the City in Roman Thought* – *From Walled City to Spiritual Commonwealth*, tr. by S. O'Donnell, Indiana University Press, 1970, pp. 21–22.

[10] All quotes from *The City of God* in this chapter and in chapter VIII are from the translation by Marcus Dods.

[11] Eric Voegelin, *The New Science of Politics*, Chicago, The University of Chicago Press, 1952, p. 88.

CHAPTER II

ERRAND INTO THE WILDERNESS:
THE CITY UPON A HILL

The American civil religion provides an excellent example of the relationship between a public philosophy, or the rationally perceived order of reality on which the society is based, and the civil theology, or symbolic, or mythic expression of the society's self-understanding as a unique people with a unique destiny. In the case of the United States these two orders gradually differentiated themselves from the Puritan view of America as a "City upon a Hill", a shining example to the world of the true, divinely ordained order of human participation in the cosmos. Since the tensional relationship between the unchanging order of the public philosophy and the dynamic, destiny-oriented civil theology is quite important for understanding European civil theology, we shall examine the development and articulation of the religious beliefs and symbols that had a direct and significant bearing on the development of the American self-understanding. America was founded on the Puritan belief that it was their vocation to establish the true order, the kingdom of God, in the New World, far away from the disorders and corruptions of the Old World. This religious belief in the possession of truth and the necessity of putting this theory into practice is decisive for the religious self-understanding and symbolization of the new society.

The first settlers to arrive in New England intended the establishment of a *novus ordo saeculorum*, a new order of the ages that would be at the same time a return to a very old and perfect order that had been lost and found and lost again. The Puritans assumed this elusive political order to be the manner of human existence proclaimed by God, and bestowed first upon the Israelites and then upon the early Christians. As William Bradford wrote in his history *Of Plymouth Plantation 1620–1647*, "It is well known unto the godly and judicious, however since the first breaking out of the light of the gospel in our honourable nation of England, what wars and oppositions ever since, Satan hath raised, . . . as being loath his kingdom should go down, the truth prevail and the churches of God revert to their ancient purity and recover their primitive order, liberty and beauty." [1] With the westward migrating Puritans, who bore the light of the Reformation to the New World, God was making a third and possibly final attempt to rescue mankind from the shares of that old deluder Satan.

23

However, what is most likely the first work to reflect seriously upon the experience of colonizing and surviving in America antedates the landing of the Puritans in New England by some ten years. In 1610 the Counsell of Virginia published in London a pamphlet with the rather polemical title *A True Declaration of the Estate of the Colonie in Virginia, With a Confutation of Such Scandalous Reports as Have Tended to the Disgrace of so Worthy an Enterprise*, a work significant for its emphasis on Divine Providence, a common theme among the Puritans which was to become one of the major symbols of the American self-understanding. The essay was propaganda designed to refute a number of pernicious rumors regarding the failure of the Virginia colony, the unhealthiness of the climate and prevalence of disease, the frequent occurrence of catastrophes, etc., by recounting impressive tales of wonder-working Providence, such as the case of the shipwreck of Thomas Gates' expedition. Gates had left England in 1609 with a fleet of nine ships in order to resuscitate the failing Jamestown colony. However, the flagship was wrecked on Bermuda (the shipwreck that inspired Shakespeare's play *The Tempest*) and the survivors managed to reach Jamestown in May 1610 only after constructing a new ship. They found the colony in a state of complete disintegration, wracked by disease, Indians, and starvation. The survivors of the colony and of the rescue expedition were just setting out on their way back to England when Lord de la Warr, the governor of "London's Plantation in the Southern Part of Virginia", arrived with fresh men and supplies. Thus was the Virginia colony miraculously preserved.

To the Counsell of Virginia such a series of events can be interpreted only as living, irrefutable proof of God's provident care for his people. That the colonists were able to survive on Bermuda after the wreck by living off the native fauna seemed much more remarkable to the early seventeenth century than to later readers of *Robinson Crusoe*. In general the early expeditions to Virginia expected to receive their sustenance from England rather than from their own hunting and agricultural skills, and when provision ships failed to arrive the colonists simply starved. Hence, such wonderful survival redounds to the eternal glory of God, who in a similar situation had "sent abundance of Quayles to feed his Israel in the barren Wilderness". God's Providence is the major theme which the Declaration constantly reiterates as the basis of the interpretation and an assurance of future success. A number of episodes in the early colonization of Virginia are recounted with the central idea of cosmic harmony and Divine Providence epitomized as follows: "He that shall but turne up his eye, and behold the spangled Canopie of heauen, shall but cast down his eye and consider the imbroidered Carpet of the earth, and

withall shall marke, how the heavens heare the earthe, the earthe heare the
corne and oyle, and they relieve the necessities of man, that man will ac-
knowledge Gods infinite prouidence. But he that shall further obserue, how
God inclineth all casuall euents, to worke the necessary helpe of his Saints,
must needs adore the Lords infinite goodness." [2] The Saints, of course, do
not journey to Virginia simply to wonder at Divine Providence; they also have
a mission in the New World, an "errand into the wilderness" – the exaltation
of the faith and the increase in temporal prosperity: "Our primarie end is to
plant religion, our secondarie and subalternate ends are for the honour and
profit of our nation . . . " [3] It is written that the Gospel should be preached
to all the world before the eschaton, and the fact that the third means of such
preaching, after apostolic evangelizing and conquest, is "marchandizing and
trade", is merely a further testimony to the wonderful economy of Divine
Providence which so happily consolidates the spiritual and temporal well-
being of the Saints. At any rate, it seems to have been taken for granted that
life in the New World had been reserved for those most deeply and sincerely
concerned with conforming existence in this world as closely as possible to a
transcendent order. Virginia, as part of the New World, has become the new
Promised Land which is reached by enduring ordeals and trials similar to
those endured by the Israelites, with a similar assurance of divine favor. We
find, then, that Providence functions as the symbol for divine ordering of and
intervention into human affairs. On the other hand, there is another aspect
of order, not yet clearly differentiated from the first, that of the colonists'
experience of their own responsible, divinely appointed role in wresting order
from chaos, to create a new world. This is essentially a demiurgic role, and is
alluded to here in the statement that the primary end of the plantation is to
"plant religion". Through the plantation the people are to transform the new
continent from a wilderness into a paradise, according to the true order.

In another early work, *Good Newes from Virginia*, by Alexander Whitaker,
we find a slightly greater emphasis on the assigned work of the colonists.
Whitaker, reflecting upon the trials and tribulations of the first colonists,
testifies to Divine Providence. "First, if we consider the almost miraculous
beginning, and continuance of this plantation, we must confesse that God
hath opened this passage unto us, and led us by the hand unto this work."
The experience of the early colonists in faring forth from the old world in
order to take possession of the new, the difficulties and hardships they had
to endure and their success in spite of such obstacles, led them to regard
themselves as acting not on their own behalf, but for the sake of doing their
"Christian worke" of bringing order and religion to Virginia. To provide

financial support for this work, Whitaker pleads with the English for contributions, exhorting them to "remember that the Plantation is Gods, and the reward your countries".[4] There is an intimate relationship between the glory of God and the bountiful returns to the investing country; apparently the Kingdom of God is inextricably linked with the eventual aggrandizement of the glory and wealth of England. However, we must note two closely related moments in the flow of thought: first, that the Plantation is God's kingdom, founded by the Chosen People; and, second, that the People's Christian work is the cultivation, or ordering of this Plantation and the spreading of the Gospel, thereby liberating the Indians from thralldom to the "divell". We find, therefore, that the order of existence in Virginia derives from two basic sources: divine providence and the responsible "Christian worke" of the English people.

Essential to the symbol of Providence is the experience of wonder at events that cannot be fully accounted for in terms of natural causes, ordinary human actions or volitions. At the heart of the Counsell of Virginia's and Whitaker's and other writers' emphasis on Providence is a profound sense that order neither is nor can be a purely human achievement, that in the newly rediscovered and almost overwhelming demiurgic experience of wresting order from chaos, paradise from wilderness, man encounters the decisive insufficiency of his own powers. It is a basic human experience that order is not self-sufficient, not self-explanatory or self-contained, nor can it be explained entirely by human agency. There is always a residue of meaning that resists translation into the terms of agent and action on the human level. It is, of course, possible to symbolize the unknown agency as chance or fate; however, the American myths and symbols, some of which have been already mentioned, are an excellent example of the compact, experiential sense of the umbilicum, the sense that order has flowed gratuitously into, and in a sense created, human existence from a trans-human source, either through the workings of Providence or through the colonists' own active, conscious implementation of order, or both.

From the beginning of their migrations the Puritans spoke in theological symbols when attempting to explain the meaning of their "errand into the wilderness", for they were conscious of acting not merely on their own behalf but for the sake of a transmundane order. In his letter to the departing Pilgrims, John Robinson used one such symbol when he exhorted them to be and to remain "the house of God". However, a more adequate and enduring symbol appears in John Winthrop's *A Modell of Christian Charity*, written on the flagship Arabella in 1630. After discussing the covenant between God and the Puritans which binds them to be a model of Christian charity, and describing the disastrous consequences of neglecting to observe that covenant, Winthrop finally advises that the only means to prevent the breaking of the covenant and to provide for future generations is to heed the counsel of the prophet Micah "to do justly, to love mercy, to walk humbly with our God. . . . So shall we keep the unity of the spirit in the bond of peace." If this counsel is followed, then "we shall find that the God of Israel is among us, and ten of us shall be able to resist a thousand of our enemies. The Lord will make our name a praise and glory, so that men shall say of succeeding plantations: 'The Lord make it like that of New England.' For we must consider that we shall be like a City upon a Hill; the eyes of all people are on us." [5] While it may be doubted that the eyes of all the world were on the small band of Puritans sailing westward to complete the Reformation in New England, what was far more important to the Puritans was that God was with them, that in their fidelity to their covenant with God they would enjoy the perfection of order and divine invincibility. Through such fidelity the Puritan community would exist at the center of the cosmos and would from there radiate divine truth throughout the world. Winthrop's symbol for this state of being is the City upon a Hill, a light to the nations, the paradigm for participation in transcendence.

The meaning of this symbol received further elaboration some twenty years later in Peter Bulkeley's *The General Covenant: or the Covenant of Grace Opened*, which stated that it was the responsibility of the people of New England, because of all that they had received, to set an example of holiness for the rest of the world. "We are as a city set upon a hill, in the open view of all the earth, the eyes of all the world are upon us, because we profess ourselves to be a people in covenant with God, and therefore not only the Lord our God, with whom we have made covenant, but heaven and earth, angels and men, that are witnesses of our profession, will cry shame upon us if we walk contrary to the covenant which we have professed and promised to walk in. If we open the mouths of men against our profession, by reason of the scandalousness of our lives, we (of all men) shall have the greater sin . . . " [6] The order of the society derives from both its faithful adherence to the will of God and his providential care and reward of its fidelity; this relationship decides the place of the society in the world as a whole. The Christian work of the people of New England is to surpass all other men in holiness for the inspiration of other men. William Bradford assigned society a similar role, although he did not use a characteristic symbol for the community. "God, it seems, would have all men to behold and observe such mercies and works of His providence as these are towards His people, that they in like cases might be encouraged to depend upon God in their trials, and also to bless His name when they see His goodness towards others."[7] There is a suggestion here that the Puritan society is an experiment — although the word itself will not be applied to America until much later — an experiment to determine whether or not a people can live in covenant with God, whether or not true order is possible of achievement in this world. Or, to put it another way, the question at issue was whether it be possible to give the Mystical Body of Christ a visible, even a political form by establishing and maintaining a Community of Saints. Should the experiment succeed it was to be hoped that the rest of the world would do likewise and thus be redeemed by imitating the City upon a Hill. On the other hand, should the experiment fail, not only God but the entire cosmos would join in execration of the Puritans' scandalous, disappointing lives. The stakes were rather high.[8]

As a result of their belief in their own regenerated righteousness, the Puritans' historical experience was one of living in a new era, new not in the sense of the merely novel, but in the sense of the rebirth or restoration to a pristine perfection through their own *metanoia*, or conversion, as in Edward Johnson's belief that the new country was "the place where the Lord will create a new Heaven, and a new Earth, new Churches, and a new Commonwealth together". The City upon a Hill was to embody the newness of perfect order, the perfection of the beginning which developed into a dominant theme in American self-reflection. As is apparent even in the 1610 work of the Virginia Counsell, the early experience was one of order being wrested and preserved from chaos by a combination of human effort, determination and righteousness, and Divine Providence.

How did the Puritans then set about establishing this City upon a Hill? What was their understanding of the relationship between the religious and the political? The first practical step in the formation of a Puritan body politic was taken on board the Mayflower in 1620 with the signing of the Mayflower Compact. Since the captain of the ship had steered the Pilgrims to Cape Cod which was somewhat north of the territory covered by the patent granted to the Virginia Company, the colonists found it necessary to enact an agreement regarding public order and authority, perhaps to follow John Robinson's parting advice that they were to become "a body politic". Accordingly, on November 11, 1620, thirty-one men gathered in the small cabin of the ship and signed the Mayflower Compact, which is worth quoting in full.

In the name of God, Amen. We whose names are underwritten, the loyal subjects of our dread sovereign Lord, King James, by the grace of God, of Great Britain, France, and Ireland king, defender of the faith, etc., having undertaken for the glorie of God, and advancement of the Christian faith, and honor of our king and country, a voyage to plant the first colony in the northern parts of Virginia, do by these presents solemnly and mutually in the presence of God, and of one another, covenant and combine ourselves together into a civil body politic, for our better ordering and preservation and furtherance of the ends aforesaid; and by virtue thereof, to enact, constitute, and frame such just and equal laws, ordinances, acts, constitutions, and offices, from time to time, as shall be thought most meet and convenient for the general good of the Colony, unto which we promise all due submission and obedience. In witness whereof we have hereunder subscribed our names at Cape Cod, the 11th of November, in the year of the reign of our sovereign Lord, King James of England, France, and Ireland, the eighteenth, and of Scotland the fifty fourth. Anno Dom. 1620.

What sort of interpretation of political existence emerges from this document beginning with a solemn invocation of God? It may be assumed that the colonists expected to live a political life as some sort of civil body politic, whether they were incorporated by royal patent or their own agreement. But what is the purpose of this civil body politic? One reason is self-explanatory: for the better ordering and preservation of the colonists. But beyond this, political existence has another superior dimension of meaning – the glory of God, the advancement of the Christian faith, and, only third, the honor of king and country. The primary consideration is the glory of God, and the establishment of the covenant in the presence of God, as well as the presence of those adhering to it.

Regarding the secondary, more concrete and specific attitude toward politics, by virtue of this compact the colonists expect to "enact, constitute, and frame such just and equal laws, ordinances, acts, constitutions, and offices from time to time as shall be thought most meet and convenient for the general good of the colony". The community of mission and experience, of having set out together to brave the dangers of emigration to an unknown land for the sake of the glory of God, the Christian faith and the honor of king and country precedes the political community. The competence of the Pilgrims to covenant and combine themselves into a civil body politic derives from the community of experience and commitment which had already constituted them a religious body. The religious order accordingly becomes the matrix of the political, which is the ground of the promise of "all due submission and obedience" to the various laws and ordinances to be enacted for the general good of the colony. It was because the colonists were a virtuous people that they were able to assume the responsibility of establishing and preserving order, while yet promising all "due" submission, a small but significant reservation. The guiding assumption seems to be that the general good of the colony will be the touchstone not only of the suitability of the laws, but also of the measure of submission to them. And this determinative general good seems itself to be constituted by not only order and preservation but also the trinity of purposes invoked at the beginning, insofar as the civil body politic exists for the sake of those ends. In short, the religious community is prior to the body politic, both temporally and metaphysically, and, on the whole, it is their existence as a church or congregation that enables the colonists to constitute a civil body politic.

Some nineteen years later the settlers of the small colony of Exeter, New Hampshire, drew up their own agreement to found a political order according to the Will of God in the "Westerne parts of America": "We . . . do in the name of Christ and in the sight of God combine ourselves together to erect and set amongst us such Government as shall be to our best discerning Agreeable to the Will of God . . . binding ourselves solemnly by the Grace and Help of Christ and in His name . . . " Here we find a further variation in the symbolization of Providence and Chosen People. The workings of Providence decree that men's earthly lives should be ordered by civil government, by the Grace and Help of Christ. On the other hand, the workings of the Chosen People appear in the colonists' decision to set up their own government which will be in their judgment agreeable to the Will of God, the ordering of their lives according to the will of God being the settlers' Christian work. Here we find the cosmos of perception, or public philosophy, and the cosmos of projection, or civil theology, only partially distinguished.

Again it is the religious faculty that discerns the Will of God which determines the political order, and it is the "Grace and Help of Christ" which serves as guarantor of that order. The political society from its very foundation is rooted firmly in the Christian faith of the members of that society, as explained in the Salem Covenant of the Pilgrims. It was such a covenant that constituted a Church, in imitation of the Old Testament, and each community or congregation established itself in independent and immediate relation with God. Once this relationship existed, the people thereby constituted was required to take all proper and necessary steps to preserve its divinely willed existence as a people, and the first of these steps was a civil body politic, to which the citizens gave due submission and obedience.

Another, somewhat more articulate political document in this respect is the *Fundamental Orders of Connecticut* of January, 1639, drawn up by the men who followed the Reverend Thomas Hooker, the Reverend Samuel Stone and John Haynes, a wealthy landowner, in a westward migration from

Cambridge to found the towns of Hartford, Windsor, and Wethersfield. This is the first American political document which has the character of a written constitution. The Preamble begins with the observation that it is according to the wisdom of Providence that the towns have been founded along the Connecticut river. Since it is a divine command that peace and order should be maintained by establishing an "orderly and decent government . . . according to God," the inhabitants of the three towns agree to "associate and conjoin" themselves "to be as one public state or commonwealth". However, political order is not the only purpose of such agreement — there is the further intent "to maintain and preserve the liberty and purity of the Gospel of our Lord Jesus . . . and also the discipline of the churches, which, according to the truth of the said Gospel, is now practiced among us".

So, overarching the political association and conjunction is a "combination and confederation", among the settlers and also with their posterity, to preserve the "liberty and purity" of the Christian Gospel, as well as the discipline of the Puritan church. The text creates the distinct impression that while the commonwealth exists through a covenant among only the living, the Christian confederation exists also with the not yet born, and is therefore not regarded as being subject to alteration at the hands of posterity. This religious commitment is the center of the Preamble as the standard and criterion of order, as is indicated in the final sentence which, after the pledge to live according to the very highest expression of truth, returns to the political level to announce that, this divinely ordained government having been once established, its founders will submit to being "guided and governed" by whatever means this public state might choose to order and dispose of the affairs of the people, as they submit to the discipline of the Puritan Church. Therefore, while the public state exists to preserve the peace and union of the people, the purpose of this preservation is the larger preservation of the Gospel and its true interpretation. The settlers of Connecticut seem to have regarded their commonwealth as existing for the sake of their religion, and their religion, or the will of God, becomes the source and standard of the laws, rules, orders, and decrees of public order. Insofar as it properly manages temporal affairs, the commonwealth both derives from and is a means of preserving the Gospel.

The significance of founding a government "according to God" can be seen in another document from later that same year, the 'Fundamental Agreement, or Original Constitution of the Colony of New Haven,' which recounts a general meeting of all the "free planters" on June 4, 1639. At this meeting the order of business was "to consult about settling civil government, according to God, and the nomination of persons that might be found by consent of all, fittest in all respects for the foundation work of a church". The meeting began with a solemn invocation of the name of God, and proceeded to consider queries concerning the Scripture as providing "a perfect rule for the direction and government of all men in all duties which they are to perform unto God and men, as well as in families and commonwealths, as in matters of the church". The assembly then agreed unanimously that the true political order must be based upon the Scriptures. The first point to be noted is the procedure of establishing order: First the political, then the religious, or ecclesiastical. But there is a difference between the two types of order, for while the civil government waits to be determined according to God, the actual question regarding the ecclesiastical order is not what it is to be, for that is already decided, but simply who will administer it. In other words, the founding of a church requires an agreement merely on persons, but the establishment of a government requires an agreement on a political order, an agreement based not on expediency but on discernment of the mind of God, for the political order emerges from the religious. Therefore, the religious order already exists in the minds of the settlers and determines the political order.

How does an assembly of ordinary mortals fathom the mind of God? On the basis of the proceedings and the propounded questions we can arrive at the conclusion that the meeting was, in effect, a formality, a ritual of foundation, for the settlers were already of one mind regarding the source of the proper order of government. This common political conviction flowed from their common religious conviction that Scripture is the source of the truth of order. The queries put|before the assembly are not really questions for debate but invitations to ritual affirmation of the belief that if Scripture provides the order of the Church it can do no less for the state which is metaphysically subordinate to the Church. In New England it is the people gathered together by divine providence which mediates the will of God to the political state, which political authority, thus constituted, and empowered, proceeds to translate the divine will into practical, concrete laws, rules, orders, and decrees.

Not surprisingly, the relationship between Church and State is difficult to define precisely, for, once established, the political authority seems to have functioned as both ancillary to and independent of the Church in the task of preserving order. On the whole, Church and State seem to have been agents of one and the same order, with the Church promoting its eternal aspects and the State the temporal. Both Church and State were subordinate to the necessities of virtue. According to Urian Oakes, "the design of our founders and the frame of things laid by them [made] the interest of righteousness in the commonwealth and holiness in the Church ... inseparable. To divide what God hath conjoyned ... is folly in its exaltation. I look upon this as a little model of the glorious kingdom of Christ on earth. Christ reigns among us in the commonwealth as well as in the Church and hath his glorious interest involved and wrapt up in the good of both societies respectively."[9] Hence, treason to the civil government is also treason to the Lord Jesus.

Order is order − there is no sensible distinction between the order of state and Church. Nevertheless, the theory that the earthly community is "a little model of the glorious kingdom of Christ on earth" would seem to absorb politics into religion. In fact, the Puritans patterned their own order on that of the Israelites, for whom politics only gradually emerged and differentiated itself from religion − Moses was certainly as much a political as a religious leader.

The point, with the Puritans, is that it is the duty of the magistrate to effect the "quiet and peaceable life of the subject ... in matters of godliness", the external manifestation or expression of internal sanctity, since the inward dispositions of the heart are beyond the cognizance of the magistrate. These matters of godliness are specified in 'The Platform of Church Discipline: It is incumbent upon the magistrate to restrain and punish "idolatry, blasphemy, heresy, venting corrupt and pernicious opinions that destroy the foundation, open contempt of the word preached, profanation of the Lord's Day, disturbing the peaceable administration and exercise of the worship and holy things of God and the like". The magistrate was even enjoined to "put forth his coercive power" should a congregation "grow schismatical, rending itself from the communion of other Churches" or "walk incorrigibly or obstinately in any corrupt way of their own".

Certainly one reason why it was necessary for the magistrate to discourage and punish "religious" crimes is that the religion was the foundation of the state, and therefore every religious crime, every religious impiety, was also a political crime or impiety inasmuch as it threatened the ground of the political order. Every state has the right to preserve and protect its own indispensable foundations, and in the case of the Puritan commonwealth this right extended even to the silencing of "pernicious opinions" that destroy the foundation of public order in both its religious and political dimensions. This is not to imply that for the Puritan religion was the servant of politics − if anything, the opposite was the case. Rather, in the Puritan scheme of things, the function of political authority was to prevent the decline or disruption of the true religion. Rigorous Puritanism faltered apart from a sympathetic government.[10]

Actually, the relation between Church and State seems to have been rather symbiotic, for if the political order was dependent upon the religious for its foundation, it provided the religious order with protection from|disturbance. The prosperity of this symbiotic relationship required that both Church and State maintain a certain measure of distinction from the other. In the *Cambridge Platform* we find a statement that Church government is in no way opposed to civil government, nor does it encroach upon the authority of public officials, but rather strengthens the power of government by inclining the people toward "more hearty and conscionable obedience". The truth is that both Church government and civil government, which is "also of Christ", may "stand together and flourish, the one being helpful unto the other in their distinct and due administrations."[11]

The belief that government "is also of Christ" seems, not surprisingly, Scriptural in origin, being derived from both Old Testament accounts of God's dealings with Israel, and from certain New Testament passages, such as the passage from St. Paul, which was the basis of the early Christians' evaluation of political authority and which appears on the title page of the 1648 edition of 'The Laws and Liberties of Massachusetts': "UUhosoever therefore resisteth the power resisteth the ordinance of God, and they that resist receive to themselves damnation." [Romans 13,2] We may reasonably assume that the framers of the laws agreed also with the preceding verse: "You must all obey the governing authorities. Since all government comes from God, the civil authorities were appointed by God . . ."

'The Laws and Liberties', which may not have been formally adopted, was a code of laws appropriate to a City upon a Hill, a society in which political and religious order exist in symbiotic relationship and in which Christianity is the ultimate source of order. The introductory section recounts God's relationship with the paradigmatic political and religious order of Israel as the basis of the political and religious order of Massachusetts, with the emphasis on the laws that God provided to his Chosen People.[12] The importance of this in the present context is not only that order proceeds ultimately from God, but that divine authorship rendered the government and the laws unquestionably the best and so perfectly formulated as always to provide clear guidelines for action. Because of their self-appointed similarity to Israel, there was no doubt in the minds of the Puritans that their civil and ecclesiastical order proceeded from God and that their laws were therefore more righteous than those of other nations. Therefore, "this hath been no small privilege, and advantage to us in New-England that our Churches, and civil State have been planted . . . together like that of Israel in the wilderness by which wee were put in minde (and has opportunitie put into our hands) not only to gather our Churches, and set up the Ordinances of Christ Jesus in them according to the Apostolick patterne . . . : but also withall to frame our civil Politie, and lawes according to the rules of his most holy word whereby each do help and strengthen other (the Churches the civil Authoritie, and the civil Authoritie the Churches) and so both prosper the better without such an emulation, and contention for priviledges or priority as have proved the misery (if not ruine) of both in some other places."

One of the major differences between the Old Israel and the New Israel is that while God himself may have set up Politicall Government among the people of the Old Israel, it is the responsibility of the people of the New Israel to frame their own civil polity and laws according to God and the standards He has established through Israel. The political order is framed according to the word of God, that is, it has no meaning or purpose in itself but only insofar as it fulfills the will of God, which is the basis of the best order. There is no understanding of political order as a separate reality possessing its own meaning: since the order and laws of God encompass everything, human laws must necessarily be part of the law of God. Therefore, there can be no conflict between the Christian and the citizen, for since the authority of God is the common denominator, or even the essence of all laws, there must prevail harmony between Church and State. The Puritans will avoid a ruinous conflict between civil and church authorities by making them mutually dependent. The City upon a Hill is distinguished by the possession of the true religion, which leads to undisturbed order.

In general, the 'Lawes and Liberties', as do most other Puritan political documents, represents a recapitulation of the Israelite understanding of politics and its intimate relationship with religion as well as an implementation of the policy later outlined in the 'Cambridge Platform', according to which the magistrate must deal with outward manifestations of religious disorder. Many of the laws, particularly the capital laws, are adopted from the Old Testament, including the original penalties. Concerning the precise duties and obligations of the political authorities, the 'Lawes and Liberties' seems to regard such authority as a partner of ecclesiastical authority in the implementation of order.[13]

In short, the Puritans were well aware of the potential disorder caused by conflict between Church and State; their prophylaxis was a policy of obviating such conflict by the preservation of each advantageous to the other. With this view in mind we may find it less startling that the Puritans should have regarded Christ as the political as well as mystical head of his Kingdom; not only is it advantageous to regard Christ as political so that He may found the political as well as the religious order of the Commonwealth, and so that the harmonious relationship of Church and State may find its ideal in the perfect integration of the two in the hypostatic person of Christ, but also because the political is simply the outward manifestation of the mystical inward order, such outward order being, of course, also very much the concern of Christ.

Unfortunately, by the third generation it was becoming increasingly apparent that the order of the City upon a Hill was as precarious and corruptible as in ordinary societies. The number of Saints, the level of religious fervor and moral righteousness declined markedly, which moved the elders and ministers of the churches to meet in Boston in 1679 to consider "what are the evils that have provoked the Lord to bring his judgments on New England," the judgments in question being an Indian war, pestilence, and fire. The consensus of the synod was that "New England had indeed fallen from the high estate in which the founders had left it." The members lamented the decline of godliness, the abounding of pride, swearing, Sabbath-breaking, laxity of discipline, and drunkenness.[14] While none of this seems justification for a jeremiad in our own less perfectionist times, three hundred years ago the disappointment of utopian expectations produced a vehement response. Perhaps the most profuse execration of the rampant moral turpitude came from the pen of Michael Wigglesworth, an otherwise mild-mannered Massachusetts minister. In his comminatory epic poem 'God's Controversy With New England', Wigglesworth presents a mythic account of the cosmic drama of the creation of order out of disorder in the New World, with the arrival of the Saints, the fall into sin, and the divine punishment. It is considered here as a mythologization of the Puritan emigration and endeavor to establish a City upon a Hill, a mythologization that shows the intimate relationship, at this early stage, between the public philosophy and the civil theology.

Wigglesworth begins the salvation history culminating in New England with the overcoming of the infernal chaos of the primitive American continent by celestial order. America is described as a vast region that had known no "English foot" until the Puritan migrations, "a waste and howling wilderness" inhabited only by "hellish fiends" and "brutish men" who worshipped Devils. While this seems a gross injustice to the people of Massassoit, Wigglesworth was not at all interested in historical or anthropological accuracy. What did concern him was the structure of the myth, the cosmic drama, the defeat of darkness by the forces of light. He goes on to describe pre-Puritan America as placed in darkness far from the light of heaven, amid shadows of "grim death" and "eternal night". America had never seen the "Sun of righteousness", Christ, the source of all peace, order, and salvation. Such is the setting. The action of the cosmic drama commences with the Puritan migration which is the sallying forth of the armies of the Lord of Hosts. The landing of English feet produces miraculous results: " . . . the darkness sad / Soon vanished away, / And all the shaddows of the night / Were turned to lightsome day," the blind received their sight, the wilderness rejoiced, the valleys, hills and woods sang the praises of God. The former "Devils den" is now irradiated with "glorious gospel-shine", for it is from here that the King of Kings will rule the nations. In this myth the Christian work of the Chosen People has been virtually absorbed by the actions of Providence, and the Puritan settlers are essentially an instrument of the divine ordering force. Those who opposed God's people in this mission were, of course, smashed to pieces, as were the Amalekites who fought against God's Old Israel. America, then, becomes a haven of perfect order for the Chosen People, while the "scourge" passed through Europe. While Europe was plunged into death and disorder only America remained securely in peace, as a kind of utopia, or parousia, a new creation redeemed through the covenant with God that seems to have implied even a transformation of human nature. In fact, the new order established in America was so radical a departure from the old as to require a suspension of the ordinary course of cosmic events to symbolize it adequately – the morning stars shone all day long, and the day continued for many years without being interrupted by darkness. This type of symbolism was the forerunner of the later symbol of the West as the source of daylight and renewal in a complete reversal of cosmic order.

Unfortunately, as Wigglesworth narrates, such perfect order did not endure, for the inhabitants did not sufficiently cherish their virtue or remain faithful to the covenant, nor did they realize that this new order was to be both a manifestation and a reward of their virtue and fidelity. They failed to fulfill their Christian work of imposing the divinely ordained order on the chaos of the new world and simply took the favor of Providence for granted. The central section of the poem is a lengthy reproachful indictment by God of his unfaithful servants in New England and his comparison of them with the sinful Israelites. He threatens the "Revolters" and "Backsliders", those who are wallowing in all manner of sinfulness, with grievous punishment if they do not return to the path of righteousness, and finally states that He will attempt to correct the sins of the people by condign punishments. The poem then returns to the voice of the author who describes the plagues and other disasters that have befallen the people of New England as divine retribution for their sins. The major theme of the poem is that of order, the divinely ordained order that is dependent on the virtue of the people for its mediation to earthly existence, and the fall from order, as well as the harmony between virtue and prosperity and between sin and catastrophe. The people represent a cosmic ordering force only so long as they faithfully obey the word of God and remain virtuous. In other words, while the beginning of the poem is a projected cosmos, a myth of divine actions as ground and explanation of human actions and experience, the central part of the poem presents the judgment that there are perceived laws and covenants and truths to which the Chosen People must conform their lives. Divine Providence is not automatically propitious. Man must conform to the required standards if he is to live in the Kingdom of God on earth, and so the myth remains subordinate to the divine command to live virtuously.[15]

Beneath the ardent Puritan endeavor to establish the divinely willed form of society we can observe the gestation of the American language, or universe of discourse, with its own system of signs and symbols derived from the matrix of the Western tradition. The New England Puritans, and the Virginia settlers before them, consciously or unconsciously selected from the Judaeo-Christian tradition those events and symbols which seemed best able to integrate their experience with the whole, with the cosmos, indeed with the history of the entire creation. Most of the Puritan symbols are elaborations on or variations of the prime symbol of the Chosen People, or the New Israel, with this symbol itself emerging from the Puritans' belief that they constituted a kind of "remnant" entrusted with the task of preserving and nourishing the true religion, the single means of participating in transcendence. It was this conviction of divine election that begot the syndrome of symbols that was to constitute a major portion of the American tradition. As an example, the Synod of 1689, convoked to deal with the distressing decline of virtue in New England, drew up an account of "the mind of the Assembly", which, according to Thomas J. Wertenbaker, explained the significance of the comparison with Israel as the foundation of the American language of self-understanding. "It was a great and high undertaking of their fathers, they said, when they ventured themselves and their little ones upon the rude waves of the vast ocean to follow the Lord into New England. To find a parallel one would have to go back to ancient history, to the journey of Abraham from Ur, or that of the Israelites from Egypt. In the American wilderness the Puritans had been the recipients of God's peculiar mercies. He had turned the desert into a fruitful land. He had cast out the heathen. 'Our fathers neither sought for, nor thought of great things for themselves, but did seek first the Kingdom of God and his righteousness.'" [16] The symbol of the Chosen People was born in an experience of departure from all that was familiar and setting forth into the unknown to recreate order from chaos, paradise from wilderness. The embarkation of the Puritans was not merely emigration, but also Exodus; the voyage to Massachusetts was not simply a sailing across an ocean, but also a journey through the vast and hostile wilderness of the Atlantic Ocean to the equally hostile wilderness of New England. As Cotton Mather was to express it in his monumental *Magnalia Christi Americana, or The Ecclesiastical History of New England*, "The most *crooked way* that ever was gone, even that of Israel's peregrination through the wilderness, may be called a *right way*, such was the way of this little Israel, now going into a wilderness."[17] The Counsell of Virginia had relied quite heavily on a comparison with Israel to explain the otherwise inexplicable survival of the colony, to create an experience of order and meaning out of what would otherwise have been subjection to a series of meaningless accidents and coincidences. Through this use of symbol the exodus from England becomes ritual – not as mere formality, but, in its deeper sense, as efficacious participation in the order of the cosmos. It is by such ritual emigrations that God's Chosen People implement the divine plan of salvation. Such an understanding of ritual as the efficacious re-enactment of events rendered paradigmatic by their own efficacy forms the root of the American language of public discourse.

For the Puritans, and, we might say, for the seventeenth century in America in general, the forces involved in the ritual are Divine Providence and the Chosen People insofar as they are involved in their Christian work. Order emerges from the complex, dynamic, synergistic relationship of the two. Once arrived in New England, the Puritans were engaged in a work of foundation, or in their own term, "edification", of the Kingdom of God, and it is foundation that provides the second major ritual in the American experience. The significance of foundation is almost entirely religious, a covenant with God to establish a society upon the order of Christian love. According to John Winthrop's 'A Modell of Christian Charity', the purpose of the City upon a Hill is "to improve our lives to do more service to the Lord and to comfort and increase the body of Christ of which we are members, so that ourselves and our posterity may be better preserved from the common corruptions of this evil world in order to serve the Lord and work out our salvation under the power and purity of His holy ordinance." And in order to realize this end, "we are entered into a covenant with [God]. . . . We have taken out a commission. The Lord has given us leave to draw our own articles;

we have promised to base our actions on these ends, and we have asked Him for favor and blessing."[18] The core of the ritual of foundation, as well as of the exodus, is a covenant between God and the People with which He is united by "closer bonds of marriage" (Winthrop) than with any other, and the foundation endures only so long as the Chosen People is faithful to the covenant. It is an assumption of the ritual of foundation that the religious order, the covenant, precedes the practical arrangements of the political order, which is established primarily to protect the religious community. The Puritans had no belief that their civil body politic was to have any meaning or destiny of its own, apart from its role of preserving the true Church. The secular is but incompletely differentiated from the sacred.

If we compare this state of affairs with Rome, we find that while the Massachusetts and Connecticut colonies possess the myths or religious beliefs prior to the foundation of cities, they do not as yet possess what we could properly regard as a civil theology, that is, a religion designed to evoke and direct piety toward the State for the sake of the State. In many respects the Puritan Commonwealth is in a condition similar to that of early Rome, where religion and politics were not truly differentiated. While the Puritans claim to draw a distinction between Church and State, both exist for the same ultimate purpose, and both derive from the will of God, or the mind of God. They are merely two independently functioning but interrelated aspects of the same ordering power. The good Christian is also a good citizen, of the right political order.

In summary, we find in the seventeenth century a very close relationship, almost identification between the cosmos of perception and the cosmos of projection. The two are seen as differentiable, although not yet fully differentiated, in the experience of disorder and decline from perfection. In this experience is perceived the rift between the colonists' Christian work, that is, their obligation to conform their lives to a certain order, and the mysterious workings of Divine Providence, which are primarily a translation into divine or cosmic terms of the actions and aspirations of human beings. In the eighteenth century, under the influence of incipient nationalism, these different perspectives began to be separately developed.

REFERENCES

[1] William Bradford, *Of Plymouth Plantation 1620–1647*, ed. by Samuel Eliot Morison, New York, Alfred A. Knopf, 1952, p. 3.

[2] *A True Declaration of the Estate of the Colonie in Virginia, With a Confutation of Such Scandalous Reports as have tended to the disgrace of so worthy an enterprise*, London, William Barrett, 1610, p. 24.

[3] *Ibid.* p. 6.

[4] Alexander Whitaker, 'Good Newes From Virginia', in *God's New Israel: Religious Interpretations of American Destiny*, ed. by Conrad Cherry, Englewood Cliffs, N. J., Prentice-Hall, Inc., 1971, pp. 36–37.

[5] John Winthrop, 'A Model of Christian Charity', in *The Annals of America* (hereafter referred to as *AA*) Vol. I, Chicago, Encyclopaedia Britannica, Inc., 1968, p. 115.

[6] Peter Bulkeley, 'A City Set Upon a Hill', in *AA*, Vol. I., p. 212.

[7] Bradford, p. 329.

[8] John Winthrop described the results of failure as follows: "If we deal falsely with our God in this work we have undertaken and so cause Him to withdraw His present help from us, we shall be made a story and a byword throughout the world: we shall open the mouths of enemies to speak evil of the ways of God and all believers in God; we shall shame the faces of many of God's worthy servants and cause their prayers to be turned into curses upon us, till we are forced out of the new land where we are going." John Winthrop, 'A Model of Christian Charity', *AA*, I, p. 115. That this became a theme of American self-reflection and self-evaluation is indicated by Edward Everett's speech on July 4, 1826: "If we fail ... not only do we defraud our children of the inheritance which we received from our fathers, but we blast the hopes of the friends of liberty throughout our continent, throughout Europe, throughout the world, to the end of time." Quoted in Harry V. Jaffa, *Equality and Liberty – Theory and Practice in American Politics*, New York, Oxford University Press, 1965, p. 116.

[9] Quoted in Thomas Jefferson Wertenbaker, *The Puritan Oligarchy*, New York, Charles Scribner's Sons, 1947, pp. 70–71. Oakes goes on to say, "Although Churches be distinct and therefore may not be confounded one with another, yet all the Churches ought to preserve Church communion one with another, because they are all united in Christ, not only as a mystical but as a political head." *Ibid.* p. 72.

[10] "That the New Englanders were correct in emphasizing the importance of State support for congregationalism is shown by the history of those groups who migrated to New Jersey, where the provincial government regarded them with suspicion if not open hostility. It was found impossible to enforce Scriptural law, to exclude Anglicans, Quakers and other 'heretics', to control education, to enforce the Sabbath law." Wertenbaker, p. 72.

[11] An even stronger statement of the divine source of the civil authority and its commission to encourage virtue and punish vice is to be found in the 1680 document 'A Confession of Faith; Owned and Consented to by 'the Elders and Messengers of the Churches'. Chapter xxiv, 'Of the Civil Magistrate', Begins: "God, the supreme Lord and King of all the world, hath ordained civil magistrates to be under him, over the people for his own glory and the public good; and to this end has armed them with the power of the sword for the defense and encouragement of them that do good, and for the punishment of evil doers."

[12] "So soon as God had set up Politicall Government among his people Israel hee gave them a body of lawes for judgment both in civil and criminal causes. These were brief and fundamental principles, yet withall so full and comprehensive as out of them clear deductions were to be drawne to all particular cases in future times. For a Common-

wealth without lawes is like a Ship without rigging and steeradge . . . ".

[13] "Whereas it is the duty of the Christian Magistrate to take care the People be fed with wholesome and sound Doctrine, and in this hour of temptation wherein the Enemy designeth to sow corrupt seed."

[14] Wertenbaker, p. 180.

[15] A recapitulation of Wigglesworth's theme appears a century later, in 1776, in the 'Address of the Convention of the Representatives of the State of New York to Their Constituents', written by John Jay. "Under the auspices and direction of Divine Providence, your forefathers removed to the evils and wilderness of America. By their industry they made it a fruitful, and by their virtue a happy country. And we should still have enjoyed the blessings of peace and plenty, if we had not forgotten the source from which these blessings flowed; and permitted our country to be contaminated by the many shameful vices which have prevailed among us."

[16] Wertenbaker, p. 72.

[17] Cotton Mather, *Magnalia Christi Americana; or The Ecclesiastical History of New-England*, [1702], New York, Russell & Russell, 1967, p. 50.

[18] Winthrop, pp. 114–115.

CHAPTER III

THE REORDERING OF THE COSMOS

For 'approximately a century after the Puritan migration the American self-understanding remained inchoate, absorbed largely in Church History, and not as yet conscious of America as a nation. The critical period for the development of the American civil religion and national consciousness was the middle of the eighteenth century, after the Eastern shore of the continent had lost its wilderness character and was, if not quite a paradise, at least settled and cultivated. In addition there had accumulated a century or more of experience of existence in the New World with its demands and its rewards, both actual and imaginable. And sufficient time had elapsed for the implanting and development of indigenous American political institutions and an America ushered in a new and probably final, unsurpassable epoch in the shape American thought became explicit during this period, beginning approximately with the Great Awakening and extending until the inauguration of the government under the Constitution.

Despite the trauma and upheaval of the Revolution, on the whole this period elaborated and expanded the kind of optimism regarding the cosmic significance of America that was expressed in the symbol of the City upon a Hill. This optimism found utterance in a number of related symbols, all of which were freighted with a sense that the discovery and development of America ushered in a new and probably final, unsurpassable epoch in the history of the world. The awareness of time and history and the structure of redemption through history have always been dominant features of American thought, although they have undergone a number of transformations. One of the most influential symbols, a development of the City upon a Hill, is that of the Parousia, the Millennium, the apocalyptic role of America in the divinely ordained culmination of history.

Millennialism in the modern world began with the Protestant Reformation, which instigated a renewed interest in reading and interpreting the Scriptures, at least partly out of a desire to understand how the Reformation fit into the divine plan of salvation. Millennialist speculation based on the Apocalypse was quite common in England in the sixteenth and seventeenth centuries, and was carried to America by the Puritans. In his study of American millennialism, Ernest Lee Tuveson writes that the source of the Puritans' belief that

43

they had been entrusted with a mission of world redemption was Protestant theology. In 1662 Jonathan Mitchel wrote that the reason for what Increase Mather called "Our fore-Fathers pious Errand into this Wilderness" was "REFORMATION," or the avoiding of corruption and the vigorous adhering to a "more Exact Profession and Practice of the contrary Truths and Rules, according to *Scripture*-Pattern". Mitchel went on to say that the forefathers intended more than Reformation. "They considered themselves in fact as advancing to the next step beyond the Reformation – the actual reign of the spirit of Christ, the amalgamation of the City of the World into the City of God." According to such a belief, earthly society was to become the abode of the Saints, the Kingdom of God, of Christ, it was to be a temporal and spatial region of perfect order. And the establishment of such an order is to be the Christian work of the Chosen People, the New Israel: " . . . as the *Prophetical* and *Priestly* Office of CHRIST, was completely Vindicated in the First Times of *Reformation*, so now the great CAUSE and *WORK* of God's *Reforming People*, is, to set up His *Kingdom*."[1]

Although the numerous millennial visions entertained in New England differed in many particulars, mainly theological, they had in general the attribute, as Tuveson points out, of rejecting the Augustinian philosophy of history, according to which history is the realm of coexistence and conflict between good and evil, with the perfection of order existing only transcendently and eternally.

One of the most important of the American prophets of the millennium was Jonathan Edwards. Although Tuveson's remark that Edwards does not envision the American colonies as *the* people through whom God will inaugurate the millennium is quite accurate, nevertheless in the context of the influence on the still nascent tradition this difference is negligible. Edwards was an electrifying preacher, perhaps best known for his fire-and-brimstone sermon 'Sinners in the Hands of an Angry God', and a prolific author of works on theology. His preaching in Northampton, Massachusetts, was largely responsible for the Great Awakening, the religious revival that swept New England in the 1740's, generating a fever pitch of apocalyptic and millennialist expectations. According to Alan Heimert and Perry Miller, "In the Awakening, Edwards believed, God had not simply promised that the millennium would begin in America, but that God had called on his American people to will a reorganized society into being."[2] For Edwards the mark of sanctity is unremitting "endeavor to redeem society" and establish the Kingdom of God on earth. Such an American Parousia seems the only logical meaning of so significant an event as the discovery of America and the planting therein of the true religion. As Edwards himself put it, "I think we may well look upon the discovery of so great a part of the world, and bringing the gospel into it, as one thing by which divine providence is preparing the way for the future glorious times of the church, when Satan's kingdom shall be overthrown throughout the whole habitable globe, on every side, and on all its continents." [3] For Edwards the only adequate explanation for the long concealment and late disclosure of "so great a part of the world" as America is that God has reserved it for a special role in the history of redemption, a role Edwards described as "the most glorious renovation of the world". He seeks to prove the reasonableness of America's having such a role in his work *Some Thoughts Concerning the Present Revival of Religion in New England*. The arguments in this work are a recapitulation of the major themes of American myth. Speaking of the Great Awakening, he reflects that "it is not unlikely that this work of God's Spirit, so extraordinary and wonderful, is the dawning, or at least a prelude of that glorious work of God, so often foretold in scripture, which, in the progress and issue of it, shall renew the world of mankind. . . . And there are many things that make it probable that this work will begin in America . . ." [4]

Edwards supports this last assertion with his exegesis of Isaiah 50,9, a favorite passage among millennialists: "Surely the isles shall wait for me, and the ships of Tarshish first, to bring my sons from afar." The distant isles are America, as "the first fruits of that glorious day". Edwards' major assumption, which he states quite explicitly, is that there is "a kind of equality in the dispositions of Providence". We might suspect, however, that this is not the ultimate assumption, which rather seems to be the more nationalistic expectation that America is not destined to remain a provincial backwater, isolated from the centers of civilization and culture in Europe, but is instead ordained for a major role in world history as sacred history. Therefore, in order to provide America with such a role, Edwards must assume that Providence organizes the course of the world's temporal existence according to the principles of bilateral symmetry, for God's glorious work of creation and redemption in the Old World is to be recapitulated, sublimated, and completed in the alembic of the New. "God has made as it were two worlds here below, two great habitable continents, far separated one from the other: The latter is as it were now but newly created; it has been, till of late, wholly the possession of Satan, ... This new world is probably now discovered, that the new and most glorious state of God's church on earth might commence there; that God might in it begin a new world in a spiritual respect, when he creates the *new heavens* and *new earth*." [5] America is a new world, even a new creation, its discovery an epochal event in sacred history, ushering in, as it does, the Parousia. Previously relegated to the dominion of Satan the new world has been plunged into chaos and barbarism, but God's plan is to transform it into a glorious spiritual kingdom.

So, just as Christ was born physically and made the "purchase of redemption" in the old world, so in the new "it is not unlikely that the great spiritual birth of Christ, and the most glorious 'application of redemption', is to begin in this." The Old World slew Christ and spilled the blood of a great many saints and martyrs. "God has, therefore, probably reserved the honour of building the glorious temple to the daughter that has not shed so much blood, when those times of the peace, prosperity and glory of the church, typified by the reign of Solomon, shall commence." [6] The inheritance has passed to a new land which is relatively innocent. Edwards is very careful to speak only in terms of the probable. He does not presume to be privy to the mind of God, but, reasoning from sacred history and scripture, finds it likely that the structure of the cosmos and universal history will adhere to the course he outlines, according to an interpretation which provides America with a properly central role. The Great Awakening is the harbinger of the recreation of the world.

Experience, both spiritual and temporal, indicates a symmetrical structure of history, with America as the site of the church's latter-day glory. Since Adam and Eve, Noah and his sons, and Christ all lived in the Old World, "it is probably in some measure to balance these things, the most glorious renovation of the world shall originate from the new continent, and the church of God in that respect be from hence". There is to Edwards an obvious parallel between the fall of the first Adam, remedied by God's glorious renovation of mankind through Christ, the second Adam, and the Roman Catholic Church, what Edwards calls "the great anti-christian apostasy", remedied by the Reformation, "the glorious renovation of the world", which is to achieve its latter-day glory in the new world. By implication America is to be the source of the third Adam who will inaugurate the glorious third age of the church's history. Note that America is to be the seat of the glory of the *Church* — Edwards does not prophesy glory for America as a political society. Thus, the coincidence of the discovery of America with the Reformation is one sign of the destined role of America in sacred history. Another sign is the transfer of the source of affluence from the old continent to the new. To the initiated this is easily understood as presaging a transfer of spiritual empire. Henceforth America, the West, will be the seat of spiritual order.

A further support for Edwards' interpretation is that the manner of the building-up of America from its pristine chaos and barbarity conform well to God's preferred method of manifesting His power; which is to begin from nothing and build up something more excellent than anything that had previously existed. "When God is about to turn the earth into a paradise, he does not begin his work where there is some good growth already, but in the wilderness, where nothing grows, and nothing is to be seen but dry and barren rocks, that the light may shine out of darkness, the world be replenished from emptiness, and the earth watered by springs from a droughty desert . . . " [7] The development of America from a barren wilderness to a bountiful paradise as an imitation and in some respects a recapitulation of God's creation of the world from nothing, reveals America as an avatar of divine power. Hence the glory of America redounds to God whose work it is. Because America is the "utmost, meanest, youngest and weakest part" of the habitable earth, the place "where the church of God has been planted last of all", it is here in America that God will begin the metastatic renewal of the habitable earth, a renewal to be marked by the commencing of a radically new cosmic order. "There are several things that seem to me to argue, that the sun of righteousness, the sun of the new heavens and the new earth, when he rises – . . . shall rise in the west, contrary to the course of things in the old heavens and earth. The movements of Providence shall in that day be so wonderfully altered in many respects, that God will as it were change the course of nature, in answer to the prayers of his church. . . . The sun of righteousness has long been going down from east to west; and probably when the time comes of the church's deliverance from her enemies . . . the light will rise in the west, till it shines through the world like the sun in its meridian brightness." [8] The new order that will flow through America to the rest of the cosmos is to have its source in the west rather than the east, a reorientation, or, more accurately an 'occidentation' of cosmic order. This 'western dawn' is Edwards' version of what was traditionally known as *translatio imperii*, or periodic movement of the seat of imperial rule. The idea of such movement is quite ancient, although it was Western Europe, in a more recent period, that decided on a specifically westward *translatio*. In America that seat of empire has at last found its ultimate resting place. Thus, America's future is not simply its own, but the future of mankind, of the world, even of the cosmos. [9]

Among those anticipating an important role for America was the philosopher and bishop George Berkeley, whose poem, 'Verses on the Prospect of Planting Arts and Learning in America', although not truly millennial in intent, was often quoted in support of a millennium's arriving in America through *translatio imperii*. The significant verse is the last.

Westward the course of empire takes its way;
The four first acts already past,
A fifth shall close the drama with the day;
Time's noblest offspring is the last.[10]

Quite the opposite of Edwards' western dawn, Berkeley's poem suggests only that America is to be the scene of maturity, the fruition of Arts and Learning. America is a child of the evening, not of the morning, and its own decline will be if not the end of time, at least the end of Western civilization. However, if the third line is ignored the verse can be used to support millennialist expectations.

The latter half of the eighteenth century saw the full creation of the American myth, the cosmos of projection which we might call the occidentation of order, gradually created through a secularized amalgamation of millennialism and *translatio imperii*, which sometimes rose to rapturous heights. In 1778, in perhaps the darkest hour of the American colonists' struggle for independence, the Reverend Phillips Payson was transported to the summit of a western Mount Pisgah from which he surveyed the Promised Land, the future home of the people redeemed from the fleshpots of Europe. "To anticipate the future glory of America from present hopes and prospects is ravishing and transporting to the mind. In this light we behold our country, . . . enjoying the purest liberty, . . . the envy of tyrants and devils but the delight of God and all good men; . . . Hail, happy posterity, that shall reap the peaceful fruits of our sufferings, fatigues, and wars! With such prospects, such transporting views, it is difficult to keep the passions or the tongue within the bounds of Christian moderation."[11]

A few years earlier, the poet Timothy Dwight expressed similar sentiments in his poem, 'America: or a Poem on the Settlement of the British Colonies: Addressed to the Friends of Freedom, and Their Country', an epic which, as may be guessed from the title, is in many respects a somewhat secularized version of the myth developed in Wigglesworth's 'God's Controversy With New England'. Dwight begins with an account of the barbarity, superstition, ignorance, and "deepening gloom" imposed upon Europe during the Dark Ages. But then, through the divinely inspired discovery of America and the Reformation, the darkness began to lift, as "AMERICA'S bright realms arose to view, / And the *old* world rejoic'd to see the new." America is given a distinctly redemptive role, as the Promised Land, the place on earth which is closest to heaven.

O Land supremely blest! to thee 'tis given

To taste the choicest joys of bounteous heaven;
Thy rising Glory shall expand its rays,
And lands and times unknown rehearse thine endless praise.[12]

Clearly America is to be the well-spring of an age or epoch of the world, an epoch whose duration is indicated by the "endless praise" which America, god-like, is to receive from lands and times which cannot yet be foreseen. Toward the end of the poem Wigglesworth's eschatological vision of meta-static perfection appears as the American destiny, quite apart, it would seem, from the godliness of the citizens. Or perhaps the godliness is simply taken for granted. In this final time America's power shall extend from sea to sea and a heavenly kingdom shall descend, shedding Light and Glory over the entire world until the actual end of the world. America is to be the navel through which transcendent ordering forces will flow into and throughout the world in order to banish all causes of discord and disorder to "their native hell." From America is to radiate the millennial reign of peace that is (according to some interpretations of the Apocalypse) to precede the end of the world. It is not difficult to see the development of this view of America as the site of a heavenly kingdom from John Winthrop's symbol of the City upon a Hill performing a similar function, albeit somewhat less millennially. It might also be mentioned that the first two lines quoted above contain an adumbration of the idea called in the nineteenth century "Manifest Destiny", the belief that the physical power of the American nation is to extend "from sea to shining sea", while the moral power of America will pervade the world. Manifest Destiny itself was essentially a secularization, a translation into political power and territorial hegemony of the implications of Winthrop's symbol.

Dwight did not cease his vaticinal labors with 'America'. In 1774 he published 'Columbia', in which the mission of America is the dominant theme. Note the echo of Berkeley in the third line.

Columbia, Columbia, to glory arise,
The queen of the world, and child of the skies:
Thy reign is the last, and the noblest of time,
Most fruitful thy soil, most inviting thy clime;
Let the crimes of the east ne'er encrimson thy name,
Be freedom, and science, and virtue, thy fame.[13]

He goes on to predict that "earth's little kingdoms" will bow before the splendor of America, which under its triumphant flag will give peace to the world. And just after the Revolutionary War Dwight reiterated the millennial theme with another epic, 'The Conquest of Canaan' in which the New World becomes the fifth kingdom of the Book of Daniel, with another echo of Berkeley's verse: "Here Empire's last and brightest throne shall rise; / And Peace and Right, and Freedom, greet the skies." We find in the succession of Dwight's epics a view of America as ushering in an earthly reign of peace and justice and happiness, an order encompassed by freedom and science and virtue. Nevertheless, Dwight does maintain the religious framework of the vision.

However, the imagery and the vision tend even more to the secular, to earthly progress toward an ideal in other poets of the Revolutionary period, such as Joel Barlow, who in his patriotic oration delivered at Hartford, Connecticut to the Society of the Cincinnati on July 4, 1787, referred repeatedly to the "American empire", which stands as the achievement of the age. "The present is an age of philosophy, and America the empire of reason. Here neither the pageantry of courts nor the gloom of superstition have dazzled or beclouded the mind." Barlow, speaking while the Constitutional Convention was sitting in Philadelphia, took it for granted that America would have a central role to play in the world if the citizens fulfilled their responsibilities. "Every free citizen of the American empire ought now to consider himself as the legislator of half mankind." At the close of his oration Barlow picks up the Reverend Payson's theme, while keeping it somewhat more within the bounds of Christian moderation. "Every possible encouragement for great and generous exertions is now presented before us. Under the idea of a permanent and happy government, every point of view in which the future situation of America can be placed fills the mind with pecular dignity and opens an unbounded field of thought. ... [T]he example of political wisdom and felicity, here to be displayed, will excite emulation through the kingdoms of the earth and meliorate the condition of the human race."[14]

While America is to be a City upon a Hill, Barlow regarded this city not as God's Plantation but as the home and the empire of reason. Barlow was more a son of the eighteenth century than of the Puritans, although he did accept those aspects of the Puritan tradition that were compatible with a view of rational progress. In the Preface to his epic patriotic poem in 3,675 couplets, 'The Columbiad', Barlow explains to his readers that the object of the poem is "to inculcate the love of rational liberty", to demonstrate that republican government is the realm of all good order and permanent peace, and that the future progress of mankind depends upon organized liberty in particular governments. Barlow's own purpose is admittedly didactic — he wishes to direct the course of American thought to appreciate republican institutions as "the great foundation of public and private happiness, the necessary aliment of future and permanent ameliorations in the condition of human nature." Barlow here advocates a somewhat Augustan policy — the use of the fine arts and particularly poetry, to create an American myth of republican institutions as the true form of order and the basis of glory. In effect, Barlow proposes the creation and dissemination of an American myth of a cosmos that has been laboring toward the perfection of republican institutions in America. When he began writing the work, originally entitled 'The Vision of Columbus', Barlow described, in somewhat Berkelian terms, his "plan for a poem on the subject at large, designed to exhibit the importance of this country in every point of view as the noblest and most elevated part of the earth, and reserved to be (the) last and greatest theatre for the improvement of mankind in every article in which they are capable of improvement."[15] The discovery, colonization, and development of America must be the culmination of history, for nowhere else will mankind ever be susceptible of greater progress toward perfection. While Barlow was no millennialist in the religious sense, he bears certain marks of the species in a secular sense, in his belief that America is to be "the last and greatest theatre for the improvement of mankind in every article in which they are capable of improvement". His poetry implicitly assumes an occidentation of order.

This theme was picked up also by other poets, such as Philip Freneau and Hugh Henry Breckenridge, who wrote the Commencement Poem for the Princeton Class of 1771, 'The Rising Glory of the West'. Here we find an explicit use of the theme of light and salvation from the West. "I see, I see / Freedom's established reign; cities, and men, / Numerous as sands upon the ocean shore, / And empires rising where the sun descends." This restructuring of space is followed by a resymbolization of the structure of time so that the present, the beginning of the consummation of history in the empire of the West, becomes "dark antiquity", the twilight of a remote dawn to the final state, America as the New Jerusalem: "Indeed, / How could I weep that we exist so soon, / Just in the dawning of these mighty times, / Whose scenes are painting for eternity.'[16] In this implicit assimilation of history to the order of day and night, the darkness of Europe yields to the dawn of a new epoch in America, which shall reach its culmination in distant future ages. The symbols of such anticipations of glory and order appear in Freneau's own poem 'America Independent', in which the poet praises America for its "triumph more divine" and its "second golden reign". Freneau was a Jeffersonian and such a tireless opponent of Hamilton in his newspaper, the National Gazette, that Washington was once provoked to refer to him as "that rascal Freneau".

While we must make allowances for the orotund nature of patriotic poetry, particularly regarding a nation which is just struggling into existence, we can still clearly discern in such poetry as that of Dwight, Barlow, and Freneau a fairly consistent and articulate myth of the meaning of America and its place in the cosmos and history. And, what is equally significant, this seems to be a conscious, deliberate creation of myth, that is, the poets write not in the white heat of non-reflective patriotic fervor, but in the tranquil recollection of such sentiments, with the intention of awakening similar sentiments in the hearts of other Americans so that they will cherish and strive for the proper ideals, those of America's greatness.

It is important that we understand the precise meaning of myth in this context. The patriotic poets were not creating a "myth", meaning a fiction or a falsehood, in order simply to manipulate the emotions of their fellow-countrymen. Rather, in their poems they spoke for the consciousness of Americans – they acted as mediums in articulating the sense of destiny that had been subliminal in the American tradition, so that providing America with such a glorious destiny would make Americans better citizens. In effect, such poems told Americans what they wanted to hear because they already, in some sense, believed it. Patriotic poems simply crystallized the aspirations of the people and gave the people a reason accounting for their faith by placing it logically within the course of cosmic order and historic development. And so the cosmos is ordered, or reordered, to accommodate the American sense of destiny. But this myth is not yet entirely separated from the cosmos of perception, the public philosophy, for it is still the responsibility of Americans to cherish certain ideals and to live up to certain standards, in short, to do their Christian work if their destiny is to be realized.

If actions, particularly the actions and policies that will determine America's future, are guided by beliefs, then those beliefs must be strengthened as much as possible, made even irrefutable, by rooting them in the very nature of things, because the source of order and center of empire has been moving steadily westward throughout recorded history, and since America is the *ultima Thule* of the West it must be the site of the culmination of history and the divine plan of salvation, with all that that implies. There seems to have been a consensus that geography is destiny: in Western man's scheme of things cosmic order moves Westward and because America is the Westernmost nation, it must unquestionably be the greatest. America is destined to be the divine ordering force for the world, a force so irresistible that future generations shall "enjoy perpetual rest", a traditional Christian obliquity for the ecstasy of union with God.

Such myth-making was by no means confined to poetry; another arena for the deployment of the myth-maker's powers was the sermon, for ministers of the same period delighted in contemplating the glories of the earthly kingdom as much as of the celestial. A typical example is the May, 1783 sermon, 'The United States Elevated to Glory and Honour', in which Ezra Stiles rhapsodized on the future magnificence of America after the approaching successful termination of the war with England. One of Stiles' principal themes is the New Israel, the New Chosen People, whose glory may be expected to be dependent upon its fidelity to God, for it is the ways of the virtuous that prosper in the well-ordered cosmos. In this the Old Israel prefigures the New: " ... the history of the Hebrew theocracy showed that the secular welfare of God's ancient people depended upon their virtue, their religion, their observance of that holy covenant which Israel entered into with God on the plains at the foot of Nebo on the other side of the Jordan. Here Moses, the man of God, assembled three millions of people, the number of the United States, ... "[17] Stiles' numerical exegesis of the Bible in accordance with America and its salvific role is not limited to the population: "It was of the Lord that 'a woman clothed with the sun, and the moon under her feet', and upon 'her head a crown of twelve stars' (not to say thirteen) should 'flee into the wilderness, where she hath a place prepared of God (Rev. xii, 1 & 6), and where she might be the repository of Wisdom, and keep the commandments of God, and have the testimony of Jesus."[18] The United States is a new experiment in human freedom and in progress toward perfect order, and there is every reason to expect that Americans will become a great people. Stiles' message was clear: that just as the secular, temporal welfare, the safety and prosperity of the Hebrews depended upon their awareness of and fidelity to the divine order, so the safety and prosperity of the United States is also a result of the intervention of God and requires fidelity to the divine will. There is reason to expect that God intends to bestow greater blessings on America than those he bestowed on the Hebrews, that will make the United State "high among the nations in praise and in name, and in honour." America has not, of course, arrived at its present auspicious condition merely by its own efforts; rather, America has been brought through the Revolution to the "dawn of Peace" by "the wonder-working Providence of God", which has led America along the ordained path. Such a structure of cosmic space and time is quite similar to that of Edwards: from eternity God has destined America to be the theater of a particular display of his power, the *Magnalia Dei*, the rising glory of America.

In his prediction that all nations will attend to and contemplate the American revolution Stiles recapitulates the City upon a Hill theme that America will be the center of the world's attention and desire and that American order, the true order, will propagate peacefully and naturally. The prophecy of Daniel is thus fulfilled, and America will become the alembic in which all human knowledge is purified and perfected so that it "may reblaze back from America to Europe, Asia, and Africa, and illumine the world with TRUTH and LIBERTY". Stiles goes on to quote John Adams: "The progress of society will be accelerated by centuries by this revolution. ... Light spreads from the day-spring in the west; and may it shine more and more until the perfect day." [19] Here again we encounter what is perhaps the prime symbol of the re-structuring of the cosmos to accommodate the anticipated role of America — the dayspring in the West.

In America the experience of a new beginning in an unquestionably far more successful quest for earthly perfection and happiness can be adequately symbolized by a repolarization of cosmic order. Just as the articulation of the significance of the life of Christ required a sudden redirecting and restructuring of time at the moment of his birth because living after Him was so radically different from living before, and perhaps just as this overwhelming experience of a new order so easily translated itself into apocalyptic symbols, so in America, the discovery of which was, in Charles Sumner's words, regarded as "the greatest event of all secular history", [20] the experience of a new beginning, of an entering into a perhaps radically different epoch in the divinely ordained history of the world, could, similarly, find an adequate outlet only in often rapturous, apocalyptic expectations and a reversal of cosmic order, a reversal as radical as the transformation of the traditional symbol of decline and death into the symbol of rebirth into new and vigorous life. The point is not that, as in Berkeley's poem, America is to be the last and noblest episode in the history of earthly empire, but, more dramatically, that America's discovery, colonization, growth, and independence are the hymeneals of the wedding of time with eternity. America is the last that is the first, the omega and alpha, and the end of an old order and the beginning of a new. In short, there is one current of the tradition of American self-interpretation which finds it essential to establish America as the center of a reordering of the cosmos.

Nor were the poets and preachers alone in their extravagant expectations. Dr. Richard Price, the friend of Benjamin Franklin, suggested that in historical importance the American revolution ranked second only to "the introduction of Christianity among mankind", an idea that anticipates Sumner's pronouncement on the historical significance of the discovery of America. In 1779, when the outcome of the Revolutionary War was in considerable doubt, David Ramsay, a delegate from South Carolina to the Continental Congress, delivered 'An Oration on the Advantages of American Independence', replete with euphoric sentiments. "When I anticipate in imagination the future glory of my country, and the illustrious figure it will soon make on the theatre of the world, my heart distends with genuine pride for being an American. What a substratum for an empire! compared with which, the foundations of the Macedonian, the Roman, and the British, sink into insignificance ... "[21] Ramsay also repeats the theme of *translatio imperii* and the occidentation of order, symbolized by the Western sunrise, a theme closely related to that of America as the savior nation. Ramsay maintains that since the Deluge "true religion, literature, arts, empire, and riches" have been slowly and inexorably moving Westward to fix their "long and favorite abode" in the new, Western world. America's independence "will redeem one quarter of the globe from tyranny and oppression, and consecrate it the chosen seat of truth, justice, freedom, learning and religion." And so America becomes the foundation of the happiness of generations yet unborn, and Americans should bear with patience their sufferings "in a cause of such infinite importance".

America is indeed become the site of the infusion of all true order into the world. It is the source of earthly happiness, the foundation of a new empire, "the chosen seat of truth". Even Jedidiah Morse, in the preface to his *American Geography*, published in 1789, painted a picture of America as nurturing the highest degree of perfection possible to man in all areas of human virtue and endeavor, and, in short, America was to be "the largest empire that ever existed", an empire, based not on coercive power, but on the irresistible metastasis of order and truth.

It is interesting to see what becomes of these ideas and symbols in the nineteenth century. One striking development, due to the rapidly accelerating Westward expansion of the American frontier, as well as the discovery of the vast mineral and other natural resources of the West, is an even further enhanced appreciation of the significance of the West in the redemption of the world, as, for example, in Lyman Beecher's sermon 'A Plea for the West'. "But if it is by the march of revolution and civil liberty, that the way of the Lord is to be prepared, where shall the central energy be found, and from what nation shall the renovating power go forth? What nation is blessed with such experimental knowledge of free institutions, with such facilities and resources of communication, obstructed by so few obstacles, as our own?.... It is equally plain that the religious and political destiny of our nation is to be decided in the West."[22] This decisive character of the West, its role in the redemption and evangelization of the world, is based on the extent of its territory and its potential for population, wealth, and political power. "The West is a younger empire of mind, and power, and wealth, and free institutions rushing up to a giant manhood, with a rapidity and a power never before witnessed below the sun." According to the tradition and evolution of the symbol, the West is the "navel" through which the salvific order will flow into the world. The transformation of the West into a symbol of resurrection and rebirth becomes a variation of the Christian experience that "death is swallowed up in victory".

Therefore, not only is cosmic order reconstructed so as to accord America a leading role, at the very source of light and life, but Scripture and sacred history are re-interpreted so as to have prophesied and prefigured this role. And this occidentation of order, with all that it implies, is in fulfillment of "the great designs of Providence", Providence being the primary American symbol for the seat of order, structure, and meaning in history, which is centered around America, or so it would seem. Indeed, if we turn back to the revolutionary period, we find, in one of the first proposals for the Great Seal of the United States, an appropriation of the Exodus to symbolize the Revolution, with the idea that those who rebel against tyrants are especially favored by divine providence.

In 1778, five years after Stiles' sermon, Samuel Langdon closed his sermon, 'The Republic of the Israelites an Example to the United States', with the fervent wish, "May the general government of the United States, when established, appear to be the best which the nations have yet known and be exalted by uncorrupted religion and morals! And may the everlasting gospel diffuse its Heavenly Light and spread Righteousness, Liberty, and Peace, thr' the whole world."[23] The United States is to be the closest approximation to perfect and enduring order the world has ever seen. Accordingly, the superior government of the United States is an indication that the government has been given by God. This translation of the cosmos into American terms goes even so far as to regard Israel as a "republic" and a rebel against tyrants in the cause of political liberty, paradigmatic for the United States.

In this chapter we have been exploring one part of the tradition, the American civil theology, or public myth, or common symbolism of the meaning of American existence as it developed during the eighteenth century. The seventeenth century had seen a civil religion that combined symbols, such as Providence, Chosen People, and the City upon a Hill, with the belief that the source of order in the Commonwealth must be the mind of God discerned by the Chosen, virtuous People. Indeed, to the Puritan mind the foundation of the Commonwealth and the destiny of the Commonwealth were simply not distinguishable. However, during the eighteenth century foundation and destiny gradually drew apart, with the latter acquiring a language, a system of symbols of its own. In other words, while the primary symbolic ingredients of the occidentation of order – millennialism, *translatio imperii*, and the City upon a Hill – placed great emphasis on the future magnificence of America, and the order which it was to spread throughout the world, such symbols and the ways in which they were used were less concerned with the source of that order and the precise principles on which it was to be based.

For its political symbols the Puritan Commonwealth had mined not Christianity, a universal non-political religion, but Judaism, the religion of a particular "Chosen" people. Therefore, even though the Christian religion of the Puritans was a potentially universal religion, the early settlers took a very special view of themselves. They were the remnant, fleeing from Europe and bearing with them the ark of the true order in which God dwells among men as they crossed the perilous wilderness of the ocean in order to transform the barren wilderness of New England into a land flowing with milk and honey.

Nevertheless, there was a tension inherent in their self-understanding, insofar as they believed themselves to possess the true interpretation of Christianity, for Christ's command was not to build an ideal political society that could be admired and emulated, but rather to "go forth and teach all nations". The tension lay between the provincialism or isolationism of that people more closely married to God than any other, and the universality of the truth which they believed themselves to possess.

The eighteenth century, mainly through the nationalism of such as Jonathan Edwards and the writers and preachers of the revolutionary period, as well as the political documents producing and produced from events, resolved this tension by differentiating between the public philosophy and civil theology. The public philosophy made explicit the universal principles of national order, while the civil theology, or public myth, became both an ecumenic and an eschatological civil theology; a myth of a world empire, at least of a moral order, and an empire that realizes the fullness of truth and order, the Kingdom of God on earth. In short, America was to be the ordering center of the final glorious regeneration of the world. The ecumenicity of the civil theology derives partly from the universal principles of the public philosophy and partly from its own elements of millennialism, which assumed that in some sense the world is to be one fold with one shepherd. The myth-makers were never daunted by the insignificance or remoteness of the American colonies, for they regarded America as the Bethlehem of the nations of the world, or, to use another image, as the remnant that preserved and cherished the truth, and would eventually radiate such truth throughout the world.

What we have seen developing here is the symbiotic relationship of two differently conceived views of the cosmos. In other words, what we might call dichocosmy (from the Greek words *dicha*, meaning apart, asunder, at variance, and *cosmos*, meaning order), or the tension between the cosmos of perception, the unchanging moral and cosmic order on which the society is built, and the cosmos of projection, the structuring of the cosmos in the dynamic image of the society's aspirations, can also be seen as a symbiotic relationship, for each reinforces the other, much as in the Puritan view of Church and State. In fact, though they have different orientations both views of the cosmos are based on the same religion, Christianity, although incorporating much from the Old Testament. Specifically, dichocosmy means the coexistence of two different but not incompatible world-views. The public philosophy, or Christian work of the people, sees God primarily as Lawgiver, setting standards of conduct and inner disposition which men are required to meet in order to avoid dire consequences. The civil theology, on the other hand, sees God as Providential Lord of History, arranging time and history so as to give the starring role to the Messianic American people. The public philosophy gives America an order; the civil theology gives it a unique identity and destiny.

The idea relationship between the two is balance, that is, identity and destiny derive from a perfect obedience to divine, unchanging law. There is, however, the danger that the civil theology emphasizing national glory will be developed at the expense of the requirements of national order. But before considering this possibility we must first consider the public philosophy as it was articulated during the latter part of the eighteenth century.

REFERENCES

[1] Quoted in Ernest Lee Tuveson, *Redeemer Nation – The Idea of America's Millennial Role*, Chicago, University of Chicago Press, 1968, pp. 97–98.
[2] *The Great Awakening – Documents Illustrating the Crisis and its Consequences*, ed. by Alan Heimert and Perry Miller, Indianapolis, The Bobbs-Merrill Company, 1967, p. 1.
[3] Quoted in Tuveson, p. 100.

[4] Jonathan Edwards, 'The Latter-Day Glory is Probably To Begin in America', in *God's New Israel: Religious Interpretations of American Destiny*, ed. by Conrad Cherry, Englewood Cliffs, N. J., Prentice-Hall, Inc., 1971, p. 55.

[5] *Ibid*. p. 56.

[6] *Ibid*. pp. 56–57.

[7] *Ibid*. pp. 57–58.

[8] *Ibid*. pp. 58–59.

[9] This idea of the Westward movement of empire was observed by Andrew Burnaby, an English clergyman, who visited the middle colonies in 1759–1760 and reported, "An idea strange as it is visionary, has entered into the minds of the generality of mankind, that empire is travelling Westward; and every one is looking forward with eager and impatient expectation to that destined moment, when America is to give law to the rest of the world." Quoted in Tuveson, p. 101.

[10] Quoted in Tuveson, p. 94.

[11] Quoted in *By Freedom's Holy Light – A Selection of Patriotic Messages by Gordon Palmer*, New York, The Devin-Adair Company, 1964, p. 155.

[12] Quoted in Tuveson, p. 104.

[13] *Ibid*. pp. 107–108.

[14] Joel Barlow, 'The Unfinished Revolution', in *AA*, Vol. III, p. 93.

[15] Quoted in Charles Burr Todd, *Life and Letters of Joel Barlow*, New York, Da Capo Press, 1971, p. 15.

[16] *The Poems of Philip Freneau*, ed. by Fred Lewis Potter, Princeton, The University Library, 1902, Vol. I, pp. 76–77.

[17] Ezra Stiles, 'The United States Elevated to Glory and Honour', in *God's New Israel*, p. 82.

[18] *Ibid*. p. 92.

[19] *Ibid*. p. 90. It is interesting to note that the millennialism appears, some forty-four years later in an even stronger form in a sermon by Lyman Beecher: "Indeed, if it had been the design of heaven to establish a powerful nation in the full enjoyment of civil and religious liberty, where all the energies of man might find scope and excitment, on purpose to show the world by experiment, of what man is capable . . . where could such an experiment have been made but in this country [?]. . . . [T]he light of such a hemisphere shall go up to heaven; it will throw its beams beyond the waves – it will shine into the darkness there, and be comprehended; it will awaken desire, and hope, and effort, and produce revolutions and overturning, until the world is free. . . . Floods have been poured upon the rising flames of Aetna. Still it burns, and still the mountain heaves, and murmurs; and soon it will explode with voices, and thunderings, and great earthquakes. Then will the trumpet of jubilee sound, and earth's debased millions will leap from the dust, and shake off their chains, and cry, 'Hosanna to the Son of David.' Quoted in Sidney E. Mead, 'The Nation With The Soul of a Church', *Church History*, Vol. XXXVI, No. 3, p. 279.

[20] On the whole Sumner seems to have expected America to conquer the world through its example as the City upon a Hill. In 1867 he published a monograph entitled *Prophetic Voices About America*, a collection of prophecies of the discovery and future greatness of America. At the end of the book he wrote, "Our country needs no such ally as war. Its destiny is mightier than war. Through peace it will have everything. This is our talisman. Give us peace and population will increase beyond all experience; resources of

all kinds will multiply infinitely; arts will embellish the land with immortal beauty; the name of Republic will be exalted, until every neighbor, yielding to irresistible attraction, will seek a new life in becoming a part of the great whole; and the national example will be more puissant than army or navy for the conquest of the world." *Prophetic Voices About America* (A Monograph from the Atlantic Monthly, Sept. 1867), p. 306.

[21] David Ramsay, 'An Oration on the Advantages of American Independence', in *American Ideas*, ed. by Gerald N. Grob and Robert N. Beck, New York, The Free Press, 1963, Vol. I, p. 226.

[22] Lyman Beecher, 'A Plea For the West', in *God's New Israel*, p. 120.

[23] Samuel Langdon, 'The Republic Of The Israelites An Example To The American States', in *God's New Israel*, p. 105.

CHAPTER IV

THE PUBLIC PHILOSOPHY

The Declaration of Independence, the first centralizing, crystalizing document in the public philosophy because of its role in the founding of the American nation, is not, of course, the actual origin of the public philosophy. By 1776 there had already existed an indigenous American political tradition for a century and a half, beginning with the Virginia House of Burgesses in 1619 and the Mayflower Compact a year later. This was an articulate tradition, possessing strong convictions regarding the meaning of political order and lacking only the sense that it was the basis of national unity, a lack supplied by the Declaration.

We have already observed that the Pilgrim society, or civil body politic, was quite consciously and deliberately created as a community of God and men by a covenant among the colonists and between them and God, and that such a body politic existed for the glory of God and advancement of the Christian faith, as well as for the more pragmatic political ends of order and preservation. The Mayflower Compact itself was not a constitution –; it established no political institutions, nor did it enact any legislation, but it served as a kind of enabling act for the necessary laws and institutions for "the general good of the colony". The text of the Compact and the commentary by Mourt, one of the signers, indicate that the Pilgrims' intent was simply to establish the proper, divinely approved form of government and then submit to it. There is, to be sure, a certain reservation in the "due submission and obedience", but this is no indication that the Pilgrim Fathers were proto-Lockians. They do not mention the protection of rights as one of the purposes of the civil body politic, for the simple reason that for the Puritans individual rights were subordinate to the glory of God, the advancement of Christianity, the honor of king and country, and the general good of the society. Indeed, for the Puritan the advancement and preservation of Christianity was itself all the protection of individual rights that was necessary, for they saw the protection of the individual as embedded in a far wider order of things and meanings. As Willmoore Kendall has pointed out, the primary concern was with the higher law that had to be applied to everyday problems, This higher law in itself was deemed sufficient protection of the individual.[1]

How far the Pilgrims, and later other Puritans, were from a belief in

61

democracy, or the control of the government by the people, is indicated by
John Cotton in his 'Letter to Lord Saye and Seele', written during the 1630's.
God has prescribed rules for the right ordering of the soul and the Commonwealth, "so far as both of them are subordinate to spiritual ends", and yet has
avoided "both the Church's usurpation upon civil jurisdiction, *in ordine ad
spiritualia* [as ordained to the spiritual], and the Commonwealth's invasion
upon ecclesiastical administrations, *in ordine* to civil peace and conformity to
the civil state". The form that God has given Church government is compatible
with any form of Commonwealth. But the best Commonwealth is constructed
closely in accordance with the Church, which is decidedly not a democracy.
"Mr. Hooker doth often quote a saying out of Mr. Cartwright . . . that no
man fashioneth his house to his hangings, but his hangings to his house. It is
better that the Commonwealth be fashioned to the setting forth of God's
house, which is His church, than to accomodate the Church frame to the
civil state. Democracy, I do not conceive, that ever God did ordain as a fit
government either for Church or commonwealth. If the people be governors,
who shall be governed?"[2] Since democracy flies in the face of a common-
sense ordering of governors and governed, and there must be someone who
is definitely the governed, and since it is obviously not the will of God, it
cannot be accepted as a valid form of government. The people, as Church
members, are to choose their governors from among their number. The role
of the Church in the political realm is to prepare "fit instruments both to
rule and to choose rulers", by educating both rulers and ruled to be godly
men, men of virtue and piety. Indeed, only godly men possess the integrity
to use wisely and preserve the liberties they possess in the Commonwealth,
these liberties being (1) to choose all magistrates, and to call them to account
at their General Courts, and (2) to choose such burgesses, every General
Court, as with the magistrate shall make or repeal all laws. The *sine qua non*
of such government is that all citizens be themselves governed by the law of
God, particularly as expressed in the Scripture. The divine scriptural law is
the foundation of the Puritan public philosophy, or what served as such, and
which can be summed up as the belief that government of Commonwealths
should rule in accordance with the will of God. This does not entail democracy, which lacks the necessary distinction between rulers and ruled.

John Winthrop agreed with Cotton that the Puritan Commonwealth had
no business organizing itself as a democracy. In his view the right form of
government, in which magistrates had the power to veto the decisions of the
people's representatives, was a mixed aristocracy, the magistrates forming a
kind of aristocracy of "gifts and experience". This type of government has

Scriptural precedent. "Now if we should change from a mixed aristocracy to a mere democracy, first, we should have no warrant in Scripture for it; there was no such government in Israel. We should hereby voluntarily abase ourselves, and deprive ourselves of that dignity which the providence of God has put upon us, which is a manifest breach of the Fifth Commandment; for a democracy is, among most civil nations, accounted the meanest and worst of all forms of government." [3] Two hundred years later Americans regarded Democracy as the glory of their nation.

Cotton's and Winthrop's regard for Scriptural precedent and the hierarchy of merit, as well as their distaste for democracy was the political theory guiding the foundation of the first colonies. There was, of course, disagreement with this philosophy, almost from the first; for example, Roger Williams was expelled from Massachusetts in 1635 for his disagreement with the Puritan policy of state enforcement of religious intolerance. Williams and his followers founded Providence, Rhode Island, as a haven for liberty of conscience. The form of government they adopted was rather simple and more democratic than the Puritans found tolerable — all the inhabitants were to choose "five disposers" to dispose of public lands as well as other public business.

However, before long even in Massachusetts Bay there was a movement for at least some degree of democracy, partly because the deputies grew restive under the authority of the magistrates who often proved to be less reliably superior in virtue and wisdom than it had been hoped. Or, to consider it from the other point of view, the ordinary colonists gradually came to be less concerned with a zealous cultivation of virtue than were the magistrates. In 1641 the Massachusetts Body of Liberties was drawn up, based on English common law and foreshadowing the Bill of Rights. It begins with a statement that order depends upon protection of what amount to individual rights. "The free fruition of such liberties, immunities, and privileges as humanity, civility, and Christianity call for as due to every man in his place and proportion without impeachment and infringement, has ever been and ever will be the tranquillity and stability of churches and commonwealths; and the denial or deprival thereof, the disturbance if not the ruin of both." [4] There follows a lengthy specification of the rights and liberties of the people which must be protected against arbitrary government. While this was not a truly "democratic" document, it did lead to the 1648 'Book of the General Lawes and Libertyes', which somewhat reduced the power of the magistrates. As the preface to the 1641 document states, the order of churches and commonwealths derives from respect for the liberties, immunities, and privileges that are prescribed for each man by humanity, civility, and Christianity — three sources of universal order. Such rights are due to man, as man, and not as members of a particular church or commonwealth. Although the protection of such rights is not the *raison d'être* of the church and commonwealth, it is a necessary condition of it.

The process of democratization continued slowly but relentlessly in New England, despite the opposition of preachers such as William Hubbard, who in May, 1676, subjected his congregation to an election-day sermon with the self-explanatory title, 'The Happiness of a People in the Wisdom of their Rulers Directing and in Obedience of their Brethren Attending Unto What Israel Ought To Do'. Among the causes of this process were the decline in religious fervor among the colonists, the constant pressure for religious toleration because of the numbers of persistent adherents of other sects infiltrating New England, and an increasing belief that the happiness of a people does not necessarily consist in submission to rulers who may or may not be wise.

Perhaps we might sum up the early American political theory, or public philosophy, insofar as it was one, by saying that government was divinely ordained for the good order of God's holy people, and was itself properly ordered by the virtue of the people and those who ruled them. This order involved the people's respect for the laws decreed by the magistrates, and the magistrates' respect for the rights of the people. The inner dynamism or tension of this period lay between those who felt that the necessary wisdom for good government lay, for the most part, only with the magistrates, and those who felt that the people themselves were capable of governing, rather than simply choosing their governors and hoping that the governors would prove worthy of their choice. This tension, with all its implications, becomes more explicit during the Revolutionary period, with an increasing emphasis on rights.

Between 1685 and 1776 America was introduced to Enlightenment thought, which served greatly to increase the importance of individual rights and to shift the divine legitimation of government to the people themselves, thus replacing theocracy with unscriptural democracy. It was, to be sure, a rather carefully principled and articulate sort of democracy, not simply mob rule. The central document setting forth the meaning of this democracy was, of course, the Declaration of Independence, which did not spring into existence in 1776 out of Thomas Jefferson's solitary reflections, but was instead the concentration of such colonial thinking as we have just seen on the nature and purpose of political society, a process of thought which was certainly influenced but not determined by the political thinking going on in England, and on the Continent.

The increasing concern for rights rather than due submission to the political authorities can be gathered from Samuel Adams' 'The Rights of the Colonists and a List of Infringements and Violations of Rights'. [1772] Adams lists the natural rights of the colonists as those to life, liberty, property, and defense of these, and goes on to say that men have the right to remain in, leave, or return to the State of Nature whenever they please. And "when men enter into Society, it is by voluntary consent; and they have a right to demand and insist upon the performance of such conditions, and previous limitations as form an equitable original compact." [5]

There are two things that should be noted here. The first is that Americans of the latter half of the eighteenth century did not compose or adopt theories about political society simply for the sake of speculation. Political theory such as this did not find expression in America until it was needed to explain and justify a sense of grievance and oppression. A preponderance of political writing during this period is polemical or exhortatory in intent, written not for the scholar but for the obdurate Parliament and King and the aggrieved citizen. While the colonists may have protested against injustice in the name of the rights of Englishmen, those rights were themselves grounded in universal, natural, God-given and inarguable rights of man. As Adams put it, "The absolute Rights of Englishmen, and all freemen in or out of Civil society, are principally, personal security, personal liberty and private property."

The second point is that even though the language of Adams' statement is that of the Enlightenment, particularly John Locke, it constitutes not a break with but a development of the American tradition in its emphasis on protecting the individual against the abuse of political authority. As far back as 1641 we find the Massachusetts 'Body of Liberties' invoking "such liberties, immunities, and privileges as humanity, civility, and Christianity call for as due to every man in his place and proportion without impeachment or infringement". This is not yet the language of natural rights, but the intent is the same — to protect the citizen against the government. On the whole the American tradition of rights is based on the assumption that no man can be presumed to be sufficiently virtuous to be allowed to rule other men without their consent.

It was only when the British government began to challenge the assumptions which the colonists had long held regarding themselves and the meaning and order of their own existence, that philosophically literate men felt called upon to make explicit and universal the philosophical principles upon which the colonies considered themselves as being founded. The claim to the rights of British subjects was gradually transformed, under the weight of British intransigence and the American sense of destiny, to the claim to the rights of men. This was, obviously, not the creation of a public philosophy *ex nihilo*, any more than the ravishing visions of the Revolutionary poets and preachers gestated in isolation from the mind of the society. The spokesmen of the public philosophy, for the most part, expounded the foundations of the society in the eighteenth century, in the language of the eighteenth century, and in the process they virtually completed the language of American public discourse.

The foundation principle is commonly regarded as the Law of Nature or the Will of God, which legislates or decrees human freedom for the sake of human happiness. In his 1775 pamphlet on America's right to legislative autonomy, Alexander Hamilton explained the role of this law of nature in the Western tradition. "Good and wise men, in all ages . . . have supposed, that the Deity, from the relation we stand in to Himself, and to each other, has constituted an eternal and immutable law, which is indispensably obligatory upon all mankind, prior to any human institution whatever." Hamilton quotes Blackstone on this law of nature, which is universally binding and is the standard of validity for all human laws and institutions. This natural law is, then, the basis of the natural rights of mankind, which are concerned with preserving and beautifying human existence. To this end men are given "an inviolable right to personal liberty and safety".[6]

As John Jay explains in his 'Address of the Convention of the Representatives of the State of New York to Their Constituents' [1776], freedom is so essential to man that its preservation is not only a right but a duty. "You and all men were created free, authorized to establish a civil government, for the preservation of your rights against oppression, and the security of that freedom which God hath given you, against the rapacious hand of tyranny and lawlessness. It is, therefore, not only necessary to the well-being of Society, but the duty of every man, to oppose and repel all those, by whatever name or title distinguished, who prostitute the power of Government to destroy the happiness and freedom of the people over whom they may be appointed to rule."[7] Dutiful protection of liberty is very closely related to, if not identical with, virtue, and we find in this Address written by Jay very strong echoes of Winthrop's observation that if the Puritans remained steadfast in their fidelity to the Covenant, ten of them, strengthened by the truth, would be able to defeat a thousand of their enemies, who stood upon the shifting sands of falsehood. And, like Wigglesworth, Jay ascribes the calamities of the colonies to the prevalence of "shameful vices", for "It is a well known truth, that no virtuous people were ever oppressed; and it is also true, that a scourge was never wanting to those of an opposite character . . . " Just as the Jews were oppressed by Egypt, Babylon, Syria, and Rome because of their wickedness, so America is oppressed by Britain as punishment for its guilt in falling away from a sense of duty to God, "If we turn from our sins, [God] will turn from his anger."

As is becoming apparent, this particular address is a traditional combination of civil theology with public philosophy. The first passage quoted is primarily public philosophy insofar as it discusses the principles of the proper order of society and civil government, but this is increasingly surrounded with an aura of Biblical imagery and civil theology, which accompanies the movement of the Address from an appeal to reason to an appeal to emotion, an exhortation to pursue the struggle and return to virtue, for "our cause of God, of human nature and posterity . . . ". At the peroration Jay sounds the persuasive theme of the occidentation of order — Americans are destined to success by the Will of God and the entire course of cosmic order. " . . . Divine Providence will not permit this Western World to be involved in the horrours of slavery. Consider that, from the earliest ages of the world, Religion, Liberty, and Empire, have been bounding their course toward the setting sun. The Holy Gospels are yet to be preached to those western regions, and we have the highest reason to believe that the Almighty will not suffer Slavery and the Gospel to go hand in hand! It cannot, it will not be." [8]

So, by the time of the Revolution, despite the emphasis on natural rights, we find that Americans were still quite concerned with the importance of the virtue of the people as the basis and legitimation of power, as is indicated by the 'Instructions from the Town of Malden, Massachusetts, for a Declaration of Independence', from May 27, 1776. "We are confirmed in the opinion, that the present age would be deficient in their duty to God, their posterity and themselves, if they do not establish an American republic. This is the only form of government which we wish to see established; for we can never be willingly subject to any other King than he who, being possessed of infinite wisdom, goodness and rectitude, is alone fit to possess unlimited power." We might note that where the virtue of the ruler can be presumed upon, no enumeration of rights is felt to be necessary. The movement for listing and protecting rights arose only as the flaws of human political authorities were experienced. An accepted right is a simply an assurance that one man will not have to suffer for the faults or vices of another.

On June 12, 1776, "the representatives of the good people of Virginia" adopted a Declaration of Rights, written by George Mason, "as the basis and foundation of government". This is a systematic presentation of the principles of human existence on which good government must be established, and its influence on the Declaration of Independence is obvious. Section one states "that all men are by nature equally free and independent and have certain inherent rights, of which, when they enter into a state of society, they cannot, by any compact, deprive or divest their posterity; namely, the enjoyment of life and liberty, with the means of acquiring and possessing property, and pursuing and obtaining happiness and safety". The assertion that all men are by nature equally free and independent is made on the basis of reason, as attested by Thomas Jefferson for one, who, in the final draft of the 1775 'Declaration on Taking Arms', closely modelled in this passage on John Dickinson's draft, wrote, "If it was possible for men, who exercise their reason, to believe, that the Divine Author of our existence intended a part of the human race to hold an absolute property in, and an unbounded power over others, marked out by his infinite goodness and wisdom, as the objects of a legal domination never rightfully resistible, however severe and oppressive, the Inhabitants of these Colonies might at least require from the Parliament of Great Britain some evidence, that this dreadful authority over them, has been granted to that body. But a reverence for our great Creator, principles of humanity, and the dictates of common sense, must convince all those who reflect upon the subject, that government was instituted to promote the welfare of mankind, and ought to be administered for the attainment of that end."

The people as a whole, or at least a majority, possesses the sole authoritative voice in the ordering of government because the people alone can be relied upon to possess sufficient wisdom and virtue to provide properly for their own happiness and safety, a conclusion apparent to "common sense". The divine right of the people to self-government is their supreme protection against the danger of suffering because of the *libido dominandi* of men ambitious enough to seize power or greedy enough to wield it for their own purposes, or simply insufficiently wise to be entrusted with power. This right functions as a remedy for the Fall which made human nature somewhat less than perfect, and as such a remedy its efficacy depends upon the extent to which the people themselves constitute an ordering force. This, in turn, depends largely, according to the more pragmatic eighteenth century view, on the potentially disordering self-interests of all the individuals, not so much cancelling each other out, but rather being sublimated into a collective self-interest. It was Hamilton, not Jefferson, who called self-interest "that most powerful incentive of human actions", but it is, albeit disguised, just as essential to Jefferson's thought.

In his *Notes on the State of Virginia*, written in 1781–82, Jefferson discussed this role of the people as best guardians of their own interests. "Every government degenerates when trusted to the rulers of the people alone. The people themselves, therefore, are its only safe depositories; and, to render even them safe, their minds must be improved to a certain degree." Jefferson did not indulge in an uncritical worship of the people – that was reserved for the nineteenth century with its often expansive development of the civil theology. Though they are the "ultimate guardians of their own liberty", they cannot guard their liberty well unless they possess intelligence and knowledge, as well as virtue. Moreover, since, as Jefferson wrote in 1774, "the God who gave us life, gave us liberty at the same time", it may be presumed that the preservation of liberty is as much a duty owed to God as an act of self-interest.

This should give some indication of the state of the public philosophy at the time of the writing of the Declaration of Independence. Among the speculative politicians (as John Adams referred to them) the consensus was that the order of government in which the people possess the supreme power is both the law of nature and the Will of God. Government exists for the happiness of the people, which it secures by protecting their rights to life, liberty, and property. That is, it arbitrates among the self-interests of the citizens. And despite the emphasis and even reliance on self-interest, virtue was always accorded an important and probably decisive role in the attainment of happiness. The public philosophy itself contains a tension between virtue and rights. Perhaps the major question that remained unanswered was to what extent virtue was a matter of disinterested righteousness, and to what extent it might, or should be, tailored to produce the sort of public happiness that was desired. Or, to put the question another way, should the society seek first the Kingdom of God in the confident expectation that all else would be given to it, or should it seek first its own more immediate goals and revise the demands of the Kingdom of God accordingly? This is, as has been pointed out, the basic point at issue between the public philosophy and the civil theology.

In 1776 the Declaration of Independence began its career as the authoritative formulation of the American public philosophy. The Declaration was not, of course, intended to be primarily a philosophical treatise, but rather a statement and justification of the reasons why the American statesmen reluctantly found reconciliation with England impossible. Nevertheless, their basic grievance was what the Declaration proclaims as the violation of their rights, not as Englishmen, but as men, that is, the violation of universal principles of political order and human nature. The significance of these principles is that they establish the Declaration as the first founding document of the American national public philosophy, the principles of a universal order on which the country is founded specifically as a nation.

The Declaration can easily be divided into three sections: first, a statement of the general principles, the alleged violation of which by George III has impelled the American people to the separation; second, a list of more specific grievances; and third, a recapitulation of the beginning. The familiar opening statement indicates that the Declaration is addressed to mankind, which is very much in the tradition of American self-understanding as responsible for its actions to the entire world, and also indicates that the Declaration has been written as an explanation to rational men of the reasons why the action of the colonies is both rational and necessary. According to divine and natural law the American people have a right to a "separate and equal station", the ability to exercise their own sovereignty. A key word in this opening paragraph is "necessary", that is, the American people find independence not only desirable, but essential for conformity to the principles regulating human life.

The principles which necessitate independence are "self-evident truths", universally applicable, but not yet universally accepted. The justification of independence by ineluctable truths provides American independence and order with an irrefutable foundation. These self-evident truths are new in the sense of being newly discovered, and they are, as embodied in the Declaration, prophetically proclaimed by the people of the United States of America, the nation which will embody them in its political existence. These truths seem to be five in number: (1) all men are created equal; (2) all men are endowed by their Creator with certain unalienable rights; (3) among those unalienable rights are life, liberty, and the pursuit of happiness; (4) to secure these un-alienable rights, governments are instituted among men and receive their just powers from the consent of the governed; (5) whenever any form of government becomes destructive of these unalienable rights it is the further, presumably unalienable, right of the people to alter or abolish such govern-ment and institute a new government, laying its foundation on such principles, and organizing its powers in such form as to them shall seem most likely to effect their safety and happiness. The underlying theme of the Declaration is order based on a proper understanding of human nature. The assumption is that human existence will be disordered if social orders are constructed on the belief that some men are created booted and spurred to rule others, and that it is quite permissible to deprive an inferior of his life or liberty or ability to pursue his own happiness. Order can be maintained, the citizens can be free and happy only if the governing principle is virtue and law, not men. No individual man can have the right to govern another, simply because as a fallible human being he lacks the necessary wisdom and virtue. Only God possesses the wisdom and virtue required of a monarch.

Moreover, self-evident truths are derived from reverence for God, principles of humanity, and common sense, all of which are, or should be common attributes of mankind along with reason. On the whole, we might infer the presupposition that the sort of government which the colonists upheld is divinely ordained, or, in the Puritan phrase, "according to the mind of God". We might also note the suggestion that the function of government is essentially providential in that it is "instituted to protect the welfare of mankind", and so it participates in Divine Providence.

One might say that the disorders of the existence of America caused, or allegedly caused by the lack of wisdom and virtue on the part of the King and Parliament of England have become so intolerable that endurance of them can no longer be justified before God and a world that expects the best of the American City upon a Hill, and thus it becomes necessary for the American people to abolish the British government as their government and replace it with a government more likely to effect their safety and happiness. The grievances against the King are essentially that he has attempted to usurp the place of the people as the source of the rights of government — he has deprived the people of their rights instead of protecting their rights.

The last paragraph, beginning, "We, therefore, the representatives of the United States of America . . . ", contains an appeal to "the Supreme Judge of the world for the rectitude" of the intentions of "the good people" of the colonies. Such separation is not only necessary, it is righteous, and such righteousness is grounded in the sense of righteousness, a suggestion that the separation and establishment of an independent government is divinely ordained. Further, the representatives are acting in the name of and by the authority of the good people of the colonies, the righteous, perhaps even the Chosen People, who are seeking the greatest possible degree of earthly happiness. The representatives of these good people "solemnly publish and declare, that these united colonies are, and of right ought to be, free, and independent states". This declaration restores the harmony between what is and what ought to be: Independence is not simply desirable, but is necessitated by an adherence to an underlying, presumably divine, order, one according to the laws of nature and of nature's God. Hence the concluding reference to a firm reliance on the protection of Divine Providence. The righteousness of their cause, grounded in the requirements of human nature, entitles the colonists to appeal for divine assistance in their endeavors. Therefore, while there does seem to be a divine sanction for government, it is mediated through the people, whose task it is to construct a public order according to the mind of God.

That the Declaration of Independence rapidly became the paradigm of American political ideas and ideals, as well as the major source of the public philosophy, is apparent from a survey of post-Declaration state constitutions. Virtually all of them reiterate in some form, often direct quotation, the ideas basic to the Declaration as a mark of their orthodoxy. For instance, the Massachusetts Constitution contains 'A Declaration of the Rights of the Inhabitants of the Commonwealth of Massachusetts', of which Article I states, "All men are born free and equal, and have certain natural, essential, and unalienable rights; among which may be reckoned the right of enjoying and defending their lives and liberties; that of acquiring, possessing, and protecting property; in fine, that of seeking and obtaining their safety and happiness." This formulation returns to that used for the first draft of the Declaration of Independence, which mentioned property rather than the pursuit of happiness as one of man's unalienable rights.

One of the most common provisions of state constitutions is that it is the duty "of all men in society, publicly, and at stated seasons, to worship the SUPREME BEING, the great Creator and Preserver of the universe". The reason for this is that "the happiness of a people, and the good order and preservation of civil government, essentially depend upon piety, religion, and morality." Accordingly, there is a form of public cult encouraged. This is not, after the Bill of Rights, a government-controlled cult, but takes the more limited form of each citizen's publicly worshipping God according to his own conscience. It is an American conviction that the good Christian is the good citizen.

The common bond of piety, public worship, and the public beliefs of the members of the commonwealth is the sense of order, partaking of both civil theology and public philosophy: as the citizens worship for the sake of becoming better men, and for the good of their relationship with God as a precondition of public order, it is more public philosophy, but as men worship for the sake of becoming better citizens it is more civil theology. There is, of course, no sharp distinction between the two. God is to be worshipped as the Supreme Being, the great Creator and Preserver of the Universe, that is, the source of order. It is God who has brought the universe out of chaos and continues to preserve it from chaos, and piety, religion, morality, and public worship represent a public commitment to the preservation of order, both in America and in the cosmos of which America is the center. Public worship unites the order of the society with the order of the universe through the beliefs and dispositions of the individual citizens.

In general, then, the principles of the Declaration of Independence form a core of political beliefs, held by the citizens of all the states, and publicly proclaimed. They are also beliefs regarding the principles of universal order: there is nothing in the public philosophy which would limit its significance or application to the United States alone. And even though these beliefs are philosophical principles we do not find here a pure public philosophy. These principles have a civil theology orientation in that they are held for the sake of the society — they have a certain pragmatic character. Nevertheless, they are universal principles of divinely ordained order according to which America is paradigmatically ordered for the sake of all mankind.

The Declaration of Independence was the culmination of the stage in the development of the public philosophy that was concerned with the struggle for independence, and as a vital part of this struggle the Declaration focusses on the rights of the citizens. The next stage came in the Constitution through the necessity of establishing an order of American existence that would endure, and the philosophical principles underlying the Constitution focus on the virtue, or lack of virtue, of the citizens.

By far the best explanation of the theoretical assumptions of the Constitution is to be found in *The Federalist*, which one recent commentator has called "the only original work of political theory ever produced by a revolution and composed by successful revolutionaries". The primary intent of *The Federalist* is the very political purpose which the Greeks called *peitho*, or persuasion, in this case by an appeal to reason. Madison, Hamilton, and Jay set out to persuade the good people of America that the Constitution was altogether reasonable — not perfect, or ideal, but flowing from and reconciling circumstances and sound principles. In the process Publius (the collective *nom de plume*) also reconciled governing philosophical principles, consisting largely of a philosophical anthropology with a civil theology that is an outgrowth of it and has characteristics of both the ecumenic and eschatological types.

For Publius the linchpin of the arguments in favor of the new Constitution is the Union, not itself a theoretical concept but rather more a symbol for the American order as a whole as well as the indispensable foundation for such an order. The importance of the Union is not simply the prevention of squabbles between separate regional confederations of states — this is its importance on the level of rational, even common-sense argument — but, far more profoundly, a decision whether or not the citizens of the states would establish themselves in history as one people. In this light, the defect of the Articles of Confederation was that it was little more than a treaty of friendship among thirteen sovereign peoples. On the other hand, even though the political forces of this first confederation favored separate, sovereign states, this state of affairs itself remained in unstable relationship with more powerful forces inclining the citizens of all the states toward "a more perfect Union". The weight of the tradition was toward one unified nation.

The paramount, self-evident importance of the Union for the future of the American people is indicated by Hamilton at the beginning of the first paper. "After an unequivocal experience of the inefficiency of the subsisting federal government, you are called upon to deliberate on a new Constitution for the United States of America. The subject speaks its own importance; comprehending in its consequences nothing less than the existence of the UNION, the safety and welfare of the parts of which it is composed, the fate of an empire in many respects the most interesting in the world." Publius' arguments for the Constitution as necessary for the preservation and prosperity of the Union are based upon the civil theology, which implied that in order to fulfill their destiny the Americans must be one people. Evidence of.Publius' reliance on the civil theology is not difficult to find. Hamilton continues by explaining his restrained reference to America as an "empire in many respects the most interesting in the world". "It has been frequently remarked that it seems to have been reserved to the people of this country, by their conduct and example, to decide the important question, whether societies of men are really capable or not of establishing good government from reflection and choice, or whether they are forever destined to depend for their political constitutions on accident and force. If there be any truth in the remark, the crisis at which we are arrived may with propriety be regarded as the era in which that decision is to be made; and a wrong election of the part we shall act may, in this view, deserve to be considered as the general misfortune of mankind."

Hamilton thus invokes a somewhat secularized version of the Puritan civil theology. The question whether men are capable of establishing good government from reflection and choice is a descendent of the Puritan question whether men can live according to the mind of God, a question decided by the covenant of the assembly. The Puritans regarded their own time as the divinely appointed era in which this question was to be resolved. And Hamilton's statement that an error could be considered "as the general misfortune of mankind" is a rather etiolated version of what the Puritans regarded as the consequences of failure. This responsibility for the welfare of mankind adds "the inducements of philanthropy to those of patriotism" in considering the Constitution. "Happy will it be if our choice should be directed by a judicious estimate of our true interests, unperplexed and unbiased by considerations not connected with the public good." In addition to the philanthropic, there are reasons touching nearer to American ambitions as a political City upon a Hill, which would indicate a serious reappraisal of the degree of responsibility involved in the decision for or against the Constitution. "By a steady adherence to the Union, we may hope, ere long, to become the arbiter of Europe in America, and be able to incline the balance of European competition in this part of the world as our interest may dictate."

This invocation of the civil theology tradition is designed to derive the arguments for the Constitution from the very roots of the American self-understanding. If Americans are whom they have always thought themselves to be, the adoption of the Constitution is the only rational, consistent course they can follow. However, this truth of order and American identity is a challenge to individual and local interests and requires some sacrifice of self-interest in the interest of the good of the whole and the discovery of truth. "The plan offered to our deliberations affects too many particular interests, innovates upon too many local institutions, not to involve in its discussion a variety of objects foreign to its merits and of views, passions and prejudices little favorable to the discovery of truth."

From this basis in the civil theology Hamilton later presents arguments for the Union from a practical point of view, such as the disorderly proclivities of human nature. Only a believer in Utopia could expect that either separate States or several confederacies could exist without conflict. "To presume a want of motives for such contests, as an argument against their existence, would be to forget that men are ambitious, vindictive, and rapacious. To look for a continuation of harmony between a number of independent, unconnected sovereignties in the same neighborhood, would be to disregard the uniform course of human events, and to set at defiance the accumulated experience of ages." We find Hamilton in this passage laying out what has become a central problem in American thought — the tension between the universal ideal of order which America embodies and its ability to live according to that order, for even the Chosen People is still composed of people. Although the important question of man's capacity for self-government may have been reserved for America to decide, in Hamilton's sober view the country represents no radical departure from the normal course of human experience. Indeed, perhaps the only hope of success lies in a judicious appraisal of accumulated human experience. America is bound by the cords of common humanity to the past as well as to the rest of the contemporary world. A choice based on America's true interests is also based on the true interests of mankind, which indicates America's role as a representative nation. America's paradigmatic role and mission are those of first embodying and perfecting the best order of human existence.

The importance of the Union advances from the practically expedient to the sacred in Madison's riposte to those who felt, for whatever reasons, that a Union could not endure. "No, my countrymen, shut your ears against this unhallowed language. Shut your hearts against the poison which it conveys; the kindred blood which flows in the veins of American citizens, the mingled blood which they have shed in defence of their sacred rights, consecrate their Union and excite horror at the idea of their becoming aliens, rivals, enemies." (14) Kindred blood and mingled blood, symbols of life, the life of Americans, consecrate the Union to that life, so that disparagement of the Union becomes "unhallowed", almost sacrilegious. The sacredness of the Union is not humanly or arbitrarily determined, but derives from kindred blood and sacred rights commonly defended. Therefore, the ultimate source of the sacredness of the Union is the source of the blood and rights, which source must be Divine Providence, or the Creator, or the Great Governor of the universe. The Union is, in a sense, transcendently sacred for the "political safety and happiness" of the American people. Hamilton calls it "that sacred knot which binds the people of America together". (15)

This rootedness of the Union in a trans-human source, in Providence, or in nature, is apparent in the second paper, ascribed to John Jay. Jay first presents a survey of the geographical conditions that incline toward Union, the fact "that independent America was not composed of detached and distant territories, but that one connected fertile, wide-spreading country was the portion of our Western sons of liberty". He then points out the numerous sociological factors — common ancestry, language, religion, manners, customs, principles of government as well as the Revolutionary War — that tend toward Union and seem to indicate that Union is the will of Providence. Jay described America as a kind of Garden of Eden, a Promised Land given by Providence to the Chosen People, the "Western sons of Liberty". The Union is indispensable if America is to fulfill its destiny. Jay points out that from the beginning of their national existence the American people have been almost instinctively aware of the importance of the Union. "A strong sense of the value and blessings of the union induced the people, at a very early period, to

institute a federal government to preserve and perpetuate it. They formed it
almost as soon as they had a political existence . . . " (2) The "very early
period", the beginning of American political existence, was some twelve years
before Jay's writing, at the time of the Declaration of Independence.

Among the blessings of and persuasive arguments for the Union is American
prosperity, prosperity being a traditional manifestation of godliness and the
correct political order. "It is worthy of remark that not only the first, but
every succeeding Congress, as well as the late convention have invariably
joined with the people in thinking that the prosperity of America depended
on its Union. . . . I sincerely wish that it may be as clearly foreseen by every
good citizen, that whenever the dissolution of the Union arrives, America will
have reason to exclaim, in the words of the poet: 'Farewell! A long Farewell
to all my Greatness.'" (2) The Union will eventually become one of the central symbols of the civil theology, a primary manifestation of the intentions,
and a linchpin of the workings of Divine Providence on behalf of America and
mankind.

But even with their emphasis on the Union, Hamilton, Madison, and Jay
are a long way from adhering to the kind of civil theology found among the
more "imaginative" patriots of the time. Hamilton explicitly warns against
the danger inherent in the apocalyptic forms of civil-theology symbolism,
describing them as "ideal theories" for promising Americans that they will
escape the human condition as it has been known everywhere else. "Is it not
time to awake from the deceitful dream of a golden age, and to adopt as a
practical maxim for the direction of our political conduct that we, as well as
the other inhabitants of the globe, are yet remote from the happy empire of
perfect wisdom and perfect virtue?" (6) Just as Jefferson in the Declaration of
Independence, Hamilton is placing the states and their actions "in the course
of human events", which is uniform, that is, human nature does not change
and America will be liable to the same disorders that have plagued other
societies. Over against the apocalyptic and utopian speculations of those who
proclaimed that America was to be the site of the New Jerusalem, or was to
usher in the final and glorious Golden Age of the world, Hamilton places
the cold, hard facts of human nature and experience and the necessity and
limitations of government. Men are driven by a *libido dominandi*, which
necessitates government to constrain them to conform to the principles of
order which serve as the public philosophy. And "in framing a government
which is to be administered by men over men, the great difficulty lies in this:
You must first enable the government to control the governed; and in the
next place oblige it to control itself. A dependence on the people is, no doubt,

the primary control on the government; but experience has taught mankind
the necessity of auxiliary precautions." These precautions consist in remedy-
ing imperfect motives by providing "opposite and rival interests" to balance
the interests already present, and according to Hamilton this procedure
"might be traced through the whole system of human affairs, private as well
as public".

Government both manifests and remedies the imperfections of human
nature. However, Publius steers a middle course and regards human nature as
also possessing a number of qualities which "justify a certain portion of
esteem and confidence", and it is on these good qualities that Republican
government is based. And so Hamilton finds the "supposition of universal
venality in human nature is little less an error in political reasoning than the
supposition of universal rectitude. The institution of delegated power implies
that there is a portion of virtue and honour among mankind which may be a
reasonable foundation of confidence; and experience justifies the theory."
This, then, is the philosophy of human nature contained in the American
~ Constitution. It is by building its public order on the solid foundation of such
truth that America will fulfill its destiny by proving the possibility of self-
government. This is the aspect of the public philosophy which concentrates
not on the responsibility of the government to protect the rights of the
governed, but on the responsibility of the citizens to be at least moderately
virtuous so as to protect the government from faction.

The importance of *The Federalist* in the present context is its articulation
of a balanced understanding of both public philosophy and civil theology.
The principles of the public philosophy are fairly easy to discern, being the
essential preconditions and structures of a republican form of government
constructed according to reason and justice, as well as a realistic appraisal of
human nature. This is a universal public philosophy, which in itself neither
distinguishes America from any other nation which might choose to adopt it
nor provides America with a unique position in the structure of time or the
course of human events. What does distinguish the United States is the fact
that it is the first country, at least in modern times, to establish its public
order upon such republican principles.

To be more precise, there are two aspects of the civil theology in evidence
here. First, the sense of mission, the sense that "it seems to have been reserved
to the people of this country" to decide whether or not men are capable of
establishing "good government from reflection and choice", whether it is
possible for reason to hold sway over accident and violence and passion.
America is the City upon a Hill, the country whose action and choices are

"philanthropic", crucial for the efficacy of the public philosophy. The Union is essential to offset the factional, disorderly tendencies of human nature. Accordingly, it must be seen as necessary, as logical, and as providentially ordained, as sacred — it must, indeed, be an object of religious devotion so as to render it unquestionable, unchallengeable. However, under both these aspects the civil theology is subordinated to the principles of the public philosophy. To put it another way, while the civil theology provides the public philosophy with an historical significance, the possibilities envisioned by the civil theology are limited to those compatible with the public philosophy. It should be pointed out that even though the philosophy of Publius must be accepted as public philosophy insofar as it is, according to a tolerably authoritative interpretation, the philosophy of the Constitution, it was to become, for the most part, latent in the American tradition, while the self-evident truths of the Declaration of Independence were to become the explicit and active principles of the public philosophy. The disadvantage of this state of affairs was that the eloquent but philosophically non-rigorous formulations of the Declaration were inherently less capable than *The Federalist* of exercising a restraining influence over the civil theology's predilection for flights of fancy, as occurred in the nineteenth century.

REFERENCES

[1] "American political society expresses itself, from an early moment, in the symbol of the supreme legislature on the one hand, and on the other of a higher law that the supreme legislature must apply to day-to-day problems. It does not express itself in terms of individual rights; or at least not in terms of individual rights against the legislature, individual rights that the legislature must respect, must not violate." Willmoore Kendall and George W. Carey, *The Basic Symbols of the American Political Tradition*, Baton Rouge, Louisiana State University Press, 1970, p. 59.

[2] John Cotton, 'Democracy Detrimental to Church and State,' *AA*, Vol. I, pp. 152–53.

[3] John Winthrop, 'A Negative View of Democracy', *AA*, Vol. I, p. 169.

[4] *Massachusetts Body of Liberties, AA*, Vol. I, p. 163. It might be mentioned that the 1641 version of the Massachusetts Body of Liberties may or may not have been adopted. It did, however, serve as a draft version of the 1648 'Lawes and Liberties of Massachusetts' which was adopted.

[5] Samuel Adams, 'Report of the Committee of Correspondence to the Boston Town Meeting, Nov. 20, 1772', in *American Ideas*, Vol. I, pp. 176–77.

[6] Alexander Hamilton, 'The Farmer Refuted, etc.', in *The Papers of Alexander Hamilton*, ed. by Harold C. Syrett, New York, Columbia University Press, 1961, Vol. I, pp. 87–88.

[7] John Jay, 'Address of the Convention of the Representatives of the State of New

York to Their Constituents, 1776', in *The Correspondence and Public Papers of John Jay 1763–1826*, ed. by Henry P. Johnston, New York, Da Capo Press, 1971, Vol. I, p. 103.
[8] *Ibid*. pp. 118–119.

CHAPTER V

THE CIVIL THEOLOGY: MYTHS OF DESTINY

We have, by the grace of God and the miracle of Providence, survived the buffetings of fate, the ill-chance of misfortune, the hatred and infections of Europe, the malevolence of kings and tyrants, in a half-century of unparalleled progress. We have, as a nation, fulfilled the initial promise of our destination, pledged by those brave and noble men who first set foot on the soil of Massachusetts and Virginia; and we have made the New World bloom in freedom, justice, and the sweetness of right. It is now to the future we look, to the next half-century's fulfillment, for our glorious destiny, ordained by God and Nature since the beginnings of time.

Ohio Orator, 1826[1]

The underlying theme of most American myth-making during the nineteenth century was an impatient preoccupation with American destiny that produced a gradually increasing concern with the projected civil theology cosmos almost to the exclusion of the public philosophy. As the above quotation indicates, by 1826 many Americans were looking forward eagerly to the divinely ordained glorious destiny of their country. The pledge of the earliest settlers that America should be as a City upon a Hill had been fulfilled magnificently, or so Americans felt. But this was no longer enough. The men of the nineteenth century could see farther into the future, and most of them saw glories and achievements beyond the visions of the seventeenth century.

This was, of course, no radical departure from the vision of the Puritans, merely a more ravishing elaboration and concentration of the belief that America was God's country and at least in the realm of myth-making a much increased tendency to reduce piety to democracy and nationalism. If progress toward perfection was the tonic theme of American self-translation into

81

myth, democracy was the dominant theme. Such democracy was not simply one form of government among others, specifically rule by the majority of the people, but a mythic participation in divine and cosmic order. According to the myth, the American nation stood high in the order of being and was God's chosen nation because it was a democracy.

With a few rare exceptions the rapturously and religiously apocalyptic version of American destiny current during the eighteenth century seems to have died out during the nineteenth century, being replaced by a generally more secularized myth of America's salvific destiny. While it is impossible to separate all the explorations of the meaning of America into well-defined categories, it is possible to discern several trends that elaborated and developed the various possibilities latent in the civil theology symbolism. We can do no more here than indicate the major variations that shaped American self-reflective myth-making during the nineteenth century and, on the whole, developed the civil theology without much reflection on the public philosophy.

There was, for example, a continuation of the belief in American history as governed by Providence. In 1834 George Bancroft published *A History of the United States*, with a purpose of justifying the ways of Providence to Americans. "It is the object of the present work", as Bancroft declared at the beginning, to explain "how the change in the condition of our land has been accomplished; and, as the fortunes of a nation are not controlled by blind destiny, to follow the steps, by which a favoring Providence, calling our institutions into being, has conducted the country to its present happiness and glory."[2] Bancroft proceeds to recount the Puritan understanding of themselves and their mission, the favorableness and "infinite mercies" of Providence, their own position as "favorites with heaven", as the "depositories of purest truth", selected "to kindle in the wilderness the beacon of pure religion which should illuminate the entire civilized world". Bancroft's interpretation is less explicitly Christian than the Puritans' own self-understanding, but it is an attempt to inspire Americans with an unshakable faith in their divine election.

Some six years before the Civil War, Henry Reed embodied this idea in two lectures entitled *The Union*, which he delivered with the general purpose of reawakening and reinforcing devotion to the Union at a time when it was seriously threatened. His purpose in delivering the lectures was that of showing that American history is not simply the work of the American people, a work which might be altered at will, but is instead the work and design of a transcendent providential deity, in which case America should not be tampered with by mere human beings. "It seems to me that there is no consideration better calculated to deepen in the mind of every reflective citizen a reverence for the Union than a just sense of its origin; . . . It was the work of time, the natural consequences of events, a growth from circumstances, or whatever other phrase may be used as a substitute for an express acknowledgment of a Providence in the destinies of mankind. It is not possible to trace the Union to any premeditated plan, the idea of any one man, or the concert of any body of men. . . . In truth the Union was not made, it *grew.* . . . The Union grew as the forest grows, and the seed was not sown by man's hand." [3] Reed's interpretation is very similar to that explained in *The Federalist*: the existence of the Union was obviously intended by Providence for the sake of man's welfare, and even immanent redemption; such a Union is essential to America's ability to fulfill its divinely ordained role, indeed the Union is part of that role. Because of this divine origin, treason to the Union is more deeply the "guilt of thankless impiety", for "this Union was the work of God". Reed was not particularly concerned with prophesying a glorious future for America; rather his purpose was essentially conservative — to strengthen the forces necessary for the preservation of the Union, concentrating on one central symbol of the civil theology, Providence, as well as introducing a note of racial or ethnic pride: the task of establishing "the highest form of political life" was reserved for the English-speaking people.

Although Reed's lectures seem to have faded into obscurity in our own time, around the turn of the century they did succeed in inspiring Robert Ellis Thompson to write his own interpretation of Providence in American history, *The Hand of God in American History — A Study of National Politics.* Far more than Reed, Thompson is very much concerned with the future, and with "the vocation of America". What interest he has in the past expresses itself in the repetition of what had become, by 1902, almost clichés, such as the traditional encomium to Washington, and the observation that Providence "seems to have kept the whole continent from discovery until Europe had reached the point of social development at which its people were competent to become successful emigrants", and Thompson does not overlook the traditional casting of America in the image of Israel: " . . . natural rights are the rights essential to the completeness of our human nature. . . . They are defined in the second table of the law which God gave to the chosen nation. . . . That law defines the foundations of national life for all time." [4]

The last seven Commandments are the public philosophy, forming the foundation of national life for all times and all nations. "The Bible is the handbook of politics", and in an earlier work, *De Civitate Dei: The Divine*

Order of Human Society, Thompson proclaimed the Hebrew nation the type of all national life. In this same book he discussed the importance of Christian as opposed to secular education in inculcating in the citizens the proper "reverence for the public order and the established authority". Divine authority is the supreme sanction of national order. America exists and participates in a Christian cosmic order which, for Thompson, manifests itself in democracy, both political and economic. "The republic will have realized its destiny when it has shown the world that no wreck of the historic forms of society is required to satisfy the reasonable demands of the many to share in the material and intellectual results of the social movement." [5] The social movement involved here is the Progressive movement, which aimed at economic democracy in the face of increasing capitalist accretion of wealth. This became identified in the minds of its adherents with the destiny of America — the equal distribution of wealth so that all men might participate to much the same degree in the sources of material being.

There are two other spokesmen for the providential view of history whom we should mention before going on to other areas: Horace Bushnell and Isaac Wise. Bushnell, in a sermon shortly after the end of the Civil War explained that it had been the fault of the American people, that is, specifically the Southerners, to regard the government as a merely human invention which they could alter or abolish at will. But "Government is now become providential — no more a mere creature of our human will, but a grandly moral affair." It is obvious that this clashes somewhat with the tenet of the Declaration of Independence that the government is founded by and upon the consent of the people, and that the people retain the right, if not the duty, to alter or abolish this government whenever they find such compatible with their best interests. It was actually the Civil War that established the limitations of the principle of self-determination — that it should not be a basis on which the country would be fragmented into a multitude of sectional interests. The principle serves the public philosophy only so long as it helps to unify, for the Union has a superior place in the public philosophy and civil theology. There will simply never be any occasion, as was accepted after the war, to alter or abolish the federal government according to any "natural right". The government is sacred. "Henceforth ... we are to revere [government's] sacred rights, rest in its sacred immunities, and have it even as the Caesar whom our Christ himself requires us to obey." [6] Now it is the government which possesses the rights to be reverenced and protected, and it is the people's sacred duty to obey. The seemingly miraculous preservation of the Union indicates God's vital interest in America's destiny, and the impossibility of man's defeating the divine will.

Another venture into traditional American symbolism of progress and providence is that of Issac Wise, in his remarks on *Our Country's Place in History* from January, 1869. After announcing that "history is Providence realized", he goes on to discuss America's destiny. "This destiny which a nation realizes in the designs of Providence, is its place in history. Furthermore, however different the destinies of the various nations, they are similar in one chief characteristic, whose name is PROGRESS." [7] For America, liberty is progress: "Liberty is the cause, progenitor, preserver and protector of all the blessings which we enjoy and impart to others. ... Liberty is our place in history, our national destiny, our ideal, the very soul of our existence." Liberty is in fact the substance of American order. In Wise's understanding it is far more a mythic symbol than a concrete political reality, for it supplies the metaphysical dynamism for America's existence. America then is the axis of human progress through her incarnation of liberty, which will insure America's glorious destiny. "Nothing can arrest our progress, nothing drag down our country from her high place in history, except our own wickedness working a wilful desertion of our destiny, the desertion from the idea of liberty. As long as we cling to this idea, we will be in honor, glory, wealth, and prosperity." [8] Fidelity to the spiritual ideal manifests itself in worldly glory and prosperity. None of Wise's ideas or symbols are new: all are derived from the matrix of American thought and simply combined in new ways. His concern with America's place in history is simply a civil-theology concern. In agreement with many of his predecessors, Wise postulates the designs of Providence as realized in human progress toward perfection.

Indeed, the idea of progress, in one form or another, seems to be central to the reflection of the nineteenth century, that is, even more significantly than in the previous two centuries. Emerson, the "high priest" of the American philosophy of individualism, was preoccupied with the idea of America as the New Beginning, as well as the related idea of America as the last attempt by Providence to ameliorate the human condition. Among his early poems are several which develop the symbolism of America as the rich West to which Empire shall come, bringing Glory and Grandeur in its wake.

> Heave gently, dark Ocean! thou bear'st on thy breast
> The hope of mankind to its home in the West
> If the tempest should bury that ship in the deep
> The fortunes of nations beside it should sleep ... [9]

Even more than America, however, each individual man is a new beginning, or, as Emerson put it, "an inlet into the deeps of Reason", a "revolution", because he is not bound to the tradition but is free to venture forth on his own. It is not the case that all thoughts have been written, that there is nothing new under the sun. America is such a radically new beginning that all past knowledge pales into ignorance – the entire universe is yet to be known. Therefore it is America's destiny to recreate, or perhaps create the world through advancing "into a new and more excellent social state than history has recorded". "It seems too easy to America to inspire and express the most expansive and human spirit; new-born, free, healthful, strong, the land of the laborer, of the democrat, of the philanthropist, of the believer, of the saint, who should speak for the human race." [10] Emerson and his contemporaries lived in the very morn of America's days – America is itself the denial and antithesis of tradition, habit, custom. Since the past is negated, and America is the future, it would seem to be the case that the history of America becomes the history of the world, a mythic idea which is at least subliminal in all American symbolism.

However, there is another, distinct branch of thought within the civil theology which prescribes America's role as one of active spreading of its order and institutions. This branch found its primary manifestation in the issues of Manifest Destiny and Imperialism. The term "Manifest Destiny" itself apparently was first used by John L. O'Sullivan in an editorial on the annexation of Texas in July, 1845. However, it was not until five months later, through its reappearance in an editorial on the Oregon controversy with Great Britain, that the phrase became popular. The editorial, 'The True Title', which appeared in the New York Morning News on December 27, 1845, purported to settle the issue by an appeal to the obviously irrefutable claim of the United States to the Northwest Pacific coast. "And that claim [to Oregon] is by the right of our manifest destiny to over spread and to possess the whole of the continent which Providence has given for the development of the great experiment of liberty and federative self-government entrusted to us. It is a right such as that of the tree in the space of air and earth suitable for the full expansion of its principle and destiny of growth – such as that of the stream to the channel required for the still accumulating volume of its flow." [11]

It was obvious to O'Sullivan that an order as perfect as that of the United States must advance to the uttermost possible limits. Were it not for the oceans, it might well have been the Manifest Destiny of the United States to overspread and to possess the whole of the earth. Certainly there were those who spoke of taking over Canada and Mexico, and even all of South America, but such fanatic imperialists were fortunately in the minority. However, the sense of this destiny lies in an irresistible natural life-force, a force beyond human control which can only be accepted and accommodated. This is a destiny contained within the very nature of American order, a destiny bestowed by Providence. Such a claim is a departure from the tradition of international law, which does not and cannot recognize "destiny" as a valid basis for territorial claims. In fact, Americans wanted Oregon, and simply developed a myth to transform their desires into the will of God, although this process may not have been conscious.

A second assumption is that order is still renewing itself by spreading to the Western extremities of habitable land. The "noble young empire of the Pacific" will be the final perfection of order, since farther Westward progress is impossible. Because America has already been entrusted with the final perfection of order, all Western settlement must be under the aegis of the American government. For another nation to appropriate to itself the Western part of North America would be to deprive America of the crown of its perfection. The idea of Manifest Destiny, although serving to rationalize America's ordinary desire for the wealth of natural resources in the West, does not originate so much in greed as in the myth of the American civil theology which was always a translation of American aspirations into the order of the cosmos. Expansion to the Pacific seems to have been vital for the American sense of identity.

O'Sullivan, somewhat of a Jeffersonian, had founded *The United States Magazine and Democratic Review* in 1837. As editor he wrote a salutatory for the first issue extolling the democratic principle, its role in America and its relation to Christianity. O'Sullivan regarded the *Review* as necessary "at the present critical stage of our national progress, for the advocacy of that high and holy *democratic principle* which was designed to be the fundamental element of the new social and political system created by the 'American experiment . . . '" In order to clarify the true meaning of democracy, O'Sullivan presents "the cardinal principles of political faith", the first of which is the principle of democratic republicanism. "We have an abiding confidence in the virtue, intelligence, and full capacity for self-government of the great mass of our people − our industrious, honest, manly, intelligent millions of freemen"[12] − this was a belief in the virtue of the people that somewhat exceeded the view of *The Federalist*.

The upshot of this abiding confidence is the belief that the popular opinion and will should be "the animating and moving spirit of all legislation", for "the vigilance of public opinion . . . is the true conservative principle of our institutions." Apart from the difficulties involved in concrete application, "the democratic theory is perfect and harmonious in all its parts". Essential to this harmony is the Jeffersonian principle that "the best government is that which governs least". Order is largely spontaneous, not imposed by governmental decrees. In fact, government, with its "fostering hands" is apt to bungle the job. "The natural laws which will establish themselves and find their own level are the best laws." This is designed as an analogy of the divine government of the Creator who, in ruling the physical world, relies upon "fundamental principles of spontaneous action and self-regulation". Order, then, would seem to require very little energy to maintain.

Thus, democracy is "the true theory of government", the "elixir of poliitcal life". It not only "contains the idea of full and fearless faith in the providence of the Creator", but it is "essentially involved in Christianity, of which it has been well said that its pervading spirit of democratic equality among men is its highest fact, and one of its most radiant internal evidences of the divinity of its origin".[13] America has not yet, of course, achieved perfect democracy – Christianity and the democratic principle are to guide mankind's development "down the long vista of future years".

This theory of democracy is an abstract political theory, consisting of the eternal truths of human order, of mankind's harmony with the order of the cosmos. It is as vital to human happiness as is Christianity, which has become the spiritual, specifically religious form of democracy. Accordingly, the "noble mission" was entrusted to America as the City upon a Hill, the mission "of going before the nations of the world as the representative of the democratic principle and as the constant living exemplar of its results. . . . For democracy is the cause of humanity. It has faith in human nature. It believes in its essential equality and fundamental goodness. . . . It is the cause of Christianity."[14] Democracy, like Christianity, is the cause of the spontaneous regeneration of the world and of the human soul, and it embodies the vision of Deutero-Isaiah of a world of perfect order and harmony.

Not surprisingly, such a view of America's "noble mission" and ideal foundation involved a rather high degree of nationalism, an expectation that, as O'Sullivan wrote in 1839, America was "destined to become the birthplace of a new society, constructed in a new spirit and on a new plan, attaining the highest reach of civilization, and ordained to work a thorough change in the structure of European government and social existence".[15] The democratic is "the last order" in the development of civilization from barbarism to "the ultimate perfection of man", and America is responsible for the first permanent existence of democracy.

And this redemptive democracy is "the supremacy of the people, restrained by a just regard to individual rights – that condition of society which secures the full and inviolable use of every faculty".[16] At the end of this article O'Sullivan returns to the relationship between democracy and Christianity in the redemptive effect each has on man. "In that ennobling influence, Christianity and democracy are one. What, indeed, is democracy but Christianity in its earthly aspect, Christianity made effective among the political relations of men."[17]

Regarding America's destiny, O'Sullivan proclaims, with Emerson, that America has little connection with antiquity, or even the more recent past – it is itself a new epoch; its birth was the beginning of a new history in which America's roots are in the future. This accomplishes, in the order of time, a reorientation paralleling the occidentation of order. America will be "the great nation of futurity" because it is founded on the perfect universal principle of equality, the foundation of order in both the physical and moral worlds.

However, it is not enough for America to be a City upon a Hill – it will become a veritable cosmos, as ancient societies tended to regard their own boundaries as the limits of the cosmos. "The far-reaching, the boundless future will be the era of American greatness. In its magnificent domain of space and time, the nation of many nations is destined to manifest to mankind the excellence of divine principles; to establish on earth the noblest temple ever dedicated to the worship of the Most High – the Sacred and the True. Its floor shall be a hemisphere; its roof the firmament of the star-studded heavens; and its congregation a union of many republics, comprising hundreds of happy millions calling, owning no man master, but governed by God's natural and moral law of equality, the law of brotherhood – of 'peace and goodwill among men.'"[18] America is simply identified with the totality of order – it is itself a temple, the cosmos, and would seem to include all of mankind, or at least all of mankind that is happy.

O'Sullivan goes on to lament the lack of a national literature commensurate with the noble spirit of republican institutions, with the "matchless sublimity" of America's position as the earthly bearer of the moral dignity and the salvation of man; the site of "a new heaven and a new earth". America is the divinely chosen saviour of the world from darkness, ignorance, and oppression, rather an old theme in the American myth. Since it is America's destiny to be the cosmos on the spiritual level, it is manifestly ordained that the nation should expand to occupy as much as possible of the actual physical cosmos. The empire of the spirit requires a foundation in a concrete, earthly empire.

The myth of Manifest Destiny naturally placed great emphasis upon the mythic meaning of the American West, which meaning continued to grow throughout the nineteenth century. One of the more significant works to appear during the 1880's was Josiah's Strong's *Our Country*, important not only because of its relation to the Social Gospel movement, but also because of its emphatic reiteration of the myth of the West, and its meaning for America and the world. Strong begins with an implicit overview of world history, with America playing a decisive role, not only throughout its existence, but even more particularly during Strong's own lifetime. "Many are not aware that we are living in extraordinary times. Few suppose that these years of peaceful prosperity, in which we are quietly developing a continent, are the pivot on which is turning the nation's future. And fewer still imagine that the destinies of mankind, for centuries to come, can be seriously affected, much less determined, by the men of this generation in the United States." [19] Strong's own time is an axis time of the world, decisive for mankind's progress toward perfection. America's position as the West in world history is actually very close to that of Christ, as a center and source of salvific order. "Like the star in the East which guided the three kings with their treasures westward until at length it stood still over the cradle of the young Christ, so the star of empire, rising in the East, has ever beckoned the wealth and power of the nations westward, until today it stands still over the cradle of the young empire of the West, to which the nations are bringing their offerings." [20]

Symbolically, then, the young empire of the West is not only the future redeemer of the world, but it is also the City upon a Hill, the earthly order admired and even worshipped by the nations of the world, the nation whose very existence implies a restructuring of cosmic order. The progress of the world, of civilization, in the direction of popular government is in the hands not only of the United States, but more particularly, the Anglo-Saxon race, which embodies the two great ideas of civil liberty and a "pure spiritual Christianity". According to Strong, these are the two great needs of mankind for the highest Christian civilization. It is the providential good fortune of the United States to occupy the latitude and longitude (North and West, respectively) reserved, within cosmic order, for the highest advances of civilization. And Strong reiterates the traditional view that according to the ineluctable logic of geography and history, America must be the site of the Golden Age. "If the consummation of human progress is not to be looked for here, if there is yet to follow a higher civilization, where is the soil that is to produce it?" [21] Since civilization progresses only in a Westward direction, and only in the North Temperate Zone, it obviously must reach its culmination on the American shores of the Pacific. All past time has moved toward the "young empire of the West", and the course of the entire future of the world flows from this empire. Some of the dangers of this type of excessive nationalism, one might say chauvinism, are more apparent in the issue of Imperialism.

The problem at the center of the Imperialism controversy that became acute at the close of the Spanish-American War was not so much whether America was going to spread its power and influence beyond its North American borders, for that was largely taken for granted, but how it was going to spread this power. The advocates of annexation saw America as destined and entitled to an active expansion through the outright appropriation of territory, so as to become a very worldly empire. There were opponents of expansion or annexation throughout the nineteenth century – they saw expansion as unconstitutional or imprudent or unnecessary or all three, and they preferred the somewhat more strongly traditional view that America was to spread its order through its shining example as a City upon a Hill. However, since whenever a decision was made it was usually the expansionists who won, their views became the dominant and shaping force. The imperialist view is essentially a development of the expansionist view.

One of the most vocal and most vociferous proponents of American imperialist annexation was Senator Albert J. Beveridge. Although he is now regarded as a jingoist, it is worth examining a couple of his speeches, because his ideas are so much a hypertrophy of the civil theology. Beveridge was as adept as some of the early English settlers at combining the propagation of truth with lucrative commercial expansion. In his 1898 campaign speech, 'The March of the Flag', he proclaims the worldly empire of America: "Therefore, in this campaign the question is larger than a party question. It is an American question. It is a world question. Shall the American people continue their march toward the commercial supremacy of the world? Shall free institutions broaden their blessed reign as the children of liberty wax in strength, until the empire of our principles is established over the hearts of all mankind?" [22] Clearly the spiritual empire of principles is to be coextensive with a commercial territorial empire, with an empire ordained by Providence. "Wonderfully God has guided us. Yonder at Bunker Hill and Yorktown His providence was above us. At New Orleans and on ensanguined seas His hand sustained us. Abraham Lincoln was His minister and His was the altar of freedom the Nation's soldiers set up on a hundred battle-fields. ... We can not retreat from any soil where Providence has unfurled our banner; it is ours to save that soil for liberty and civilization." [23] Since whatever America does is a manifestation of the will of Providence, American conquest of the world is a religious crusade to save the world for liberty and civilization, for the truth of order. America's destiny to achieve the supremacy of the world means that the United States is to be "the sovereign factor in the peace of the world", that is, America is to be the linchpin of world order, an order that spreads not by example but by conquest and annexation, all providentially guided. In fact, American expansion has taken on the characteristics of a natural force designed to realize God's plan for human existence.

But his speech in Chicago opening the Republican Campaign for the West in 1900 is an even better example of the kind of "reasoning" that was used to rationalize nationalist desires as the will of God, using the traditional symbols of the civil theology. By September 1900 the major question was what to do about Cuba, considering that one of the declared reasons why the United States had gone to war against Spain was to aid the Cubans in their struggle for independence from Spain. Beveridge was a rather strong advocate of the annexation of Cuba, a position he justified with the assertion that "annexation to the greatest nation the world has ever seen is a prouder Cuban destiny than separate nationality". An American administration in Cuba would accomplish "the work of regeneration"; on the other hand the withdrawal of American order from Cuba would result only in rampant disorder: "The United States needs Cuba for our protection, but Cuba needs the United States for Cuba's salvation." In light of the fact that annexation as a program of "reason and righteousness", would be almost entirely for the Cubans' benefit, as well as being necessary for the providentially decreed spread of American order, the resolution of the Congress to grant independence to Cuba is an "unnatural experiment". "What war and nature − aye, what God hath joined together, is to be put asunder."

The salvation of America from wilderness and savages represents in microcosm the salvation of the world from disorder through the evolution of order. And it is the task of the American people to spread civilization and order from their own seminal nation. The ultimate purpose of Providence is the unification of mankind "into one vast and united intelligence", a purpose to be achieved by colonization, where coexistence with an inferior race is possible, or displacement where the inferior race is not capable of existing under civilization. Beveridge indulged a certain flair for rapturous demaguery: "Our flag! Our institutions! Our Constitution! This is the immortal order in which American civilization marches." Moreover, the Americans are impervious to the corrupting effects of power because of their abundant virtue and wisdom. "In the end, the judgment of the masses is right." The dangerous extent of Beveridge's utopian speculations is apparent in his declaration that the American people, destined to be the "master people" or the "master Nation" of the world, are locked in the eternal cosmic duel between order and disorder. Nevertheless, American mastery of the world is a divinely ordained "splendid and holy" destiny, and irresistible. In Beveridge's rhapsodic vision America is to assume the role of "that Almighty Being . . . who presides in the councils of nations", when America will be the final arbiter of all disputes, and will single-handedly protect the commerce of the world. Such a "high and holy destiny" is inevitable for America, the *ultima Thule* of the West: "AMERICAN INSTITUTIONS FOLLOW THE AMERICAN FLAG".[24]

While Beveridge's ideas are somewhat extreme, they are certainly outgrowths, however tumescent, of the matrix of the American civil theology. His vision of American destiny is a secularized version of Jonathan Edwards' apocalyptic, religious expectations, and there is nothing in such a view of America's glorious future that is not latent in the patriotic sermons of the previous two centuries. Tension with the tradition arises primarily with the City upon a Hill image — physical force is to accompany and reinforce the light of the truth. In this respect William Jennings Bryan, speaking against Imperialism in 1900, showed himself more in tune with the restrained spirit of the tradition, although his view of America's destiny is quite similar to that of Beveridge. Bryan felt that Imperialism was not part of the American destiny, that it was imposing arbitrary government on people who should rule themselves. "I can conceive of a national destiny surpassing the glories of the present and the past — a destiny which meets the responsibilities of to-day and measures up to the possibilities of the future. Behold a republic, resting securely upon the foundation stones quarried by revolutionary patriots from the mountain of eternal truth — a republic applying in practice and proclaiming to the world the self-evident [proposition] that all men are created equal. . . . Behold a republic, gradually but surely becoming the supreme moral factor in the world's progress and the accepted arbiter of the world's disputes — a republic whose history, like the path of the just, 'is as the shining light that shineth more and more unto the perfect day'".[25]

As far as America's future predominant position in the world is concerned, Bryan agrees with Beveridge. He disagrees in believing that this destiny is to be fulfilled by America's perfecting its own internal order, its adherence to the cosmic principles of truth: by perfecting itself America will catalytically metamorphose and redeem the rest of the world. By unselfishly rejecting imperialistic aggrandizement America will win the love, admiration, and trust of the other, less morally advanced nations. In short, America is to achieve a dazzling success as a City upon a Hill as, by its example, it preaches the gospel of the best political order to all nations.

The question of territorial expansion and the means thereof was not new, since it dated back at least to the Louisiana Purchase of 1803, and achieved a particular importance in the Mexican War and the treaty that ended it, as well as the dispute with Great Britain over the Northwest Territories. However, all expansion into contiguous territory on continental North America was encompassed by the commanding symbol of Manifest Destiny, of Westward expansion, intimately related to central symbols of the civil theology. But overseas territorial expansion was another matter, requiring justification through development of another symbol of the civil theology — America's high destiny as a world empire. Within the structures of its self-understanding American expansion usually emerged as a divinely willed manifestation of and means to the ultimate salvation of humanity, entrusted to the wise and virtuous leaders of the American people.

Yet in the midst of the glorious myths of Manifest Destiny and an ocean-bound republic it was precisely the rapid expansion during the nineteenth century that brought on the major crisis of the civil religion in the divisive issue that caused the Civil War — the spread of slavery. To be precise, expansion did not create the problem but merely revealed the difficulty that was already present, had been present in fact since 1619 when the first slave-ship docked at an American port. If the Founding Fathers were responsible for creating the nation, Abraham Lincoln was responsible for recreating it and re-establishing it upon the solid foundation which apparently had been lacking. In this respect the political thought of Lincoln serves as the conduit through which the public philosophy passes to the twentieth century.

The significance for the public philosophy of the issues dividing the country emerges clearly from the long debate between Lincoln and Stephen Douglas during the decade preceding the war. It is obvious that, although on the surface the debate concerned the containment or the expansion of slavery, the deeper issue was whether or not the nation was going to have a public philosophy as a basis of unity, or whether the basis of unity was going to be merely territorial contiguity. The solution that Douglas proposed would, at best, have preserved the body of the Union while killing its spirit. As Harry Jaffa points out in his superb study of the Lincoln-Douglas Debates, *Crisis of the House Divided*, "The long political duel between Stephen A. Douglas and Abraham Lincoln was above all a struggle to determine the nature of the opinion which should form the doctrinal foundation of American government. No political contest in history was more exclusively or passionately concerned with the character of the beliefs in which the souls of men were to abide."[26]

And as Lincoln often pointed out, the decisive disagreement was between those who thought that slavery was morally evil and should at least be contained if not abolished, and those who believed that slavery was morally good and should be extended. This was no crack in the national foundation that could be simply papered over. It was, indeed, a rift within the very foundations of the world, as Lincoln told the audience in the debate at Alton. "It is the eternal struggle between these two principles — right and wrong — throughout the world. They are the two principles that have stood face to face from the beginning of time, and will ever continue to struggle. The one is the common right of humanity and the other the divine right of kings."[27]

What was the nature of the wrong opinion advocated by Douglas in the genuine hope of saving the Union? The name which Douglas gave to this principle was popular sovereignty. He described it in a speech delivered in Chicago in July of 1858 as the foundation principle of self-government. "If there is any one principle dearer and more sacred than all others in free governments, it is that which asserts the exclusive right of a free people to form and adopt their own fundamental law, and to manage and regulate their own internal affairs and domestic institutions."[28] Or, yet more explicitly, "Whenever you put a limitation upon the right of any people to decide what laws they want, you have destroyed the fundamental principle of self-government."[29] According to Douglas, self-government is the rock upon which the national unity is built, and the only principle upon which the Union can be preserved. At the Jonesboro debate he said, "I now come back to the question why cannot this Union exist forever divided into free and slave States, as our fathers made it? It can thus exist if each State will carry out the principles upon which our institutions were founded, to wit: the right of each State to do as it pleases, without meddling with its neighbors."[30] The basis of the Union is in Douglas' view a kind of live and let live principle that amount to a moral indifferentism. In fact, Douglas chose to limit the public philosophy exclusively to that part of it concerned with rights rather than with virtue and responsibilities. This exclusive concentration on the great principle of rights easily leads to conflict, for it is almost entirely based on self-interest, in this case the self-interest of the stronger.

In the Sixth Debate at Quincy Douglas returned to and expanded this naively optimistic outlook, seemingly oblivious of the incredible irony of his prediction that "under that principle the United States can perform that great mission, that destiny, which Providence has marked out for us. Under that principle we can . . . make this the asylum of the oppressed of the whole earth." [31] In constrast with Douglas' strange belief that a popular sovereignty voting slavery up would inspire the oppressed of the world with hope in America as the land of freedom, Lincoln takes the more realistic and consistent view. "I hate [this declared indifference to the spread of slavery] because it deprives our republican example of its just influence in the world; enables the enemies of free institutions with plausibility to taunt us as hypocrites; causes the real friends of freedom to doubt our sincerity; and especially because it forces so many good men among ourselves into an open war with the very fundamental principles of civil liberty, criticizing the Declaration of Independence, and insisting that there is no right principle of action but self-interest." [32] Lincoln goes on to reveal the self-contradiction between the interpretation of popular sovereignty that allows for slavery and the whole public philosophy. "If the Negro is a man, why then my ancient faith teaches me that 'all men are created equal', and that there can be no moral right in connection with one man's making a slave of another." [33]

The Declaration of Independence is the source of Lincoln's "ancient faith" that the Negro, as a man, is included in the governed whose consent is required for a government's power to be just, as Lincoln stated in his Peoria speech of 1854. "Now the relation of master and slave is *pro tanto* a total violation of this principle. The master not only governs the slave without his consent but he governs him by a set of rules altogether different from those which he prescribes for himself." [34] The only way to avoid the self-contradiction is to deny that the Nego is a man, which leads to a number of other problems, and is a rather difficult position to defend. All in all, the belief that slavery is a positive good is ruinously self-contradictory. The principles that all men are created equal and that for some men to enslave others is a sacred right of self-government "are as opposite as God and Mammon". A public philosophy of rights also requires a public philosophy of virtue and mutual responsibility.

It was Douglas' position that these principles could stand together, not through reconciliation, but through indifference. But this was not to save the country, but to cast it adrift from its moorings in any eternal principle. Thereafter the order of the country would be purely arbitrary – whatever the majority of voters of each state thought it should be, based most likely on the shifting sands of self-interest. In other words, what this principle of popular sovereignty means in practice, particularly as applied to slavery, was a policy of moral indifference, most obviously exemplified in Douglas' oft-quoted statement that he "did not care" whether slavery "was voted up or voted down". In effect, each individual community became as a god, determining good and evil for itself. "I deny the right of Congress to force a slaveholding State upon an unwilling people. I deny their right to force a free State upon an unwilling people. I deny their right to force a good thing upon a people who are unwilling to receive it. The great principle is the right of every community to judge and decide for itself, whether a thing is right or wrong, whether it would be good or evil for them to adopt it."[35]

But how can a sound public order be established if the people democratically decide for themselves that evil is good? Douglas' argument, based upon a Jacksonian trust in the virtue of the people, necessarily implies that questions of good and evil are not to be a matter of vital concern, except insofar as popular sovereignty is the *summum bonum* and must be maintained, for the lack of it is evil and the cause of disorder. If one man chooses to enslave another, not only is no third man to be allowed to interfere, he should not even wish to do so. The great principle is that there be no great unifying principle, no moral consensus, no public philosophy for the nation. Lincoln attacked Douglas on this very point in the Seventh Debate. " . . . where is the philosophy of the statesmanship based on the assumption that we are to quit talking about [the slavery issue], and that the public mind is all at once to cease being agitated by it? Yet this is the policy here in the north that Douglas is advocating – that we are to care nothing about it! I ask you if it is not a false philosophy! Is it not a false statesmanship that undertakes to build up a system of policy upon the basis of caring nothing about *the very thing that every body does care the most about*? – a thing which all experience has shown we care a very great deal about?"[36]

We have quoted Lincoln's statement that the root of slavery is a tyrannical principle and that insofar as popular sovereignty leads to slavery it contradicts its supposed basis in freedom. As Jaffa points out, "The doctrine of popular sovereignty as preached by Douglas was of the essence of the Caesarian danger; it was a base parody of the principle of popular rights. It implied that whatever the people wanted they had a right to, instead of warning the people that the rights which they might assert against all the kings and princes of the old world were rights which they must first respect themselves."[37] Lincoln often argued that in its ability to deny freedom to the Negro the principle of popular sovereignty undermined the basis of the freedom of all Americans. Such a principle, far from being salvific, was instead self-contradictory, and, had it been adhered to, it would have led inexorably to the death of the spirit animating American national existence.

It might be mentioned that, as Jaffa points out, the difficulty with which

Lincoln and Douglas wrestled is found embedded in the Declaration of Independence itself, which, in proclaiming that all men are created equal, mandates the consent of the governed as the legitimation of the power of government. The difficulty then is that the equality of all men does not entail the ability of the popular will infallibly to choose the good. The Declaration fails to mention the importance of morality, but what it does imply is that unalienable rights that belong only to the stronger are scarcely unalienable rights. Douglas' position represents a rather selective interpretation of the Declaration.

Lincoln chose the equality principle as morally superior to an unfettered and undirected popular sovereignty. On his way to Washington to assume the presidency, Lincoln spoke on the Declaration in Independence Hall on Washington's Birthday: "I have often inquired of myself, what great principle or idea it was that kept this Confederacy so long together. It was not the mere matter of the separation of the colonies from the motherland; but something in the Declaration giving liberty, not alone to the people of this country, but hope to the world for all future time. It was that which gave promise that in due time the weights should be lifted from the shoulders of all men, and that *all* men should have an equal chance." [38] Lincoln thus chose to combine the principle of equality with the attempt to educate the public opinion in the truth for only the truth could save the country. Without this great moral principle the Union was not worth saving. In the sense of the Biblical injunction, the true political order comes from seeking first the Kingdom of God and its righteousness — national salvation requires a return to the true moral principles on which the nation was founded. And the civil theology, the sense of national destiny must be founded upon the solid principles of morality and righteousness. The civil theology cannot stand on its own. Lincoln definitely saw himself as having a prophetic role in calling the nation back to its true righteousness.

It should be apparent from our previous discussion that in using the symbols of the Old and New Testaments Lincoln was delving into the American civil-theology tradition. But he departed from much of that tradition by using such symbols not to encourage belief in America as the site of the New Jerusalem, but rather to call the people back to righteousness as a necessary condition for their being an example to the world. He subordinated these symbols, not to the passions and desires for better things in the future, but to cold, sober, unimpassioned reason. He predicted no millennium or Golden Age, no ravishing glorious destiny for America, but sought, in effect, an integration of the civil theology, or tradition of American myth, with the public philosophy, or tradition of reflection upon the proper political order as based upon reason and sound philosophical and theological and moral principles. And he integrated these two traditions within the overriding framework of a Christian understanding of the meaning of human existence and experience. His political religion is a public philosophy that dominates a civil theology, for the limits of the civil theology, or mythic vision of the American destiny, are determined by the vision of truth embodied in the public philosophy. Lincoln understand probably better than anyone in nineteenth-century American public life, the true balance of public philosophy and civil theology — the importance of the latter for a sense of national identity, and yet the necessity of subordinating it to the former, for American destiny does not descend gratuitously from heaven but is wrought by the Christian work of the righteous American people.

And so Lincoln re-established a unified civil religion in which a public philosophy emphasizing duty and virtue was the root of a civil theology promising that America would realize its destiny of being the land of freedom. Here the public philosophy prescribes the conditions of order. The tensions of the dichocosmy are reduced to a minimum. Unfortunately, Lincoln's spiritual heirs lacked some decisive element of his wisdom, for the myth of the Golden Age continued to play a large role well into the twentieth century.

REFERENCES

[1] Quoted in Russel B. Nye, *This Almost Chosen People — Essays in the History of America Ideas*, Michigan State University Press, 1966, p. 195.

[2] George Bancroft, *A History of the United States*, Vol. I, Boston, Charles Bowen, 1834, p. 4.

[3] Henry Reed, 'The Union', *Ninth Annual Report of the Board of Regents of the Smithsonian Institution*, Washington, Beverly Tucker, Senate Printer, 1855, p. 158.

[4] Robert Ellis Thompson, *The Hand of God in American History — A Study of National Politics*, New York, Thomas Y. Crowell & Co., 1902, p. 166.

[5] *Ibid.* p. 223.

[6] Horace Bushnell, 'Our Obligations To The Dead', in *God's New Israel*, pp. 204–05.

[7] Isaac M. Wise, 'Our Country's Place in History', in *God's New Israel*, p. 220.

[8] *Ibid.* p. 228.

[9] Quoted in Loren Baritz, *City on A Hill — A History of Ideas and Myths in America*, New York, John Wiley & Sons, Inc., 1964, p. 261.

[10] Ralph Waldo Emerson, 'The Young American', in *The Complete Works of Ralph Waldo Emerson*, Vol. I, New York, Wm. H. Wise & Co., 1929, p. 113.

[11] John L. O'Sullivan, 'The True Title', in *God's New Israel*, p. 129.

[12] John L. O'Sullivan, 'The Greatest Good of the Greatest Number', *AA*, Vol. VI, pp. 333–34.

[13] *Ibid.* p. 338.

[14] *Ibid.* p. 339.

[15] John L. O'Sullivan, 'America and the Perfectability of Man', in *AA*, Vol. VI, p. 502.

[16] *Ibid.* p. 506.

[17] *Ibid.* pp. 508–509.

[18] *Ibid.* p. 510.

[19] Josiah Strong, *Our Country*, ed. by George Herbst, Cambridge, The Belknap Press of Harvard University Press, 1963, p. 13.

[20] *Ibid.* p. 40.

[21] *Ibid.* p. 208.

[22] Albert J. Beveridge, 'The March of the Flag', in *American Forum – Speeches On Historic Issues 1788–1900*, ed. by Ernest J. Wrager and Barnet Baskerville, New York, Harper & Brothers, 1960, p. 353.

[23] *Ibid.* p. 357.

[24] Albert J. Beveridge, 'The Star of Empire', in *God's New Israel*, p. 153.

[25] William Jennings Bryan, 'Imperialism' in *American Forum*, p. 368.

[26] Harry V. Jaffa, *Crisis of the House Divided*, Seattle, University of Washington Press, 1959, p. 308.

[27] *The Lincoln-Douglas Debates of 1858*, ed. by Robert W. Johannsen, New York, Oxford University Press, 1965, p. 319.

[28] *Ibid.* p. 22.

[29] *Ibid.* p. 28.

[30] *Ibid.* p. 129.

[31] *Ibid.* p. 276.

[32] Abraham Lincoln, 'Against the Extension of Slavery' (Peoria Speech), *AA*, Vol. VIII, p. 277.

[33] *Ibid.* p. 279.

[34] *Debates* p. 279.

[35] *Ibid.* pp. 27–28.

[36] *Ibid.* p. 315.

[37] Jaffa, p. 274.

[38] *Abraham Lincoln – Selected Speeches, Messages, and Letters*, ed. by Harry Williams, New York, Rinehart & Company, Inc., 1957, p. 137.

CHAPTER VI

CHRISTIANITY AND THE CIVIL RELIGION

Before turning to developments in modern European philosophy, let us recapitulate the structures of civil religion as exemplified by the Roman and American civil religions. We have divided civil religion into civil theology and public philosophy, and said that the first is primarily mythic, and serves to order the dynamic, temporal existence of the society, to give it meaning and destiny, to interpret its historical experience, and to locate that experience within the ongoing history of the world. The public philosophy, on the other hand, is primarily a body of philosophical principles and serves to found the order of the society in immutable divine or cosmic principles of stability. In effect, the principles of the public philosophy provide the form which allows a society to be, to appear in space, and not only to occupy space but to order it. Moreover, the public philosophy, by its very nature, integrates the society not only with the order, or form, that allows the cosmos to be, but also with every other society that perceives the cosmic order according to similar principles. It is, simply, the means by which the society interprets itself according to pre-existing, unchanging standards.

The civil theology stands in tension with this, seeking to satisfy another human need, that for movement, change, progress, a sense of unique identity. In itself, the civil theology is the mythic, symbolic ordering of the temporal existence of a society and its integration with the order of a cosmos perceived as primarily dynamic. According to our analysis there seem to be two basic views of civil theology. One is the pragmatic point of view, the idea, found in Livy and Polybius, that the gods and the myths of the civil theology are merely fabulations, superstitions concocted by the statesmen and inculcated in the people with an eye to controlling the masses and maintaining public order. These myths possess no truth beyond a pragmatic truth, unless they can in some way be reconciled with philosophical principles regarded as true, such as Varro and Cicero attempted. This view of civil theology regards public myths essentially as an artificial civil theology, for its myths are imposed from above — they are created, invented by the statesmen or politicians or demagogues and virtually imposed upon the masses.

The other regards civil theology as a mythic expression by the people themselves of their sense of identity — it is a creation of a cosmos in which

101

that particular people has an important role, and perhaps even the most important role. In contrast with the public philosophy, the civil theology provides a framework by which the society interprets the cosmos according to the actions, needs, and desires of the society. The movement of the cosmic forces is not haphazard but purposive, directed toward the perfection of cosmic being, of which the glory of the particular society is a necessary and perhaps sufficient cause. In general the civil theology interprets the society through the actions of psychic cosmic dynamic forces — in ancient societies these forces were symbolized as anthropomorphic gods; in America the major symbol for the central cosmic force is Divine Providence. We might suspect that only such psychic forces are adequate as a foundation for temporal political existence. It is no mere coincidence that Epicurus, who drained the cosmos of all psychic force, retired completely from political life and concerns, or that Communism which replaces psychic or mythic force with blind, material, immanent force, aims at the elimination of all political order; or, for that matter, that Thomas Hobbes, whose cosmos is similarly devoid of the psychic, should reduce politics to the coercive containment of the passions. The civil theology grounds the psychic forces of the society in the underlying psychic forces of the cosmos. Therefore, in a case such as America, the nation's endurance through time is ordered, that is, the significance of events is illuminated and appreciated in terms of the designs of Providence, which themselves are interpreted according to the theology that the nation in question exists in a relation to the divine, psychic, cosmic ordering force that is, if not exclusive, at least unique. This popular mythic civil theology could be considered as the natural civil theology.

It should be apparent that both civil theology and public philosophy are essential, although the level of their respective development in any particular state may vary enormously. The public philosophy provides the necessary sense of community in Being while the civil theology provides the apparently equally necessary sense of dynamism, of uniqueness, identity, and destiny. A society possessing public philosophy alone could be only such as Plato's Republic or Augustine's City of God — a society of wise men, unchanging, perfectly attuned to transcendent order, and incapable of full realization in this world. But the danger of civil theology is obvious in those societies where it comes closest to existing in pure form — Nazi Germany and Soviet Russia. Both were built upon an untempered belief that they were the center of the cosmos and the measure of human existence. The proper balance of the two is not self-sustaining, but must be actively and consciously maintained by interpretations of events and a view of the future tempered by the essentially conservative public philosophy, as well as an integration of the public philosophy with some sense of purpose, of movement toward a goal, rather than simply preservation of the past.

For the moment we must consider that the most stable relationship of civil theology and public philosophy is that of the least tension between them, such as we find, for example, in the thought of Alexander Hamilton, James Madison, and John Jay, and also Abraham Lincoln. Here we find that it is America's destiny to demonstrate whether or not men are capable of establishing for themselves a public order in accordance with the principles of the public philosophy. There are no grandiose visions of a glorious apocalyptic future, of an eschaton, of the Kingdom of God in America, of the remaking of man. Yet such a civil theology is important for it provides Americans with an awareness that their achievement has a purpose beyond itself – it is ultimately for the benefit and improvement of all humanity by demonstrating the advantage of constructing a government so as to allow the citizens to regulate their own existence according to the principles of the public philosophy. The implantation of the public philosophy serves as the gyroscope, the guiding and limiting force of the civil theology. Perhaps the extreme point of limitation can be found in the very nature and existence of the public philosophy, which in its essential character as natural law with the attendant philosophical anthropology, is basically a form of Christianity, and is cognizant of the ineluctable immanent non-perfectability of men. Hamilton, among others, was quite aware of this non-perfectability of men, and was careful to delineate a civil theology that was paradigmatic but not eschatological. It seems that the civil theology can be exalted to the level of eschatological expectations only at the cost of draining the public philosophy of its truth.

From Lincoln's disagreement with Douglas and its basis in the public philosophy it should be apparent that it is indeed valid to distinguish certain principles and symbols that truly establish the society in order, from those principles and symbols that lead to disorder. Lincoln spoke for the true public philosophy, which the American people were in danger of abandoning without perceiving that this would also mean the loss of the civil theology, certainly in its traditional meaning of America as an example of virtue and human excellence. Similarly it is possible for the civil theology to consist of or promote symbols that ultimately lead to disorder through a distortion of reality. One such problem has occurred through the use of the Christian myth as the basis of the civil theology.

If we examine the symbols and structures of the American myth from the earliest settlers until the point of highest development we find that in its essentials the American myth is a version of the Christian myth, that is, America is the light sent from Divine Providence, the light shining in the darkness of the oppressed world and sent to redeem it, to lead the world into paradise. The import of the Old Testament imagery of the Puritans is the eventual advent of the Messiah, and the symbolism soon incorporated the belief that Americans were the Chosen People who would bring forth the political Messiah. There are quite a number of fairly explicit references to the Christ-role of America. Perhaps the most extreme statement, but the one which also sums up nineteenth-century American Messianism, is to be found in Herman Melville's *White Jacket*: "[W]e Americans are the peculiar, chosen people – the Israel of our time; we bear the ark of the liberties of the world. Seventy years ago we escaped from thrall; and, besides our first birthright – embracing one continent of earth – God has given to us, for a future inheritance, the broad domains of the political pagans, that shall yet come and lie down under the shade of our ark, without bloody hands being lifted. God has predestinated, mankind expects, great things from our race; and great things we feel in our souls. The rest of the nations must soon be in our rear. We are the pioneers of the world; ... Long enough have we been skeptics with regard to ourselves, and doubted whether, indeed, the political Messiah had come. But he has come in us, if we would but give utterance to his promptings. And let us always remember that with ourselves, almost for the first time in the history of earth, national selfishness is unbounded philanthropy; for we cannot do a good to America, but we give alms to the world." [1] American history is a condensation and recapitulation of all previous salvation history, from the Exodus to the wandering through the desert to the arrival at the Promised Land which happened to be occupied by the Canaanites, the pagans, to the bringing forth of the Messiah. All of this is ontogenetic recapitulation of phylogeny: what is new, what exceeds previous development is that "national selfishness is unbounded philanthropy", which became one of the essential ideas of the imperialists. With the advent of the political Messiah in America, the mechanism for the cyclosis of democracy, or the substance of cosmic order, has been virtually perfected; any good done to America will necessarily be distributed in its benefits throughout the world. It would seem, then, that America is incorruptible, immune to the normal consequences of selfishness; indeed, America is so pure that in the crucible of its national soul, selfishness is transmuted into a virtue – if not charity, at least philanthropy.

It must be kept in mind that the major foundation of the American tradition of self-reflection was provided by the New England Puritans who migrated to North America in order to complete the Reformation by establishing a society run strictly according to the principles of true religion. Accordingly, they transformed their own lives and deeds into myth by appropriating the symbols and structures of the Judaeo-Christian salvation history for the framework of the interpretation of their own experience of founding the City of God, the City upon a Hill, the New Jerusalem, From the founding of the City the political dimension of American existence seems to have been justified only in religious, Christian terms among the exponents of the American myth. While the precise degree of emphasis on Christianity varies quite a bit, it remains consistently as the prime *raison d'être* of America from the early Puritans who sought to live as much as possible according to the mind of God, to Jonathan Edwards who preached the apocalypse of the New Jerusalem in America and sought to prove his theory by an exegesis of the Old Testament and God's customary methods of dealing with the world and its inhabitants, to the poets and preachers of the Revolution, and onward even to the twentieth century. In short, through the Reformation, particularly in England, and the Puritan migration, the locus of the social dimension of Christian order was conferred upon America as a nation, with its political and historical existence becoming the means of progress toward the City of God.

We have seen the structural significance of the Christian myth for the American sense of order, meaning and destiny. From being the New Israel, the Chosen People, America eventually became, symbolically at least, the New Christ, that is, not only a people possessing a unique relationship with God, but a people incarnating the divine presence in the world, the avatar of God, the Son of God, a people with a salvific mission to all mankind. And the American Gospel is Democracy in its most cosmic sense, Democracy as the substance of cosmic order. It is through participation in Democracy that man attains the fulness of earthly happiness, just as it is through acceptance of the Gospel that man attains the fulness of happiness in heaven.

One of the major difficulties of the Christ image is that it is inevitably accompanied by apocalyptic, often earthly millennarian expectations, some deriving directly from the specifically Christian structures of history, others from America's position as the West, the last frontier for the development of civilization. And it would seem that America was founded amid eschatological symbolism: the metaphor of the Chosen People, or the New Israel certainly suggests the turning of the wheel full circle, the rondure of the world at last completed. Nowhere in Puritan use of such symbolism is there an intimation that God has plans for a third Chosen People, for this would mean either that the Puritans had overestimated their own importance or that they were simply doomed to failure. It is the Americans who have been chosen to complete the work of redemption begun in Israel and continued by Christ, and eventually America came to embody within itself both Old and New Testaments by being both Israel and Christ, the Christ of Democracy.

Another difficulty with the use of the Christian myth must be noted. The "natural habitat" of Christianity is the solitary soul, for it is only in the depths of the soul that a person experiences the redemption revealed by Christianity. And it is the solitary, loving, humble relationship with a trans-cendent God which functions as the vital principle of Christianity – without this profound inner faith, all external observances and myths are dead. Hence, it would seem that an attempt to translate Christianity into a national or polit-itical religion, a civil theology, will succeed is transporting only the external structures – symbols, images, metaphors, eschatological expectations – structures that in themselves lack the vital principle of the Christian experi-ence which is impossible on the national, political, collective level, but can be shared only in the Mystical Body of Christ, or the City of God, which means the transcendence of politics. There is, in the eschatological development of the American civil theology, a tension between the myth as the vision of the earthly impossible and politics as the art of the possible. Therefore, either the society must be transformed into the City of God, or the vital principle of the myth must be supplied by a surrogate experience of rebirth and redemption, a political *metanoia* that was a major theme of the writing, preaching, and reflecting of the eighteenth century, although the precise sense of rebirth lacked a unifying symbol. As we have seen, America adopted both courses, for in America political Christianity required a rebirth or resurrection to a new life which was shared by all Americans, and ultimately shared with all mankind. During the nineteenth century the primary symbol for the American Gospel became Democracy, which has been the guiding idea, or at least the justification, behind the assurance of American virtue, the vigorous expansion into and development of the American continent, expansion beyond the confines of North America, crusades against the enemies of liberty. Beyond its role as a surrogate Gospel, Democracy has been functional almost as an imperial idea requiring expansion to the Pacific, to overseas colonies, the moral expansion to spread the democratic way of life until all nations are democratic. This is not to imply that the imperialism of America is primarily territorial – that has been only a manifestation of the much deeper moral imperialism of the civil theology. This sort of imperial expansiveness is not due to anything peculiar or internal to democracy as such, but to its symbolic Gospel role, that is it must be preached to all nations. The result of this use of democracy as the vital principle of the American myth is that continued progress in perfecting and propagating democracy is required in order to insure the vitality of the Christian myth. It is up to democracy to sustain the sense of purpose, meaning, and destiny, and therefore democracy does indeed function as the American faith. The drawback is the demand of such democracy for constant growth, ceaseless internal renovation, particularly if external expansion into and renovation of the world appears not feasible. Such progress toward perfection insures the "credibility" of the myth.

The spiritual substance of America is, as we have seen, a form of Christianity, and so the Great Experiment is not merely political, that is, the question at issue is not simply that of whether or not men are capable of governing themselves. The question is, rather, the far more crucial one of earthly happiness, of the restoration or achievement of an order which will allow men to experience their existence in this world as ordered and meaningful. And the issue here is that of the validity, or efficacy, of the Western order which is Christianity. What emerges from a study of the tradition is that America was neither meant nor experienced as simply a body politic, but was instead intended to be primarily a religion, an ideal realization of Christianity in its immanent efficacy. In the course of human events America was to be the savior nation manifesting and communicating the meaning of Christianity for earthly happiness. In short, in America Christianity was not to be seen as a religion of consolation, counselling patience amid the trials and tribulations of this world until the attainment of an uncorruptible heavenly reward, but was instead so to order society as to allow every man to exist in a kind of foretaste of celestial bliss. This anticipated realization of hitherto unimagined earthly happiness is the primary idea crystallized in the symbol of the "dayspring of the West", as well as all the Christ symbolism — America was to be for earthly happiness what Christ was for heavenly happiness. The renovation of the soul required for entrance into Heaven becomes, through America, the renovation of the world so that all men might enter into earthly happiness. Thus America has always regarded itself as having some kind of mission, although the interpretation of the mission and of the means for carrying it out have varied. But it has always been regarded as a mission of immanent salvation, of leading mankind to freedom, prosperity, and happiness.

In summary, we find in America the development of a public philosophy and civil theology by a people in the midst of their actual historical experience. There is first of all, an open public philosophy, by which is meant that man is seen as having a divinely ordained place in a cosmos ruled by God, and it is up to man to live according to the order of the cosmos. There are rights to be respected and virtues to be cultivated. Existing in varying degrees of tension with this is another, dichocosmic, and yet also symbiotic order. The American civil theology is essentially the Christian myth of redemption and the experience of divine favor and providence. This myth exists in several forms. The first is that of Publius and Lincoln, according to which the myth rests directly on the public philosophy and is almost an outgrowth of it. In this case the American mission is seen as completely dependent on American virtue. This is the paradigmatic civil theology, for it could be used by any nation that chose to build itself upon the same public philosophy. The only difference would be that America would have the distinction of being the first nation to show the world that men are capable of governing themselves and living in freedom. The next form is that of spreading the ideal American order throughout the world so that all peoples will share in the benefits of democracy. This is both paradigmatic and ecumenical – the vision is of an empire of democracy united under the leadership of the United States. The last form sees America as the culmination of history, the Kingdom of God on earth, the new Christ, the complete immanent redemption of man. This is paradigmatic, ecumenic, and eschatological. In general, the American civil theology resonates from the paradigmatic to the eschatological – it has for a good part of American history tended toward the eschatological in answer to the need for a strong unifying force for an expanding and increasingly pluralistic nation. The eschatological is most at variance with the public philosophy, for it is here that the most dynamic myth is opposed to the unchanging principles of the public philosophy. Nevertheless, as long as the eschatological civil theology remains grounded in the open public philosophy it will not become a serious problem.

The danger of hypertrophy of the civil theology occurs when the eschatological civil theology slips from its moorings in the public philosophy and the myth posits eschatological redemption without the prerequisite responsibility and righteousness. Here the dynamic view of history and human existence takes over – righteousness becomes a function of the redemptive mission. Without the restraining influence of the unchanging principles of the public philosophy, the eschatological civil theology reduces the cosmos to dimensions co-extensive with the society and its aspirations. In short, the cosmos closes. The result is that the myth of order degenerates into a mere "myth" of grandiose expectations and the national consciousness of responsible action decline to a national solipsism. All of these structures are quite important for understanding the nineteenth-century, ideological civil theologies developed not by historical societies but by isolated individuals. Civil theologies developed in modern European philosophy follow these structures with one crucial difference — the repression of the public philosophy.

REFERENCE

[1] Quoted in Loren Baritz, *City On A Hill*, New York, John Wiley & Sons, Inc., 1964, p. 287.

CHAPTER VII

HOBBES: THE RELIGION OF TERROR

> *We have his own word for it that fear*
> *dogged [Hobbes'] steps. He was afraid*
> *of 'Nights darkest Shade,' of thieves, of*
> *persecution by his enemies, of death,*
> *which he called 'a Leap in the Dark.' His*
> *critics liked to say that his fear was a*
> *sort of inner confession of sin. It was his*
> *conscience plaguing him for his atheism.*[1]

It may seem somewhat strange that an "atheist", or someone capable of being suspected of being an atheist, should concern himself with the question of the religious foundation of the state, but Hobbes was actually the first in the modern trend of dissociating traditional religious belief and civil religion in the search for a non-traditional foundation for the state, although he endeavors to conceal the dissociation. In fact, Hobbes's interest was not so much religious as political – the preservation of political order in the midst of the replacement of Christendom with a collection of national states. In this situation "Hobbes saw that public order was impossible without a civil theology beyond debate; it is the great and permanent achievement of the *Leviathan* to have clarified this point."[2] It was the decline of Christianity as a force in some way guaranteeing the political order of Christian states that led Hobbes to seek a remedy for this problem through a reinterpretation of Christianity as a civil theology. In this chapter and the next we shall consider the metaphysical structures of Hobbes' civil religion.

The various political works that Hobbes produced all had one essential purpose – to prevent any repetition of "the disorders of the present time", by which he meant the Civil War and the execution of Charles I. In Hobbes' view civil war is nothing less than the death of the Commonwealth, and as self-appointed physician to the public order he diagnosed the cause of death as the citizens' ignorance of the causes of disorder. In other words, the patient died, not because death was inevitable, but because he did not know the correct method of preserving his health in the first place. And because citizens are unaware of such ignorance no Commonwealth is immune to civil war.

The cause, then, of the mortal illness of civil war, is that men do not know "the causes, neither of war nor peace, there being but few in the world that have learned those duties which unite and keep men in peace, that is to say, that have learned the rules of civil life sufficiently. Now, the knowledge of these rules is moral philosophy. But why have they not learned them, unless for the reason, that none hitherto have taught them in a clear and exact method?"[3] The prophylactic for the political disorder of civil war is a clear and exact method for transmitting moral philosophy so that ignorance of the rules of civil life will no longer be possible. As "the rules of civil life", moral philosophy for Hobbes is concerned not with the order of the soul but with the coherence of the body politic, and its "utility" lies in its ability to prevent such calamities as civil war, from which "proceed slaughter, solitude, and the want of all things".

The possibility of such calamities arouses fear in the human psyche, fear of violent untimely death, of isolation and helplessness, and of destitution. Not only the continuation but the tolerability of life in this world depends upon the preclusion of all these calamities. Since the Commonwealth is the only possible bulwark against an existence more to be feared than desired, the life worth living must be lived within the confines of the Commonwealth.

The teaching of moral philosophy by a clear and exact method is actually a radical departure from Western tradition. Aristotle had pointed out at the beginning of the *Nicomachean Ethics* that mathematical clearness and exactness are not possible in moral philosophy because human actions and affairs simply do not admit of the same precision as mathematics. Therefore the attainment of clearness requires Hobbes rigidly to eliminate anything and everything not susceptible of such certitude. This requirement has an enormous effect on all areas of Hobbes' thought from the true relationship between political and ecclesiastical authority to the nature of spirit and its relationship to matter. Put another way, the quest for certitude profoundly alters the final end of human existence and endeavor, and the attempt to wring from moral and political reality a degree of exactness and certitude exceeding their capacity becomes then a symptom of Hobbes' transvaluation of values.

Beginning with what he regards as the primary level of human existence, sensation, Hobbes proceeds to define the human world in terms amenable to the precision attainable in mathematics (geometry) and the natural sciences. In short, he reduces the ontological world to bodies in motion, both quantifiable, which leaves the human mind isolated from and alien to the world. In this rather crude scheme of things, the cause of sensation is the collision between the motion of an external body and the sense organs, and while such an immediate contact may be plausible in the case of taste and touch, Hobbes' vague reference to a "mediate" pressing in the case of seeing, hearing, and smelling leaves a great deal of clarity and precision to be desired. But, then, it is not physiological clearness and exactness that Hobbes is searching for.

The pressure received by the external body is further mediated by the "nerves and other strings and membranes of the body" to the brain and heart, where the action provokes a reaction, for the heart resists the pressure, and the endeavor of the heart outward to counteract the inward pressure in some unexplained way creates the illusion of the perception of something external. All sensible qualities, or sense-data, exist in external bodies only as unknown motions that force themselves upon human sense organs, or, in other words, all sensible qualities are really only the "fancy" of the mind. Sensation is not perception but only an epiphenomenon of the conflict of physical forces, and it is significant as a symptom of man's alienation from the world, rather than as the means of any kind of union with it. Needless to say, the images and conceptions in the mind, produced by resistance to the motions of external bodies, tell us nothing whatever about those bodies themselves. It is, in fact, doubtful that there is anything to be known about these bodies other than that they are possessed of motion and devoid of qualities — Hobbes never posits any kind of noumenal world lying behind the phenomenal.

Sensation, then, is born of violence — the external world's constant invasion of the human body — and "fancy" is the psychic manifestation of the body's equally constant assertion of its own order against the disorder and dissolution with which the external world threatens it. Order is precarious, and the universe is altogether indifferent to human existence.

While there is considerable inconsistency between Hobbes' theory of sensation and his physiology of the passions, the latter does extend the isolation of the human mind from the external to the isolation of each individual from all other individuals. The passions arise from the motion and agitation external bodies produce in the heart, and from the relation between this motion and the vital motion. The hindering of the vital motion produces pain, its enhancing pleasure. The former is primarily the passion of fear, the latter all those passions that draw a man toward external objects, although, strictly speaking, men are of course drawn not toward the external objects but toward their fancies of them. The net result is the further alienation of the human psyche from an external world in which everything real is reduced to quantifiable terms. It is not surprising that for Hobbes the passions seem to have far more a physical than a psychic character.

For Hobbes all of men's actions are controlled by passions rather than by reason. Indeed, the will itself is a passion — the last in any given series of passions affecting a person — and therefore all actions and decisions are virtually determined by agreeable and disagreeable phantasms. One of the more serious consequences of Hobbes' psychology is that the human personality is deprived of a center. No man possesses the inner strength to order his own passions, but is instead at their mercy. The hypothetical, and logical, result, assuming the removal of all political and social restraints, is the plunging of all men into the state of nature, the war of all against all, for with the exception of fear, all the major passions are forms of the *libido dominandi* over the means of maintaining and enhancing life. It is a secure and comfortable life that functions as the highest good for Hobbes.

As the reciprocal of his search for clearness and exactness in moral and civil theology Hobbes quite explicitly rejects the traditional understanding of the *summum bonum* or highest good, which as something beyond man's control, does not lend itself to precision, and he thereby rejects the tradition itself. The passage in question reads: "For there is no such *finis ultimus* nor *summun bonum* as is spoken of in the books of the old moral philosophers. Nor can a man any more live whose desires are at an end than he whose senses and imagination are at a stand. Felicity is a continual progress of the desire from one object to another, the attaining of the former being but the way to the latter. The cause whereof is that the object of man's desire is not to enjoy once only, and for one instant of time, but to assure forever the way of his future desires." [4] We shall consider some aspects of this rejection of tradition here, but most will be reserved for the following chapter.

Since Hobbes was certainly well-acquainted with Aristotle, we can assume that he was aware of Aristotle's explanation of the significance of the highest good as "that which is always desirable in itself and never for the sake of something else". (*Nicomachean Ethics* I, 7) Aristotle understood the highest good, or happiness, as "activity of soul in accordance with virtue", and continues, "But we must add 'in a complete life.' For one swallow does not make a summer, nor does one day; and so too one day, or a short time does not make a man blessed and happy." The highest good constitutes a state of being in which man lives consistently according to the best part of his soul.

Superficially Hobbes agrees with this — he too maintains that happiness must endure for it to be considered happiness. However, he has relocated happiness. Where Aristotle placed it in a life of virtue, Hobbes places it instead in "a continual progress of the desire from one object to another", without end, something that Aristotle found irrational and the antithesis of the highest good, and that Plato regarded as the definition of human misery. To cover his tracks Hobbes misrepresents the traditional position, implying that one swallow does make a summer, that the highest good is not lasting but ephemeral, that once it is achieved there is nothing further to be desired or enjoyed, that there is then no further reason for life or motion and so man sinks into death. Thus the highest good becomes something to be shunned and even feared, while "a perpetual and restless desire of power after power" becomes the acme of human felicity. Oddly enough, it is precisely because the traditional highest good can be attained that Hobbes rejects it. The philosophy of human nature that accompanies the highest good is incompatible with the clear and exact rules of civil life which Hobbes chooses to regard as the only means of human salvation.

Nevertheless, Hobbes cannot build a philosophy on nothing, and his disingenuous denial of the highest good accomplishes neither its annihilation nor the elimination of man's desire for an absolute. Human beings still require some sort of ultimate end as a basis on which to order their lives and experiences, and Hobbes attempts to supply this need with a different sort of ultimate end, actually a combination of a *summum malum* and a *pseudo summum bonum*. The former is death, specifically physical death to distinguish it from the death of the soul which Christian philosophy traditionally regarded as the worst evil, and the latter is what Hobbes calls "a commodious life". Human beings, then, find felicity in fleeing death and pursuing a comfortable life, for it is first to avoid death and second to achieve affluence and comfort that men do what they do. With the elimination of reason as a governing force over the passions the worst evil and greatest good inevitably collapse from the spiritual to the physical level, as will be discussed more fully in the next chapter.

Just as on the physical level sensation is the manifestation of the body's resistance to invasion from without, so on the psychological level fear is the manifestation of resistance to the unlimited desires of others. It is in this way that the state of nature is self-contradictory — since all men have a right to everything, the result is that no man can acquire secure possession of anything including his life. The intensity of desire that is manifested produces in others an equal if not greater intensity of fear. Instead of being a state of felicitous gratification of desire, the state of nature is a dreadful condition of constant fear of the possibly superior power of the other equally rapacious men. In the state of nature, not only are men incapable of happiness but they become subject to the evils they fear most — slaughter, solitude, and destitution.

In Hobbes' terms the state of nature can also be regarded as a condition of universal madness from which men escape to the relative sanity of society. "In sum, all passions that produce strange and unusual behavior are called by the general name of madness. . . . And if the excesses be madness, there is no doubt but the passions themselves, when they tend to evil, are degrees of the same."[5] Since men are necessarily governed by passions in the state of nature, where human nature reveals itself for what it truly is, men are by nature mad. Sanity exists only in society and is entirely dependent upon the forces society musters to control the passions. And the madness raging below does break out from time to time in society: "to have stronger and more vehement passions for anything than is ordinarily seen in others is that which men call madness", and "madness is nothing else but too much appearing passion".[6] Society can chain but not tame the beast. It is not difficult to see that man's desperate condition can be remedied only by a calculated application of the negative passion, fear, as an antidote to the positive, insatiable desires for some form of power. The remedy requires that men fear the consequences of the indulgence, not of others' desires, but of their own desires. The goal is to concentrate fear against a more limited opponent, so the fear will be superior. Were men not subject to fear they would remain forever in the madness of the state of nature, for it is fear alone that renders this condition intolerable. Were it possible that one man could be manifestly stronger than other men he would be able to impose his desires upon them and thereby cause them to live in terror of him rather than fear of each other. But because no man is significantly or securely stronger than any other man, Hobbes presumes that for the most part men agree to live in terror of one man rather than fear of everyone — this for the sake of the survival of all. "As for the passions, of hate, lust, ambition, and covetousness, what crimes they are apt to produce is so obvious to every man's experience and understanding as there needeth nothing to be said of them, saving that they are infirmities, so annexed to the nature, both of man and all other living creatures, as that their effects cannot be hindered but by extraordinary use of reason, or a constant severity in punishing them."[7] Given the irrational nature of man, the severity of punishment would seem to be the more efficacious measure.

As alluded to previously, the state of nature is the condition in which men are their naked selves, so to speak, and therefore because of the unremedied infirmities of their nature constantly subject to the greatest evil and incapable of achieving what they regard as the highest good. When all men are thrown upon the slender resources of their own strength and invention there is no possibility of civilization with its benefits – no agriculture, trade, architecture, arts, letters, science, and, in short, nothing that makes human life pleasant.

Therefore, quite apart from the possibilities of salvation in some future existence it is obvious to Hobbes that in this world man desperately needs a remedy for his madness, a salvation from his tendency to fall, through civil war, into an existence which is solitary, poor, nasty, brutish, and short. Since the cure for the illness requires an accurate diagnosis of its causes, Hobbes is forced to consider the question of how human existence arrived at such a deplorable condition. How did human nature come to be characterized primarily by madness?

Tracing human nature back to its origin, Hobbes locates the beginning of all disorders in the primordial disobedience to authority of Adam and Eve (disobedience to authority being the greatest sin). "Whereupon [Adam and Eve] having both eaten, they did indeed take upon them God's office, which is judicature of good and evil, but acquired no new ability to distinguish between them aright." [8] Since Adam's sin of disobedience man's nature is 'fallen', which for Hobbes means both that man is condemned to the divine office of judging good and evil on the basis of ignorance of good and evil and that he has virtually no power in himself capable of governing his passions. Because of man's fallen condition, then, we can look on the state of nature in Augustinian terms as the earthly city which resulted also from the rebellion of Adam and Eve. It is the realm in which men are governed by pride, self-will, selfishness, in short, by their egoistic passions. No true community of men is possible because there are as many conflicting wills as there are men.

Hobbes' view of present human nature is then somewhat ambivalent. Man is alienated from himself, other men, and a pleasant life because he has fallen into madness – he has become less than human through the supremacy of his passions. He has, in fact, become both a divine and a purely natural being. This lower aspect of man's existence shall be designated by the concept *corporeality*, by which is meant man's existence as a body controlled by the passions. Yet man is also divine or nearly divine through his acquired office of judging good and evil, although he lacks the required knowledge. This is a combination of natures leading to disorder and fear, and it is from this intolerable existence that Hobbes proposes to save man.

Before proceeding we must introduce a concept to characterize this ambivalence, namely *anticosmy* from the Greek words *anti*, meaning opposite, over against, and *cosmos*, meaning, here, the metaphysical order of being. In this context anticosmy will mean first the dissolution of reality into two contradictory metaphysical orders and second, the attempt to harmonize these incompatible premises with all the resulting ambiguity, ambivalence, and metaphysical dislocation. This differs from dichocosmy in that the two orders of being are not only different but contradictory, so that, logically, both cannot be true.

Anticosmy here refers to the contradictory premises that man is fallen and in need of salvation, and that man is capable of assuming the divine office of human salvation. These derive from contradictory metaphysical orders, for according to the first man is a creature in a universe ruled by God, but according to the second he is the functional equivalent of the supreme being, if not the supreme being himself.

Such ambivalence is not limited to this case but pervades all levels of Hobbes' thought. On the epistemological level, for instance, it may be asked, if all man's knowledge comes through the senses, how can man ever know that what he perceives has no existence outside his mind? How does Hobbes know that the reality of a body and the way it appears to the mind are quite different? Hobbes is postulating both that all human thought is entirely dependent on and subjected to whatever motions exist outside the mind, and also that the mind is sovereignly capable of ordering and transcending sense-data. Therefore, Hobbes' epistemology is self-contradictory. The second premise requires that the mind be capable of exceeding the limits of human knowledge as laid down in the first premise.

Furthermore, part of the difficulty of unravelling man's relationship with nature in Hobbes' thought derives from the fact that he uses the word "nature" in two contradictory senses: as chaos, unruled, undirected, without a common power. This is the sense of the state of nature from which man needs salvation; and secondly, as the art whereby God made and governs the world. This is the sense of what Hobbes calls the laws of nature, those rules by which social life is to be governed in order to maintain the social order, and thereby provide men with salvation in the form of the "highest good". Human existence, or human nature, is experienced as chaos in nature, which is outside the custom and convention of society. Outside of nature, within the shelter of society, man discovers the laws of reason, or the laws of nature − those rules which dictate the requirements for maintaining the social order.

We find further illustration of the curious ambivalence of Hobbes' thought in the Introduction to *Leviathan*: Here Hobbes introduces his political philosophy by explaining that human art can imitate the divine art of nature in the ability to make an artificial animal. But then instead of comparing the artificial with the natural Hobbes reduces the natural to the artificial. "For what is the heart, but a spring, and the nerves, but so many strings; and the joints, but so many wheels, giving motion to the whole body, such as was intended by the Artificer?"[9] The implication is that the artificial is prior to the natural, and the sense of organic unity is completely lost in the reduction of the body to a machine. There is a similar effect on the political level: " . . . by art is created that great LEVIATHAN called a COMMONWEALTH, or STATE . . . , which is but an artificial man, though of greater stature and strength than the natural, for whose protection and defence it was intended; and in which the sovereignty is an artificial soul, as giving life and motion to the whole body; the magistrates and other officers of judicature and execution, artificial joints . . . "[10] Society, as a macroanthropos, should be organic, yet man himself is nothing but a machine. Hobbes compares not the artificial with the organic, but the organic with the artificial, and implies the complete reduction of the organic to the artificial, and in fact, his Commonwealth does function as a machine rather than a living organism.

Now, since Hobbes begins with contradictory premises, it seems obvious that any salvation which he proposes will have to be in some way an attempt to harmonize these contradictories: man's fallen, dirempted nature of corporeality and divinity, of purely natural man and fallible god, must in some way be unified — the anticosmy must be concealed if it cannot be resolved. How can such a unification be accomplished?

We can see Hobbes' answer to this in the structure of the state. The marks of man's fallenness are the madness of ungoverned passions on the level of corporeality and the necessity of judging good and evil in ignorance on the level of divinity. Clearly, regarding corporeality, salvation requires control of the passions, but regarding divinity the solution is not so simple because there are two alternatives: removal of the office of judicature altogether or replacing ignorance with the divine knowledge necessary to carry out the office. Interestingly enough, Hobbes chooses both, as we shall see, and this further anticosmic salvation is the structure of the commonwealth.

Therefore, in order to understand the structure of salvation we must first elucidate the structure of civil society. We have already quoted Hobbes' statement that the effects of the infirmities of man's nature are to be hindered only by "extraordinary use of reason, or a constant severity in punishing [the passions]". Obviously, such extraordinary reason and power of punishing cannot exist in the state of nature; their existence constitutes the common power in the commonwealth. And, according to Hobbes, the only way to establish a common power capable of protecting the citizens against injuries by foreigners and each other and so enabling the citizens to live the sort of comfortable life that men regard as felicity, is for the men who wish to leave the state of nature "to confer all their power and strength upon one man, or upon one assembly of men, that may reduce all their wills, by plurality of voices, unto one will: which is as much as to say, to appoint one man, or assembly of men, to bear their person; . . . and therein to submit their wills, every one to his will, and their judgments to his judgment".[11] Hobbes regards this action as meaning more than mere consent or concord; it is "a real unity of them all in one and the same person", achieved by every man's agreement with every other man. It is, in fact, not a unity but an identity. Since men make such mutual covenants not out of any mutual love or concern or a desire to share in a more lasting order, but only for the prolongation and enhancement of each one's private, egocentric existence, there is no basis for unity of wills. There is instead only identity of wills, in view of the fact that the unifying force of the Commonwealth is terror of the sovereign, not a common terror, one in which the citizens might share, but merely a similar terror. The only lasting basis for unity is shared love, but the only thing that all the members of the Commonwealth love is the security and comfort of their own private existences. The public forum of the society exists only through the space opened by terror.

And, indeed, Hobbes' term for the sovereignty is not such as to evoke either love or unity. "This is the generation of that great LEVIATHAN, or rather, to speak more reverently, of that mortal god to which we owe, under the immortal God, our peace and defence. For by this authority, given him by every particular man in the Commonwealth, he hath the use of so much power and strength conferred on him that, by terror thereof, he is enabled to form the wills of them all, to peace at home, and mutual aid against their enemies abroad . . . "[12] The Leviathan is, like Satan, the Lord of the Proud, for all men are characterized primarily by pride, the desire to be godlike to themselves and to other men. So, by Hobbes' own admission, there can be no true union of wills but only the submission of the wills of the citizens to the all-powerful will of the sovereign, which is also the divine will.

Structurally, the sovereign is a divine reason ruling over the passions, an "extraordinary use of reason". Reason thus becomes a power standing above the passions and alienated from them, a power that alleviates but does not resolve the conflict of the passions and keeps this conflict within the bounds of "order". Reason is alienated from the passions in that, without the persuasive power of terror, reason would have no influence over the passions.

The Commonwealth, then, is an anticosmy, for beneath this divine reason, the members are still corporeal, still governed by passions, for entry into society involves no regeneration of an ordered human nature, but there is the difference that it is now terror that rules men, terror that induces them to identify their personal wills with the will of the mortal yet divine sovereign, and, in Hobbes's view, because the citizens variously agree to submit to the absolute sovereign and identify themselves with him, they are the true authors of his presumably rational actions and decisions. Logically, then, as the author of the actions of the sovereign each citizen lives in terror of himself while simultaneously sharing in the divinity of the sovereign and obeying only himself. Thus, in the sovereign each citizen is both "saved" creature and saving knowledgeable god, and so through the mediation of the Commonwealth each citizen becomes a kind of hypostatic union of purely natural man and powerful God. In the state of nature all men wish for absolute power to protect their own existences, and it is in the Commonwealth that they finally acquire it, so long as they are obedient to the will of the sovereign, which is also their own will; the citizens are free and powerful to do only in accordance with the will of the sovereign, and so the natural man finds his peace in the citizen.

The structure of salvation, then, is that in order to remove themselves from the intolerable fear of the state of nature men covenant to establish a mortal god who wields enough terror to inhibit the mad passions of the members of the Commonwealth; it can be seen that through the social compact men create their own "mortal god", as in the Commonwealth they create their own cosmos as a refuge from the horrors of the real cosmos. That is, instead of choosing to live justly out of love for the true God men can choose only to live justly out of terror of the mortal god. This limitation of human abilities is a logical conclusion of Hobbes' rejection of the *summum bonum*. In the Christian tradition the highest good is eternal life with God, made possible by the assistance of divine grace to regenerate corrupt human nature. Hobbes, however, has eliminated divine grace and man must cope as best he can with frailties of his own nature.

But there is another aspect of man's social and political life which is of equal importance and which brings us to Hobbes' civil religion. The metaphysical structures of the civil religion will be discussed more fully in the next chapter, but it is necessary here to present the basic features of the state religion which Hobbes proposes. This aspect is man's religious life as expressed by his membership in the Church. As far as Hobbes was concerned the Church and the Commonwealth must be identical and the sovereign must be undisputed head of both. Any other state of affairs produced the possibility of disagreement and disunity, which in turn produced the possibility of a fall into the state of nature and civil war through the nullification of man's self-salvation. Therefore, in order to reinforce the walls of the salvific Commonwealth Hobbes proposes a state religion, the major purpose of which lies in its ability to enhance the unity of the members of the Commonwealth already "united" in the person of the absolute sovereign. "Seeing a Commonwealth is but one person, it ought ... to exhibit to God but one worship, which then it doth when it commandeth it to be exhibited by private men, publicly. And this is public worship, the property whereof is to be *uniform*; for those actions that are done differently by different men cannot be said to be a public worship. And therefore, where many sorts of worship be allowed, proceeding from the different religions of private men, it cannot be said there is any public worship, nor that the Commonwealth is of any religion at all."[13] Just as the civil society requires an identity of wills, so it also requires a uniform public worship as a force of social cohesion. Since God's power is supposedly the sanction of the Commonwealth, a uniform public worship rather closely relates a reverential attitude toward God with a reverential attitude toward the political order in the minds and hearts of the members of the Commonwealth. The precariousness of order requires that such uniform public worship be mandatory and that it be determined by the absolute sovereign who speaks for the Commonwealth as a whole.

In order to avoid any conflict of interest between Church and State, Hobbes absorbs the Church into the State and establishes the sovereign as head of both and as speaker of the will of God. "I define a Church to be: a company of men professing Christian religion, united in the person of one sovereign; at whose command they ought to assemble and without whose command they ought not to assemble." [14] Since a profession of the Christian religion requires nothing more than a belief in Jesus as the Christ, the significance of public worship is far more political than religious; in fact it might be said to be completely political, designed simply to remind the citizens whom it is they must obey. A Church is called such not particularly because of a shared faith but because of the identity of wills: it is called a Church "because it consisteth of Christian men, united in one Christian sovereign". And the identity of wills that makes the Commonwealth is also absolutely essential to make a Church. "But if the Church be not one person, then it hath no authority at all; it can neither command nor do any action at all; nor is it capable of having any power or right to anything; nor has it any will, reason, nor voice, for all these qualities are personal." [15] In other words, if the members of the Church do not submit themselves unconditionally to the one person of the sovereign there is no Church, no ecclesiastical authority. The Church springs into being only when it is headed by the sovereign of the Commonwealth.

The Church is absorbed by the sovereign and the universal truth of Christianity is swallowed up in the particular truth of the civil society. This complete identification is necessary to preserve order and prevent the disagreements and disturbances that lead to civil war. If there is no authority, either spiritual or temporal, in a Commonwealth save the absolute sovereign, there will be no problem of conflicting loyalties – to State or to Church. Since there can be no common power over the State and the Church they must be identified.

The precariousness of order in this world is indicated by the fact that Hobbes actually proposes a kind of double cosmology, presenting the cosmos under two separate aspects which he uses to reinforce corresponding aspects of the Commonwealth. This particular phenomenon is an example of dichocosmy, for the two cosmoi are not contradictory as in anticosmy, but merely different and contrasting. The first cosmos, a justification of absolute arbitrary sovereign power, is termed "the kingdom of God by Nature", and he uses it to solve the problem of determining whether or not the commands of the civil sovereign are compatible with the law of God, an important question since the citizens are bound to obey the sovereign in everything that does not violate the law of God. As Hobbes puts the question in another context, "the difficulty therefore consisteth in this, that men, when they are commanded in the name of God, know not in diverse cases whether the command be from God, or whether he that commandeth do but abuse God's name for some private ends of his own." [16] It is this difficulty that often leads to sedition and civil war.

As Hobbes describes it, the cosmos is a Commonwealth divided into friends and enemies of God on the question of divine sovereignty. "Whether men will or not, they must be subject always to the divine power. By denying the existence or providence of God, men may shake off their ease, but not their yoke. . . . They therefore that believe there is a God that governeth the world, and hath given precepts, and propounded rewards and punishments to mankind, are God's subjects; all the rest are to be understood as enemies." [17] The real significance of this Kingdom by Nature is that men are necessarily subject to the divine power, an unlimited power that is the source of God's unlimited right. "The right of nature whereby God reigneth over men, and punisheth those that break his laws, is to be derived, not from his creating them, as if He required obedience as of gratitude for His benefits, but from his irresistible power," [18] and it is from this irresistible power that God derives "the right of afflicting men at his pleasure." This right He possesses "not as Creator and gracious, but as omnipotent." Although Hobbes occasionally uses the language of loving God because of His goodness it is obvious that in the face of such arbitrary omnipotence fear is quite likely to drive out love, especially since Hobbes has always regarded fear as the one passion capable of overcoming love and desire, even the strongest; and since fear is the response to power, it would seem that unlimited power would arouse a virtually unlimited fear. In fact, this view of God is a tale designed to put the citizens in the proper frame of mind for fearing and obeying the sovereign.

Hobbes then proceeds step by step to explain that it is the law of God that men should worship Him in public and that the most perfect worship is obedience to His law and that only the civil sovereign can determine the proper modes of uniform public worship. Hobbes concludes the chapter with a brief discussion of God's natural punishments for transgressions of His laws. Hobbes has not, of course, really addressed the question of what men are to do if the word of the civil sovereign should contradict that of the divine sovereign, but seems to proceed on the assumption that *vox regis vox dei*.

And this is indeed the belief that he wants to convey, because as long as there is a possibility of disagreement between the will of God and the command of the sovereign there is the possibility of civil war. In the Commonwealth the absolute sovereign alone can determine good and evil, and the citizens partake of divinity and avoid the state of nature by identifying with the sovereign, which they express by obedience. Therefore, for Hobbes, it is a "fault to take upon us to judge of good and evil; or to make judges of it such private men as pretend to be supernaturally inspired, to the dissolution of all civil government".[19] It belongs only to the sovereign to make laws, which are the rules of discerning good and evil. The individual has no moral responsibility whatsoever beyond blindly obeying the sovereign. "Another doctrine repugnant to civil society is that whatever a man does against his conscience is sin; and it dependeth on the presumption of making himself judge of good and evil."[20] As head of the Church the sovereign purportedly knows the will of the transcendent God and transmits it to the Commonwealth infallibly, although since God's power in this world is altogether eclipsed rather than manifested by the power of the sovereign, the sovereign's prophetic authority seems somewhat doubtful.

It follows that in order to maintain the sovereign's absolute power the citizens must be forbidden to have any private relationship with the transcendent God, for allowing any such private relationships means participating in divinity without the mediation of the Commonwealth, which opens the door to rebellion against the mortal god in the name of the eternal God. Christian men must take their sovereign, their "mortal god", to be also "God's prophet", which means that he is the only means of communication between God and the citizens, the sole channel through which the waning reality of transcendence can seem to have any influence on the world. If men do not wish to accept this, "they must either take their own dreams for the prophecy they mean to be governed by, and the tumor of their own hearts for the Spirit of God; or they must suffer themselves to be lead by some strange prince, or by some of their fellow subjects that can bewitch them by slander of the government into rebellion, without other miracle to confirm their calling than sometimes an extraordinary success and impunity; and by this means destroying all laws, both divine and human, reduce all order, government, and society to the first chaos of violence and civil war."[21] The only alternative to accepting the political authority as the *persona* for the divine authority is a divisive conflict that leads to another Fall, a return to the state of nature or primordial chaos. This derives from the character of the passions. While a relationship with God through the sovereign produces terror, the passion which least inclines men to break the laws, a direct relationship with a transcendent God manifests itself in the Commonwealth as pride (not humility), which most inclines men to disobey the laws and come into conflict with the sovereign authority. In other words, the pride of men and their claim to divinity can be controlled only by cutting them off from transcendence. The logical conclusion from this is that in order to preserve the Commonwealth, man's salvation from the state of nature, the transcendent God must be pushed out of the world. Hobbes' discussion of the Kingdom of God by Nature has already served to support and increase the authority of the sovereign by making it obvious that his powers are in the image of the absolute power of the transcendent and eternal God, and therefore irresistible, or at least not lawfully resistible. The point of the Kingdom by Nature is temporal, political power. The second step in the process of replacing the Christian cosmos with the salvific Commonwealth, the second part of the dichocosmy, is the elimination of transcendence from the world, while trying to make it appear that this is not, in fact, what is being done.

Hobbes' term for the removal of transcendence for the sake of further increasing the stability of the Commonwealth is the Kingdom of God by Covenant. In order to enhance his own authority in what he is doing he prepares for the removal of transcendence by a discussion in the section 'On Religion' in which he tries to make it as clear as possible that what he has to say about religion is very much according to God's own wishes.

First he states that the gods of the pagans were created by the human fear of the unknown, specifically the unknown causes of their good and evil fortune. On the other hand, the knowledge of the true God derives from men's desire to know the causes of natural bodies and phenomena – their inquiries in this area led them to a knowledge of the necessary First Cause. The pagans then cultivated religion "according to their own invention", the believers in the true God according to "God's commandment and direction". But, although the means differed the purpose was the same: "to make those men that relied on them the more apt to obedience, laws, peace, charity, and civil society". The meaning of religion seems limited to its political usefulness. The pagan use of religion Hobbes calls "human politics" because it is concerned with the relation between an earthly king and his subjects. The other, "divine politics", contains "precepts to those that have yielded themselves subjects in the kingdom of God". Hobbes continues this distinction between the merely human politics and the divinely ordained politics by explaining that the founders of pagan religions took great care to pretend to the people that the true origin of their religion was the god himself, as Numa pretended to receive instructions from the goddess Egeria (Hobbes had obviously read Livy), but that the founders of the true civil theology of the kingdom of God needed no such pretenses because instructions did indeed come from the true God, by supernatural revelation. The paradigm of divine politics is, of course, Isreal, which was the first Kingdom of God by Covenant. So, just as the founders of the pagan religions, Hobbes claims divine authority for his decrees, although he has taken great care to give the impression that what he says is indeed God's own truth.

As Hobbes sees it, the Kingdom of God by Covenant, which is a real, not a metaphorical kingdom, is a civil kingdom, as it was in its first appearance among the Jews. The meaning of this kingdom is "a Commonwealth, instituted (by the consent of those which were to be subject thereto) for their civil government and the regulation of their behaviour, not only towards God their king, but also towards one another in point of justice, and towards other nations both in peace and war." [22] In this kingdom the political and religious orders are identical. However, the Israelites rejected this original Kingdom of God by Covenant when they clamored for a human king of their own so that they could be like other nations. The prophets foretold that the kingdom should be restored by Christ, and it is the restoration of this kingdom that is prayed for in the Lord's Prayer.

At this point Hobbes resorts to some prestidigitation to make it appear quite obvious that Christ's kingdom can be found now in this world only in a limited form in civil Commonwealths, until the fullness of Christ's kingdom arrives in the Second Coming. After pointing out that to accept the Gospel, or in other words, "to promise obedience to God's government", means entering the kingdom of grace, and that by grace is meant that "God hath gratis given to such the power to be the subjects (that is, children) of God hereafter when Christ shall come in majesty to judge the world", Hobbes then shows that Christ now reigns only through political authorities. "If the kingdom of God ... were not a kingdom which God by His lieutenants or vicans, who deliver His commandements to the people, did exercise on earth, there would not have been so much contention and war about who it is by whom God speaketh to us."[23] Hobbes has already made it quite clear that the vicars who communicate God's will to the people can only be the civil sovereigns. Therefore, to belong to the kingdom of God in this present world one must be an obedient member of a Commonwealth and must take his sovereign to be, for him, the only representative of God on earth. Men can belong to "the City of God" only within the Commonwealth, for civil society provides the only experience of salvation possible. In support of this position Hobbes quotes Christ's statement that His kingdom is not of this world, and says that since the Kingdom of God (by Covenant) is wholly in the next world that will exist on earth after the Second Coming, the Church as an independent organization is in no sense the Kingdom. He calls the belief that the Church is the Kingdom "the greatest and main abuse of Scripture, and to which all the rest are either consequent or subservient". By this he means the universal Church, as a power requiring obedience, cannot exist, because "there is no power on earth to which all other Commonwealths are subject". By the word *other* Hobbes denies the heterogeneity of political and ecclesiastical authority. Since Hobbes has defined a Church as a Commonwealth it can have no other meaning, for temporal authority has engulfed the spiritual. As Hobbes suggests, "it is impossible a Commonwealth should stand where any other than the sovereign hath a power of giving greater rewards than life, and of inflicting greater punishments than death." A universal Church could only undermine political authority through the ability to promise the citizens a greater reward than physical life and to threaten them with a greater punishment than physical death; therefore a universal Church would simply destroy man's salvation as Hobbes has arranged it. For Hobbes there is no distinction between temporal and spiritual government — there is only government which is vested in the sovereign, who is also chief pastor and sovereign prophet. Ecclesiastical authorities can advise, teach, admonish, but they have no compulsive power to enforce obedience to their commands and therefore they are not adequate for maintaining order. The crucial point is that since ecclesiastical authorities do not have the power to protect men against calamities, civil sovereigns alone have such power and should be obeyed. And "seeing then our Saviour hath denied his kingdom to be in this world, seeing he hath said he came not to judge, but to save the world, he hath not subjected us to other laws than those of the Commonwealth." [24] The Church can proclaim only the coming kingdom of glory.

Hobbes cheerfully admits that this is a "literal interpretation of the kingdom of God", and as such it provides us with a proper understanding of the *holy* as the analogue of *public* or the *king's*. And since the latter two ideas arise by covenant or consent, so also the holy belongs to the Kingdom by Covenant and signifies "propriety gotten by consent". The distinguishing characteristic of this kingdom is that it is based on consent, unlike the kingdom by nature based on God's overwhelming power.

Nevertheless, Hobbes does not limit the requirements for salvation entirely to obedience to the sovereign. Not wanting to seem entirely an atheist, naturally, Hobbes does announce that "the *unum necessarium*, only article of faith, which the Scripture maketh simply necessary to salvation is this, that *Jesus is the Christ*", and he proceeds to quote numerous scriptural passages in support of this rather limited interpretation of the Christian faith, seemingly completely lacking in *caritas*. Actually there is one other thing required for salvation – not love of God but fear of the sovereign – "all the obedience required to salvation consisteth in the will to obey the law of God, that is to say, in repentance . . . " But since the law of God is known or at least interpreted only by the sovereign, repentance amounts to the will to obey the civil laws. Elsewhere he says, "All that is necessary to salvation is contained in two virtues, *faith in Christ*, and *obedience to laws*. The latter of these, if it were perfect, were enough to us." [25] Perfect citizenship is the ticket to salvation. Again a bit of legerdemain, for Hobbes rather strongly suggests that perfect obedience to the commands of the civil sovereign, which obedience is of course motivated far more by terror than by any more positive feeling, would alone suffice for salvation, making any concern for faith and the inner life superfluous. Christianity seems to be necessary only because men are not perfectly obedient.

All of this being the case, what has Hobbes accomplished? First of all, he has proposed a two-pronged dichocosmic "civil faith" in the Kingdoms of God by Nature and Covenant. The Kingdom provides reinforcement for the authority of the sovereign, for God Himself is described as an absolute sovereign who brooks no rebellion, a sovereign whose absolute power gives him dominion over everything and the right to do whatever he pleases. God is a civil sovereign writ large in whom the proper attributes of sovereignty are the more easily discernible. This is meant to be the cosmos of perception.

The Kingdom of God by Covenant, which is designed as the equivalent for the cosmos of projection and which is based on consent rather than coercion, is designed to accomplish something more complex, which is actually precisely the opposite of what it purports to achieve. The roots of this kingdom are in Hobbes' search for clearness and exactness and his rejection of the highest good, both steps he found necessary in order to assure a monolithic social order. The principle behind both steps is the limitation of reality to only those things susceptible of human control. The logical consequence of the rejection of the *summum bonum* is the banishment of transcendence from the world, which is what the Kingdom by Covenant accomplishes. God is permitted to have influence over men in all things that affect external actions only through the civil sovereign. The old civil kingdom of God was rejected by the Israelites, and the full restoration will be realized only when Christ returns to earth in glory. In the meantime God rules only by proxy, and since the citizens of the Commonwealth are forbidden to have any private relationship with God that might in any way prejudice their thoughts and actions against the absolute sovereign, God is left with no direct power whatsoever in the world. But Hobbes is careful to depict God as being quite in accord with this state of affairs. And even though the Kingdom by Nature presents God as omnipotent, the actual meaning of the Kingdom by Covenant is to reduce God to powerlessness in the world.

And so we have the most basic anticosmy, the most fundamental contradiction in being of all, for we are left with the necessity of reconciling, or achieving some type of hypostatic union of two sets of divine attributes, corresponding to the anticosmy in Hobbes's view of man. On the one hand, there is a God of absolute power who thereby has complete control over the world, and as the God of nature would be expected to be capable of providing man with the salvation he required in the state of nature. But, on the other hand, convention reverses this relationship — man acquires the power to save himself and any independent action of God is seen as a threat to this salvation, and therefore within the microcosmos of the Commonwealth man, or more specifically the absolute sovereign, is omnipotent, and God is powerless. This view of God as a threat to the necessary human order returns in Saint-Simon and in Comte.

In order to provide civil society with a unifying force in "a civil theology beyond debate" Hobbes has found it necessary to separate God from the world, to make God at best superfluous and at worst a hindrance to the salvific order of society. For him there seems to be no middle ground between chaos and a very rigidly controlled and enforced order. Hobbes has, of course, thrown out the baby with the bathwater — in order to remove all possible causes of disagreement, particularly religious disagreement, he has also found it necessary to cut man off, in his earthly life, from all possible assistance by divine grace. Man is left to remedy the consequences of the Fall on the basis of his own slender resources.

So, it would seem that to Hobbes the only possible solution to the problem of providing an unquestionable foundation of the social order is to convince the citizens that they can achieve their eternal salvation only by regarding the civil sovereign as their mortal god. It is the sovereign who promises them the reward of eternal life if they obey his commands. And since no traveller returns from that bourne beyond the grave the sovereign need fear no refutation. Such is the cunning of the legislator.

The fact that Hobbes' work was so universally excoriated by his contemporaries indicates that they saw through Hobbes' deception to the atheistic core of his philosophy which the abundance of scriptural quotation was meant to conceal — the sort of procedure that Lucretius had recommended in *De Rerum Natura* for gaining acceptance of an unpalatable doctrine. Just as one might try to induce a reluctant child to drink wormwood by smearing the edge of the cup with honey, so Lucretius begins his description of a rather cold and indifferent and unstable cosmos with an invocation of *alma Venus*, and so Hobbes dissolves his atheism and cosmos indifferent to man in rather liberal does of Scripture, but to no avail for his cure is worse than the disease, or so his contemporaries perceived it. Later generations, however, began to find the wormwood more to its taste.

In summary, Hobbes has reorganized the cosmos so as to place the Commonwealth in the center. The edifice is supported by a foundation of opposing forces, contradictory assumptions, which themselves rest upon no common ground. He has made it quite clear that the cost of unquestionable social unity is at least practical atheism, which, however, he has carefully disguised as the true religion, so that men will be fooled into believing that by obeying the sovereign in all things they will achieve the greatest fulfillment that human nature is capable of in this world. Such seems to be the only way to achieve an "ideal" order in a society not composed of wise men. The ultimate bases for these structures of Hobbes' thought, and their significance, require further analysis of Christian philosophical anthropology, and Hobbes' relation to it, in the next chapter.

REFERENCES

[1] Samuel I. Mintz, *The Hunting of Leviathan*, Cambridge, At the University Press, 1962, p. 1.

[2] Eric Voegelin, *The New Science of Politics*, Chicago, The University of Chicago Press, 1952, pp. 162–63. It should be noted that in paragraph 2 of his *New Science* Vico characterizes that science as "a rational civil theology of divine providence". However, he is referring not to a civil religion but a study of the workings of divine providence in "the economy of civil institutions". Therefore, the focus of Vico's 'civil theology' is God rather than political order. *The New Science of Giambattista Vico*, ed. by Thomas Goddard Bergin and Max Harold Fisch, Ithaca, N.Y., 1968.

Also, in his book *Thoughts on Machiavelli* (Glencoe, Ill., 1968), Leo Strauss interprets Machiavelli as teaching that "the imitation of ancient Rome would consist in using Christianity as a civil religion" (p. 110). "Society would be in a state of perpetual unrest, or else in a state of constant and ubiquitous repression, if men were not made incorrupt by religion, i.e., if they were not both appeased by religion hopes and frightened by religious fears. Only if their desires are thus limited can the many become satisfied with making those small demands which can in principle be fulfilled by political means. Religion as reverence for the gods breeds deference to the ruling class as a group of men especially favored by the gods and reminiscent of the gods." (pp. 230–231). This view of religion is much closer to that of Livy and Polybius than to that of Varro and Cicero and as such is more limited. It is concerned with the expedient and pragmatic truth rather than with conforming the society to an eternal or transcendent truth.

[3] Thomas Hobbes, *De Corpore*, [1655], in *The English Works of Thomas Hobbes*, ed. by Sir William Molesworth, Bart., I, London, 1839, p. 8.

[4] Thomas Hobbes, *Leviathan*, [1651], Vol. XXIII of *The Great Books of the Western World*, ed. by Robert Maynard Hutchins, 54 vols., Chicago, 1952, Part I, ch. 11, p. 76.

[5] *Ibid*. i, viii, p. 68. All further quotes are from the *Leviathan*.

[6] i, viii, pp. 68–69.

[7] II, xxvii, p. 141.

[8] II, xx, p. 112.

[9] Introduction, p. 47.

[10] Introduction, p. 47.

[11] II, xviii, pp. 100–101.

[12] II, xviii, pp. 100–101.

[13] II, xxxi, p. 163.

[14] III, xxix, p. 198.

[15] III, xxxvi, p. 181. In its fundamentals, Hobbes' view of the sovereign as the head of the church and as ordering a uniform public worship is not new. These two principles were the basis of the Elizabethan Religious Settlement of 1559, which consisted of two acts, the Act of Supremacy, and the Act of Uniformity. The Act of Supremacy of 1559 was an echo of the Act of Supremacy of 1534 which "declared the king and his successors to be 'the only supreme head in earth of the Church of England, called Anglicana Ecclesia".' (Carl S. Meyer, *Elizabeth I and the Religious Settlement of 1559*, St. Louis, 1960, p. 24). According to the second Act of Supremacy, "all foreign authority [i.e. papal authority] within the Queen's dominions was abolished: ecclesiastical jurisdiction was annexed to the Crown; ecclesiastical commissions were to be appointed, by whom

the oath of Supremacy provided by the Act was to be enforced on those liable to take it
... " (Henry Norbert Birt, O.S.B., *The Elizabethan Religious Settlement*, London, 1907,
p. 86). The Act of Uniformity bestowed spiritual power on the ruler and established an
order of prescribed, even mandatory rituals for a uniform worship throughout the realm.
One can see that the central issue here was that of eliminating a source of conflict and
disorder within the realm, rather than of enjoining belief in the true religion.

16 III, xliii, p. 240.
17 II, xxxi, p. 160.
18 II, xxxi, p. 160.
19 II, xxix, p. 149.
20 II, xxix, p. 149.
21 III, xxxvi, pp. 187–88.
22 III, xxxv, p. 178.
23 III, xxxv, pp. 179–180.
24 III, xlii, p. 218.
25 III, xliii, p. 240.

CHAPTER VIII

THE CHRISTIAN TRADITION AND HOBBES'
CIVIL THEOLOGY

At this point it is necessary to introduce a second major theme with some extensive development to deepen the analysis of Hobbes' and later thinkers' view of salvation and civil religion. This particular theme is based on the value of the Christian tradition of philosophical anthropology as the matrix of thought and a necessary precondition for any further philosophical questioning and reflection.the essential assumption of the idea of a philosophical tradition is that common or shared human experience over an extent of time has an unimpeachable claim to some degree of validity. Human wisdom and insight into experience are not limited to any particular person or country or century, and therefore one cannot claim all of the past to be in error. Disagreement with particular ideas current in the past or held by particular persons in the past is, of course, not only possible but probably essential to the growth of the tradition, but only on the condition that the vital principle of the tradition is accepted. It is this vital principle, this agreed-upon foundation of the meaning of human existence, that is the basis of dialogue among philosophers of all centuries. The tradition is an organism that grows and develops only so long as the source of its life remains intact.

When, however, the vital principle of the matrix of the tradition is rejected, when a fundamental insight of the past is declared to be illusory or obsolete or superfluous, the result is a series of deformed structures required to discredit and compensate for the rejected insight, for human experience, which does not change, must then be accounted for in different terms. The question which will guide the following discussion, as an exercise in philosophical pathology, is that of the effect of this rebellion against the tradition on the thought of the rebel, or the structural and functional changes that accompany an attempt at a profound alteration of the traditional interpretation of man and his experience.

Here we are dealing specifically with the rebellion by Hobbes, referred to in the previous chapter, in his rejection of the *summum bonum*. Hobbes' philosophical project is the rejection of the Western, essentially Christian philosophical tradition and its replacement with a method yielding certitude, clarity, and exactness, in defiance of Aristotle's long-respected dictum that such a method violates the limits of inquiry into moral and political reality.

132

In this endeavor Hobbes follows the precedent of Francis Bacon, who concluded in his *Novum Organum*, after deploring the errors and imprecisions of the past, that the only possible means of arriving at truth is to start all over from the beginning with a very consistently applied method guiding the mind at every step of the inquiry. The important idea here is beginning again from the foundations. "It is idle to expect any great advancement in science from the superinducing and engrafting of new things upon old: We must begin anew from the very foundations, unless we would revolve for ever in a circle with mean and contemptible progress." [1] What Bacon set out to achieve in and through the sciences, Hobbes seeks for moral and political philosophy: to begin anew from the very foundations with a new method. What Hobbes fails to take into account is that, although the new empirical method is the one that is proper to a science that properly limits itself to empirical discoveries, the empirical method is not congruent with the subject matter of moral and political reality. The immediate metaphysical consequences of this desire for certainty are the reduction of nature to quantifiable bodies in quantifiable motion and the corresponding reduction of reason to the ability to calculate sense data, or the phantasms it imposes on the external world.

But the most important consequence of the desire for certainty is the excision of the vital principle of the old tradition, the highest good. The most important results of Hobbes' rejection of the highest good can be understood only in relation to the tradition of Christian thought. Here we are concerned not with the intricacies and disputations of Christian philosophy, but simply with the heart of the Christian interpretation of the "ultimate" experience and with the Christian philosophical anthropology built upon this experience – the desire for salvation through union with God. In order to understand Hobbes' distortion of Christianity and its effect upon his thought as a whole we shall turn to an examination of one of the best Christian articulations of the basic human experience of the need for salvation, the writings of Augustine of Hippo, primarily his *Confessions*. This is worth investigating at some length because the search for salvation in modern philosophy can be understood as a reinterpretation of the same experience which Augustine examines in completely spiritual and apolitical terms.

The *Confessions* is Augustine's reflection on and reliving of his life until the time of his conversion, with the object of searching for the inner order of his experience which makes that experience intelligible, not only for him but for all men. As Augustine reflects on his infancy he gains insight into the basic structure of human existence. Through his observations of other children he projects himself backward in time and describes the emergence of his consciousness as being first of all an awareness of need with a desire for satisfaction. The infant's lack of language, however, prevents him from expressing his demands and so produces only frustration and rage at adults who do not perceive and satisfy all wishes.

This isolation of inarticulate helplessness and dependency on others for supplying needs is an easily remediable level of isolation — that of the simple inability to communicate one's wishes. But a deeper, far more radical and vitiating level is incipient in Augustine's realization that the infant lives only to satisfy these desires, that it is willful, egocentric, and selfish, and regards others only as a means to its own satisfaction, which characteristics constitute the sins of infancy, for the "innocence" of the infant is due to its weakness rather than to the goodness of its will. Such qualities are, of course, quite acceptable in an infant, becoming a serious problem only if they persist into adulthood.

When he reaches boyhood, Augustine begins to exchange the inarticulate isolation for membership in the society of men through learning to speak, but his ensuing surrender to custom and convention serves only to intensify rather than mitigate his isolation: "But we are carried away by custom to our own undoing and it is hard to struggle against the stream. Will this torrent never dry up? How much longer will it sweep the sons of Adam down to that vast and terrible sea which cannot easily be passed, even by those who climb upon the ark of the Cross? . . . this hellish torrent . . . (I, 16)"[2] In the infant, radical isolation is merely nascent because an infant is as yet incapable of acting responsibly. Only if the cause of this condition is not corrected as the child matures does he become entrenched in the habit of selfishness, and the problem then becomes critical because it prevents the adult from ever acting rationally, for the sake of a highest good. "For the rule of sin is the force of habit (*violentia consuetudinis*) by which the mind is swept along and held fast against its will" (VIII, 5). Augustine is not far from equating enslavement to custom with enslavement to sin, and if we seek the cause of enslavement to sin, we find, in Book XIV, Chapter 13 of *The City of God*, Augustine himself struggling to explain the origin of sin within the soul. He begins his analysis with the statement that the sin which is outwardly manifest has its beginning in the hidden depths of the soul. Speaking of Adam and Eve, Augustine says, "our first parents fell into open disobedience because already they were secretly corrupted; for the evil act had never been done had not an evil will preceded it." All sin begins in an evil will, which is the hidden source of manifest evil. "And what is the origin of our evil will but pride?" As "the craving for undue exaltation (*perversa celsitudino*)", pride stands the established order of existence on its head: "And this is undue exaltation, when the soul abandons Him to whom it ought to cleave as its end (*principium*), and becomes a kind of end to itself. This happens when it becomes its own satisfaction." When the soul becomes proud and begins to please itself too much, when it finds its satisfaction in itself rather than in God, when it seeks to become its own god, its own *principium*, its own ground, to be in and of itself by asserting its own will in defiance of God, paradoxically, it succeeds only in surrendering its will to the *violentia consuetudinis*, the hellish torrent of custom and convention. This particular strength—submission syndrome is the symptom of the most critical stage of isolation.

The allurement of this non-reflective life of pride and enslavement becomes apparent in Augustine's account of the pear-stealing escapade of his adolescence. One of his bitterest regrets regarding his early life is that he *was* enslaved to convention, that he was "anxious to be pleasing in the eyes of men". His desire to be accepted and esteemed led him to be ashamed of being less dissolute than his companions, and ultimately only increased his radical isolation. That pride manifests itself in the desire for human approval only attests to its essential impotence, for the desire for approval never allows a permanent fulfillment or satisfaction, but always requires conformity and reassurance; its logical conclusion, according to Augustine's reflection on his experience, is simply "nothing". Nevertheless, the experience of nothingness is eclipsed by "the thrill of having partners in sin" (II, 8), the illusion of escape from radical isolation by the expedient of entering a "society" in which the causes of such isolation, pride and selfishness, masquerade as a basis of union. The intensity of the "thrill" is in direct proportion to the degree of intensification of the radical isolation which actually results from such irresponsible self-indulgence. Insofar as the stream of custom and convention entices men thus to surrender blindly to its current, Augustine regards it with horror as a "hellish torrent".

For Augustine, man's social life in the earthly city is both the escape from inarticulate isolation and the intolerable intensification of the radical isolation. Membership in such a society is an exercise in futility, a self-condemnation to the madness of a vicious circle, for in order to flee the anguish of radical isolation men throw themselves desperately into precisely those activities which increase such isolation. To pause to reflect upon themselves is to be tormented by the void of their isolation, their orientation toward nothingness: they must remain in constant frenetic action for the sake of satisfying one desire after another. Such a life is essentially non-reflective and non-rational: the greater the enslavement to the mundane self and the more radical the isolation, the more superficial and chaotic the existence, and the less men are aware of their true selves. This is man's fallen, proud, unredeemed condition, his attempt to be his own satisfaction, and his consequent condemnation to the isolation-society tension, or vicious circle.

In Augustine's experience the conversion, or salvation, from the critical isolation-society tension finds a primary manifestation in the modulation of speech from the demand to the question. The demand, as existential posture, is self-exalting: rooted in pride, it speaks in monologue. The question, on the other hand, is self-abasing: it is rooted in humility and speaks in dialogue. The questions which gestate in and are born of humility are not so much admissions of ignorance as confessions of love for Him who is questioned, and they are asked with the hope for a response rather than the demand for an answer. The questions of humility are expressions of a dependence lovingly and wonderingly embraced, as can be seen in Augustine's questions: "Why do you mean so much to me? Help me to find words to explain. Why do I mean so much to you, that you should command me to love you? And if I fail to love you, you are angry and threaten me with great sorrow, as if not to love you were not sorrow enough in itself". (I, 5) Questions such as this adumbrate the significance of Augustine's turning from isolation to solitude. Paradoxically, solitude is embraced with the realization that one is *not* alone but exists through the grace of Another, that the matrix of meaning is the unknown — or the not yet revealed — and that, properly understood, death is the practice of life.

From the passages quoted above we might, perhaps, construct a description of Augustine's discovery of solitude parallel to and yet contrasting with the description of his discovery of isolation: little by little he began to realize that he did not know where he was or who he was. He could not make his wishes known because he did not know them, and he became aware gradually that He alone who could fulfill Augustine's deepest desires was within him while Augustine was outside himself. "I have learnt to love you late, Beauty at once so ancient and so new! I have learnt to love you late! You were within me, and I was in the world outside myself. I searched for you outside myself and, disfigured as I was, I fell upon the lovely things of your creation. You were with me, but I was not with you." (X, 27) In solitude Augustine's problem becomes not one of penetrating the world by expressing and making demands, but instead that of penetrating the depths within himself by tendering questions, for the God Whom Augustine encounters within himself knows everything about him there is to know: " . . . there are some things in man which even his own spirit within him does not know. But you, O Lord, know all there is to know of him because you made him" (X, 5). Therefore, Augustine experiences solitude as, on the whole, the inversion of isolation, for the difficulty is not that of expressing his desires but rather of learning them.

Hence, whereas isolation is the ground of a monologue which manifests a self-exaltation and is directed toward others in constant flight from the self, solitude or humility is the ground of a dialogue which manifests self-abasement and is carried on first of all with God and then with other men, in order to deepen the awareness of God, others, and the true nature of the self. This dialogue of solitude, then, becomes the basis of community, and the solitude-community tension parallels inversely and redeems the isolation-society tension.

Since we have found that there are two levels of isolation and that the structure of the discovery of solitude parallels inversely the structure of the discovery of isolation, we might ask now if there are also two levels of solitude. So far, we have seen Augustine's experience crystallized primarily in the question which parallels the demand. This constitutes the first level of solitude, the solitude of darkness or of inquiry. Beyond this is the second level, the radical solitude of light or of response; between this and the first level the relationship is that of the tension of dialogue. Augustine very carefully describes his own awed entrance into this solitude of light: "Under your guidance I entered into the depths of my soul [*intima mea*] ... and ... with the eye of my soul, such as it was, I saw the Light that never changes casting its rays over the same eye of my soul, over my mind. ... What I saw was something quite, quite different from any light we know on earth. ... It was above me because it was itself the Light that made me. ... All who know the truth know this Light, and all who know this Light know eternity ... " (VII, 10) To continue the inverse parallel, while isolation is marked by the constant attempt to penetrate the world in pursuit of satisfaction, solitude is marked by the discovery that one is oneself penetrated by the *summum bonum*, the source of one's fulfillment.

Inasmuch as solitude is attained through the awareness and acceptance of the unknown depths of the soul, we must now probe some of the experiences in and of these depths in order more fully to explicate the difference between solitude and isolation. First of all, we must note that solitude, for Augustine, is devotion to the quest for true innocence, the possession of a good will, a will that is completely united with the will of God through grace, while isolation is abandonment to the guilt of pride and egocentricity. Secondly, within the experience of both innocence and guilt there are further contrasting structures of experience, one of the most significant of which lies in the peculiar articulation of the hidden and the manifest within and beyond the soul.

In solitude the soul experiences itself as the threshold of transcendence. "What, then, do I love when I love God? Who is this Being who is so far above my soul? If I am to reach him, it must be through my soul. But I must go beyond the power by which I am joined to my body and by which I fill its frame with life." (X, 7) In solitude the hidden *summum bonum* is that which is beyond the grasp of the soul and which the soul restlessly seeks. This is not, however, to say that the soul is transparent to itself: indeed a thematic question of the *Confessions* is "Quis ego?" (Who am I?), and Augustine confesses quite candidly, "The field of my labours is my own self. I have become a problem to myself, like land which a farmer works only with difficulty and at the cost of much sweat." Augustine regards the dissolution of the opacity of his soul to itself as a function of his growth toward union with God. "I shall therefore confess both what I know of myself and what I do not know. For even what I know about myself I only know because your light shines upon me; and what I do not know about myself I shall continue not to know until I see you face to face and 'my dusk is noonday'" (X, 5).

The man who chooses isolation elects a self-understanding which excludes all that is hidden and dependent upon grace for revelation. By pleasing himself too much and attempting to be his own *principium*, man contrives to conjure away all his problems, all questions which he himself cannot answer, contracting his soul to the minimal size which can be illuminated by his own unaided reason. Such questions as Who am I? Whence have I come? he represses from his consciousness in order that he might seek his identity in monologue, in continually proclaiming to the world who he thinks he is; Augustine seeks his identity in dialogue, in seeking the highest good, the transcendent source of his being: understanding of God and understanding of self are complementary.

So far we have found that in solitude the soul is open in dialogue, while in isolation it is closed in monologue. Solitude, or the discovery of the true self in personal relationship with the transcendent God, is experienced as the search for innocence and for the *arché*, or *principium*, or Ground of one's being, for innocence is union with the Ground. This search in solitude, this realization of the highest good, is further characterized by experiences of death and time which are quite different from the experiences in isolation.

There are three senses of death in Augustine's reflections: the first, the primary death, the separation of the soul from the body, is the universal punishment for original sin, befalling the just and the unjust alike. What Augustine calls the second death, the eternal separation of the soul from God, is the *summum malum*, the worst evil imaginable, because it is the closest to actual annihilation. This is reserved for those who persist in rejecting God in favor of themselves, who prefer isolation, and it is itself just short of the ultimate isolation of non-being. The third kind of death is more difficult to explain; Augustine himself characterizes it in a very compact expression which occurs in the context of his account of the anguished final stage of his conversion: "I was beside myself with madness that would bring me sanity. I was dying a death that would bring me life" (*insaniebam salubriter, et moriebar vitaliter*). This death, the *mors vitalis*, is essentially the transformation of the egocentric, proud, isolated self into the redeemed, humble, solitary soul which accepts grace and places all its love in God; it is the separation of the soul from what it thinks or wishes itself to be. Unlike the other deaths, especially the second death, the *mors vitalis* is a resurrection in itself, for it is a turning, a *metanoia*, a conversion from nothing to the plenitude of Being. It is an experience which can never be defined, but only inadequately described in dialogue, as *fides quaerens intellectum*. It is redemption, the reversal of the Fall, and as such it is the necessary initiation into the truth and the highest good. Therefore, all men must die two deaths, either the primary and second, or the primary and the *mors vitalis*.

In the second death the members of the earthly city attain the greatest possible degree of isolation, whereas in the *mors vitalis* men turn away from nothing toward the greatest possible participation in Being. Thus, the second death and the *mors vitalis* balance each other and are inversely parallel: they are enantiomorphs, or mirror-images of each other. One is the turn from Being toward nothingness, while the other is the turn from nothingness toward Being; one regards death as the end of all satisfaction, while the other regards it as the beginning of all fulfillment, for in both cases the attitude toward the primary death is determined by the choice of the second death or the *mors vitalis*. This brings us to the experience of time.

In isolation time is experienced as the fourth dimension of a self-enclosed human existence, as the dimension of existence in which desires are satisfied. The experience of time becomes the experience of the tension between desire and satisfaction, and time becomes the definitive dimension of human existence insofar as men devote themselves exclusively to satisfying their desires. Time itself becomes an object of desire, for men crave endless time to avoid death and seek, in hope and terror, the ultimate satisfaction that eludes them – ironically, achievement of such satisfaction would be the prelude to death. The problem with earthly, selfish desires is not that they are insatiable but precisely that they can be satisfied. Human nature is not content with desires that can be satisfied, and when it attempts to be so, temporal existence becomes a frustrating experience of constant unfulfillment.

In solitude the experience of time becomes permeated with the presence of eternity. There is the sense that time is contained in and is subordinate to eternity — that eternity is the measure of time and time is an elementary level of participation in eternity. Unlike the second death, which is a self-condemnation to an eternity experienced as unending time, that is, unending separation from the object of desire, the *mors vitalis* becomes a surrender to an experience of time as, in Eliot's phrase in *Little Gidding*, "a pattern of timeless moments". The deepest experience of time becomes a participation in eternity, but there is yet a deeper experience which transcends temporal existence to find in the tension in between time and eternity the locus of the growth of a desire which can be fulfilled only by being increased; Augustine enters into the love of God only when his soul "clings to an embrace from which it is not severed by fulfillment of desire". (X, 6) This is the experience of time as theotropic, as pointing to its hidden source.

For Augustine the hidden source is the tensional component of the manifest, the hidden is the "psyche", the animating source of all that exists. Time, also, as a manifest dimension of human existence, is experienced as both in tension with and a participation in eternity. Accompanying this experience is a sense of immortality, a sense that one is already, in some sense, living in eternity. Therefore, while isolation is the rebellion against all existential tensions, solitude is essentially the discovery and acceptance of the tension within the soul toward transcendence, in the sense both of self- and cosmic-transcendence. It is this psychic tension to which Augustine refers in the famous passage at the beginning of the *Confessions*: "you made us for yourself and our hearts find no peace until they rest in you". (I, 1).

Perhaps we might reformulate the distinction between isolation and solitude: the hearts of all men are restless and dissatisfied, but the world is divided between those men who attempt to satisfy themselves and those who are aware that only God can satisfy them. The former speak only to make their desires known, while the latter speak only to learn what it is they desire. This corresponds to the exhaustive division of mankind into the earthly city and the City of God.

From the analysis thus far it is apparent that Augustine's philosophical anthropology is characterized by a kind of bilateral symmetry, that is, the whole of human reality is constituted by the two cities which relate to each other as right to left in that they have opposite orientations and are mirror-images of each other. The importance of this symmetry becomes clearer if we further investigate and characterize the contrasting aspects.

Those who choose the earthly city elect to live according to their earthly desires, according to themselves, their own uncontrolled passions. This choice is rooted in pride, the belief that one can be the source of one's existence. Concomitant with this assumption is the illusion that one has or should have a divine control of reality, and this illusion manifests itself in human action and motivation as the *libido dominandi*, the lust for rule, for control of existence. This is, of course, life according to the lie that man can be self-sufficient metaphysically. Since men in the earthly city all live egotistically, according to their own private and conflicting desires, there is no true society in the sense of community, but only an aggregate of individuals who live by custom and convention. Men are made unsocial by the pride at the root of sin, and through sin they fall into the *summum malum*, the second death, the eternal death of the soul. The earthly city is the realm of the fallen, unredeemed human nature.

By contrast, those who accept salvation through the grace of God choose to love God to the contempt of themselves, that is, they live for and in *amor dei*, love of God, rather than *amor sui*, love of self; they find their delight in the will of God rather than in their own desires, while the grace of God assists their reason to control and order their passions. This is the *oboedientia caritatis*, the obedience of charity, which is the basis of all true concord and community, for the members of the community achieve perfect union in their love and acceptance of the will of God, and are, therefore, truly social. The lives and hearts of such men are humble in that these men adhere to the order of reality according to which God is the source, the *principium*, of existence, and in such humility is found the truth. The members of the City of God live in hope of possessing God, the *summum bonum*, and this hope, assisted by grace, directs their reason so that their whole temporal life is ordered for the sake of achieving eternal life with God. Since the lives and wills of all the members of the City of God are ordered toward one and the same end, it is the realm of true peace, justice, and order.

We can schematize this bilateral symmetry as follows:

earthly city	*City of God*
nature	grace
summum malum	*summum bonum*
passions	reason
amor sui	*amor dei*
libido dominandi	*oboedientia caritatis*
pride	humility

    conflict   peace
    unsocial man   social man
    lie   truth

Since the Fall, human reality is thus bilaterally symmetrical in accordance
with the two and only two fundamental options open to men, choice of God
or choice of themselves. Both aspects are necessary for the whole, but were it
possible for only one to exist it would have to be the City of God, for that is
oriented toward Being, whereas the earthly city is oriented toward nothing.
These, then, are the essential structures of the Christian experience of need
for salvation, and graced response.

Hobbes is, of course, working with the same basic human need for salvation
– the difference is that he translates salvation into considerably different
terms. Since, as we have seen, Hobbes separates happiness from the traditional
highest good and identifies it with "a continual progress of the desire from
one object to another", a condition in which Aristotle, Plato, and Augustine
would have found anything but felicity, it becomes apparent that Hobbes'
rejection–distortion of the highest good condemns man to the vicious circle
of isolation and society, a fact that Hobbes attempts to conceal not only by
his misrepresentation of the traditional view of the highest good, but also by
his replacing it with a human final end of his own choosing: "The final cause,
end, or design of men (who naturally love liberty, and dominion over others)
in the introduction of that restraint upon themselves, in which we see them
live in Commonwealths, is the foresight of their own preservation, and of a
more contented life thereby."[3] This is the substance of Hobbes' salvation –
escape from death into the good life, in this case, a "commodious life" – and
it is predicated upon the absence of conversion in the traditional sense. Rather
than man's changing his life so as to conform to the order of reality, the order
is changed to conform to man's desires. As far as anything beyond this goes
Hobbes simply announces that the salvific pole of Augustine's bilateral
symmetry does not and cannot exist, at least not in this life, and he thereby
destroys the symmetrical order of the Christian interpretation of experience.
Indeed, in Hobbes' view, reality has no true order and men have no ability to
choose a life of virtue.

Hobbes uses the state of nature to portray this condition of isolation, and
in so doing he carries the implications of the earthly city to their ultimate
conclusions. The state of nature is, quite simply, the war of all against all, a
condition of intolerable fear because all men are driven only by their ungoverned desires and passions. Because all men are approximately equal in
strength and capabilities, they are all suspended in the uncertainty engendered

by the continual danger of violent death at the hands of their rapacious fellow men. Because each man is concerned only with expressing his own needs and desires and is completely isolated from every other man, this existential attitude is entirely one of monologue, an attitude of demand rather than of questioning. Men naturally find such an existence intolerable — it is an earthly experience of the horror and ultimate isolation of the second death as envisioned by Augustine. Like Augustine, Hobbes diagnoses this as madness, which, however, he attempts to cure through submission to an absolute sovereign rather than through surrender to God.

However, this is the problem of the loss of the *summum bonum* as it exists on only a very superficial level. If we probe deeper the problem ramifies into much greater complexity. For this we must return briefly to our previous observation regarding Augustine, that together the realms of the highest good and greatest evil exhaust human existence — they are completely and mutually exclusive, for they represent the fundamental orientations of human existence. The question then arises as to what happens when a thinker attempts to eliminate an aspect of reality which has been regarded as essential by the Christian, Western tradition. Is it possible to generate an integral view of reality from a bifurcated half of a previous view? Or, does the bifurcated half necessarily regenerate the corresponding structures of the rejected half?

In order to determine whether the result is generation or regeneration we must examine Hobbes' philosophy to see whether or not there are structures which correspond to the structures of the *summum bonum* for Augustine. Let us first, however, examine the structure of the *summum malum*, since this is the decisive aspect of human existence. For Hobbes, the most basic human experience is that of chaos and fear — the primordial reaction to chaos. His thought encompasses only the primary death, which has, however, assumed the status of the *summum malum*, the fall into non-being, with human nature reduced to such incorrigible egocentricity that the *mors vitalis*, with its accompanying experiences of order and peace, becomes inconceivable. The state of nature is a condition of both superficial and radical isolation — by entering society men reduce this condition to one of radical isolation rendered more or less tolerable by disguising it as a comfortable life, which has the decisive advantage of freedom from the constant fear of murder. Time is experienced not as being in tension with eternity but rather as both the ground of the resistance to death and the measure of earthly desires and their satisfactions. Because of the terrifying and constant imminence of the state of nature, even in society, the experience of order is not then susceptible of discovery, but order must instead be imposed on an otherwise recalcitrant, chaotic reality. Man must come to regard himself as the sole source of his own order, and the order which he is able to impose on reality is experienced as quite precarious. Just as Hobbes erects an absolute sovereign to preserve political and social order, so in order to preserve the psychic order necessary to acceptance of his system he establishes an absolute premise for all thought: there is no *summum bonum*. To insure that men will not think the unthinkable or ask undesirable questions, Hobbes assures them that the only possible effect a *summum bonum* could have on human life would be its termination. Just as the *summum bonum* is reduced to the *summum malum*, so the greatest evil — existence according to one's egocentric desires — becomes the means to Hobbes' equivalent for the highest good — the preservation of life in some degree of comfort.

Within the pervasive chaos of the Hobbesian universe the only appropriate mode of human existence is in the tension between isolation and society, which is antagonistic and destructive, for men who are caught in this tension are necessarily devoted to themselves and are, therefore, not truly social. Just as a true community, for Augustine, is composed of men who have discovered and embraced their own solitude, so a viable society, within the strictures of Hobbes' thought, is composed of men who are fleeing the horrors of their own isolation. They seek salvation from the unpleasant aspects of radical isolation, not from such isolation itself — which is not overcome or integrated within a social order but merely concealed by the artful device of basing a society on individual isolation through limiting the expression of selfishness. In other words, pride and egocentricity, the cause of isolation, masquerade as the basis of a society which is established to protect the selfish interests of the members. While Augustine's cure for madness required conversion, *metanoia*, a complete reorientation of the psyche, Hobbes' cure instead prescribes changing the world so that men will not experience their existence in it as one of intolerable madness.

Insofar as the problem is that men are mad because they are condemned to divinity without the requisite knowledge, with only their passions to guide them, there are two possible means of salvation — either men should receive the necessary knowledge or simply surrender the divine office of judging good and evil. We have found that Hobbes incorporates both into the Commonwealth in which the sovereign is the mortal god, created by the mutual covenants of the men who become the citizens of the Commonwealth. Since any disagreements with the sovereign immediately raise the specter of disorder and return to the state of nature, men conform to his will from the sheer desire for self-preservation. As the force that preserves men from the *summum malum* and enables them to achieve the surrogate *summum bonum* the power of the sovereign thus functions as an equivalent for grace.

However, if we probe somewhat deeper, we find that Hobbes's Commonwealth, as the realm in which men are rescued from the evils of the human condition, is a transmogrification of the City of God. The preservation of the Commonwealth becomes a functional aspect of the highest good in that for the sake of order and existence all men's actions are to be oriented toward this preservation for the preservation of their own existences. In Augustine's thought, the turning from the greatest evil to the highest good leads through the *mors vitalis*, the death of the fallen man. In Hobbes we find an equivalent for the *mors vitalis* in the making of mutual covenants, which signals the death of unlimited passions and the turning toward the absolute power of the sovereign, the equivalent for grace, as the salvation from the greatest evil. Through these covenants men then enter an existence, not according to truth, but according to convention. The equivalent for loving obedience to the eternal God becomes the terrified obedience to the mortal god.

Therefore, it seems quite reasonable to maintain that inasmuch as his thought contains equivalents for the structures of the City of God, albeit in a distorted form, the attempt of Hobbes to reject the *summum bonum* has failed, and the result has been a kind of regeneration of the old, rather than a generation of something new. However, the concept of regeneration is somewhat inadequate in this context, since the replication of the bilateral symmetry occurs only in a mutated or distorted form. For taking account of the distortion a more adequate concept is that of *repression* which is, in the Freudian understanding, the continued rejection from consciousness of some experience or aspect of reality which is regarded as undesirable. That which is repressed is shoved into the unconscious, where it exerts a disturbing influence on the actions of the person, usually emerging in strange and distorted forms which Freud called displacement-substitutes, and which function as replacements for the rejected aspects of reality.

In the case of Hobbes we encounter a kind of philosophical repression in which the idea of the *summum bonum* is rejected and pushed into a philosophical unconscious. The repression itself is rooted in a philosophical contraction in which the psyche elects monologue over dialogue and replaces metaphysics with epistemology as the basis of order: all that can be known are the contents of the human mind, which accordingly become the source of truth and order. Since Hobbes is seeking certainty and the *summum bonum* precludes all certainty, he attempts to eliminate it: as a philosopher of the monologue he speaks only to say what he wants reality to be. However, the

highest good reappears within the structure of his philosophy as a syndrome
of displacement-substitutes which preserve the bilateral symmetry. We can
schematize the syndrome of displacement-substitutes as follows:

earthly city	City of God	Commonwealth (Church)
nature	grace	power of sovereign
summum malum	summum bonum	escape from summum malum
passions	reason	calculating reason
amor sui	amor dei	terror of mortal god
libido dominandi	oboedientia caritatis	obedience of terror
pride	humility	submission
conflict	peace	minimal disorder
unsocial man	social man (community)	mutual covenants
lie	truth	convention

It is important to note that isolation remains unredeemable in Hobbes'
scheme: society is merely an aggregate of isolated, egotistic individuals, and
its purpose is only to protect the lives and interests of the individuals, to
promote the art and technology necessary for their comfortable life. Individuals still live according to their self-interest; they have merely moderated
the exercise of it for the sake of self-preservation. Since man is nothing but
passions and selfish desires, the statements he makes and the questions he
asks are necessarily egocentric. The psyche is a self-enclosed world having no
relationship with a transmundane God and community is therefore impossible.
For Hobbes nothing is hidden within man's soul, for all that man could ever
know about himself is manifest, or becomes manifest upon self-reflection.
The hidden relationship between the *summum bonum*, the *deus absconditus*
(hidden God), and the secret depths of the soul, what Augustine calls the
fundus arcanus (secret ground) – the *intima*, the *homo interior*, the *abyssus*
– this relationship is simply obliterated in Hobbes' thought, or rather not
so much obliterated as repressed and replaced with the "deep" of one's
"cogitations and experiences". By repressing the *summum bonum* Hobbes
transmogrifies the dialogue between God and the soul into merely the citizen's
agreement to obey the sovereign in return for the security of his protection.
Loving humility has been replaced by terrified submission.
This rejection of the highest good is, then, the ultimate source of Hobbes'
anticosmy. Oddly enough, it is only when man is reduced to a purely natural
being that he can be seen as a "god" capable of saving himself from the
unpleasantness connected with the purely natural condition. One of the
ineluctable attributes and perhaps the distinguishing characteristic of the
natural man is pride, or the *libido dominandi*, which by definition includes

the desire to be a god unto oneself. Removing man from a relationship with God, and indeed from anything that transcends his self-interest inevitably dissolves the human soul into a self-contradictory state, as both beast and god. The Aristotelian view of man as a composite of reason and desires has broken down into a conflict between an impotent reason and a snarling beast. There is no possible harmony in the soul between reason and the passions for Hobbes.

The resolution of the tension of this schizophrenic psyche requires a pseudo-conversion, a pseudo-humility to mask or inhibit pride, to sublimate the pride into fool's gold. Hobbes' dichocosmy then is the ideology of pseudo-humility, a pretty tale designed to persuade the citizens that pride is best turned to submission for reasons that are far from arbitrary, but are grounded in the very structure of the cosmos. The dichocosmy of the Kingdom of Nature and the Kingdom by Covenant is then a pseudo-public philosophy and civil theology, respectively, to balance submission to necessity and free choice, a cosmos of power and a cosmos of covenant, a cosmos of submission to God with a cosmos in which men have a destiny as partners with God. In itself this dichocosmy of the two kingdoms is not radically different from the corresponding structures of the American civil religion. What distinguishes Hobbes' approach is that the dichocosmy is embedded in a philosophical anthropology which denies the relationship with God and grace — two things which are part of the tradition from which the American civil religion emerged.

The dichocosmy provides grounding and legitimation for the political order by presenting a cosmic order which is actually alien to the purely natural man. The dichocosmy then helps in the conversion of the natural man into the citizen. It is the surrounding anticosmy that decides the character of Hobbes's thought, and we find that, insofar as it represses the highest good, it is a cosmos of projection built upon a complete denial of the cosmos of perception. On one level we can say that the anticosmy is what happens to a civil theology when the public philosophy, with its restraining force, is completely denied. The truth of the public philosophy, of the rational perception of the divine order and of man in humble relationship with God, does not, of course, cease to be — it exerts a decisive influence on the structures of the civil theology, which is why we find the civil theology composed of displacement-substitutes for the rejected public philosophy. The power of the public philosophy is here manifested by the fact that Hobbes cannot do without a final end of human existence — there must be something men desire for its own sake, and if it is not God or virtue then it must be a comfortable life, and everything attached thereto.

Surrounding the dichocosmy we find an anticosmy which is a kind of personal civil theology, or, to borrow a word from Eric Voegelin, an egophany, a projection of the ego onto the cosmos, a manifestation of the ego and its private desires in such a way as to conceal the truth. Egophany is actually the equivalent, on the level of the individual, of a hypertrophied civil theology, or an eschatological civil theology, or we could also say extreme nationalism. It is an attempt by an individual to remake the cosmos in the image of his own psyche. Hobbes' philosophy as a whole, as a reduction of human aspirations to physical comfort, is a remaking of man according to Hobbes' own private view as the new moral philosopher, and, therefore, it begins in a distortion of the truth.

The state religion Hobbes proposes is, specifically, a paradigmatic civil theology, for it contains nothing but the honor of being the first which would provide an identity or destiny for a particular nation. But this paradigmatic civil theology is embraced by an eschatological egophany, eschatological in the sense that it promises the realization of an earthly salvation, through man's own efforts. In giving meaning to earthly society Hobbes has transferred to it all meaning. The civil theology is a form of Christianity, but it is ultimately determined by the re-interpretation of Christianity as a legitimation of political sovereignty, accomplished through the loss of the traditional highest good. Unlike an historical people which speaks from within and seeks to interpret its collective experience, and must hold some things in common even to exist as a people, the individual philosopher is able to abstract himself from experience and create a world and a society within his own mind. In this case the civil theology of the proposed society is not an interpreter of experience, but a determiner of it. Hobbes' philosophy, then, is a displacement-substitute for Christianity, as his salvific society, as the realm in which men are both bestial and divine, is a displacement-substitute for the hypostatic union of the Incarnation. The dichocosmy is a legitimation of the anticosmy, according to which man is both beast and god, and it is because Hobbes' rejection of the highest good reduces man to an unhappy combination of the two types of being which Aristotle regarded as by nature non-political that his civil theology, or more broadly his civil religion, is a failure: it is based on a rejection of man as man.

REFERENCES

[1] Francis Bacon, *The New Organon and Related Writings*, ed. by Fulton H. Anderson,

New York, The Liberal Arts Press, 1960, p. 46.
[2] Saint Augustine, *Confessions*, tr. by R. S. Pine-Coffin, Baltimore, Penguin Books, 1961. All quotations from the *Confessions* are from this translation.
[3] *Leviathan*, p. 99.

CHAPTER IX

ROUSSEAU: THE RELIGION OF SELF-LOVE

> *Rousseau's passionate belief that men are naturally good, which he once said was the fundamental principle of his ethical writings, was less an intellectual conviction than a reversal of his innate fear that he was bad. By throwing the fault on society he was able at once to satisfy his need for condemnation and to shelter himself in a comfortable myth.*[1]

Rousseau was very much like Hobbes in that his philosophy is largely a reflection of his personality, perhaps in his case even more strongly a remaking of man in his image. But Rousseau's writings on philosophical anthropology and political theory are much more than an elaboration of and justification or compensation for his own idiosyncrasies. They are also a revaluation and interpretation of the experience of the need for salvation, and Rousseau's civil religion is merely one aspect of a complex proposed interpretation of salvation.

Rousseau had obviously read Hobbes since he discusses his theories on a number of occasions, including his discussion of civil religion where he indicates that he will correct the mistake which Hobbes had made in attempting to develop a civil religion a century earlier. According to Rousseau, Hobbes was the only Christian writer who had perceived "the evil" and its proper remedy, the reunion of Church and State, "and the restoration throughout of political unity, without which no state or government will ever be rightly constituted".[2] But Hobbes had erred in trying to incorporate christianity into his system — he did not realize that with its "domineering spirit" Christianity would never consent to be subordinate to the State. Nevertheless, Rousseau maintains that "it is not so much what is false and terrible in [Hobbes'] political theory, as what is just and true that has drawn down hatred on it." Hobbes was unpopular because he courageously pointed out the evil in men's most cherished beliefs.

Rousseau describes this evil in terms quite similar to Hobbes, yet different in some important respects. "Jesus came to set up on earth a spiritual kingdom, which, by separating the theological from the political system, made the State no longer one, and brought about the internal divisions which have never ceased to trouble Christian peoples." Since there has always been a political authority, "this double power and conflict of jurisdiction have made all good polity impossible in Christian States; and men have never succeeded in finding out whether they were bound to obey the master or the priests."[3] Rousseau, obviously less concerned with making his conclusions palatable to devout Christians, unhesitatingly blames Christ for the inner conflicts of Christian citizens. It was Christ's creation of a spiritual kingdom that separated the theological system from the State, thereby imposing on the citizens the painful duty of attempting to serve two masters, which has meant in practice, that good political order has never been possible in Christian states. And since, "all that destroys social unity is worthless; all institutions that set man in contradiction to himself are worthless",[4] Rousseau finds it necessary to correct Christ's work.

On the whole Rousseau considers Christianity, at least in its traditional form, as a purely spiritual, otherwordly religion that emasculates men, incapacitating them for any truly effective action in this world. "We are told that a people of true Christians would form the most perfect society imaginable. I see in this supposition only one great difficulty: that a society of true Christians would not be a society of men." Christians are naive and easily taken advantage of by their more worldly-wise and less virtuous opponents.

Yet Rousseau begins from a somewhat more favorable view of Christianity, or the "religion of man", the Christianity of the Gospel, completely different from its contemporary interpretation. "By means of this holy, sublime, and *real* religion all men, being children of one God, recognize one another as brothers, and the society that unites them is not dissolved even at death."[5] The only drawback of this "real religion" is that it is apolitical and therefore provides the political order with no reinforcement or further legitimation. In fact, by making men conscious of another world Christianity distracts them from their earthly, political duties. In short, Rousseau sees the need for religion, that will transform Christians into zealous and patriotic citizens.

At first blush this seems rather an unlikely conclusion to be reached by a man who regarded the social order as a realm of "oppression and misery", and who saw all the evils of human existence as arising from social life. Nevertheless Rousseau managed to combine with his love of solitude an intense devotion to patriotism, *le zèle patriotique*, although it is unclear whether it was his country or the emotion that he loved. In the *Confessions*, written a number of years after the *Social Contract*, Rousseau describes his awakening feelings of patriotism when he returned to his native Geneva after an absence of many years, during which time he had been baptized as a Catholic, although not entirely at his own will.

According to Rousseau his reception was so warm that in response he gave himself up entirely to "patriotic zeal". Unfortunately, as a Catholic, at least on paper, Rousseau was not eligible for the benefits of citizenship in the cradle of Calvinism, and so he decided, on the basis of patriotic zeal, to revert to Calvinism. "I thought the gospel being the same for every Christian, and the only difference in religious opinions the result of the explanations given by men to that which they did not understand, it was the exclusive right of the sovereign power in every country to fix the mode of worship [*culte*], and these unintelligible opinions; and that consequently it was the duty of a citizen to admit the one [*le dogme*], and conform to the other [*le culte*] in the manner prescribed by the law." [6] Rousseau concludes that there cannot be two ways of being a Christian "for a reasonable man", and so, implicitly, the good patriotic citizen is also the good Christian.

Rousseau was himself obviously of two minds on this question of the solitary versus the patriotic life. *A Discourse on the Origin of Inequality*, a panegyric to the natural, non-social man is prefaced by a Dedication to the Republic of Geneva, a civil society. In this Dedication Rousseau congratulates Geneva on being a happy combination of natural equality and social inequality in conformity with natural law. Geneva seems to have the best of both worlds, and in fact it does serve as the paradigmatic society for Rousseau, who seems in his philosophy to be searching for a way to reconcile man's natural goodness with the advantages of society. But this does not explain how Rousseau himself bridged the gap between the natural and the social man and why he was able to find his ideal in Geneva.

Rousseau seems to begin from a basic dilemma which he states rather explicitly at the beginning of *Emile*, his pedagogical work. The problem is the conflict between the man and the citizen, or between the natural man and the social man, and the need to reconcile these opposite tendencies within the individual. "He who would preserve the supremacy of natural feelings in social life knows not what he asks. Ever at war with himself, hesitating between his wishes and his duties, he will be neither a man nor a citizen. He will be of no use to himself nor to others." [7] As far as Rousseau is concerned these contradictions between self-centered wishes and society-imposed duties are the cause of "our inner conflicts". "Drawn this way by nature and that way by man, compelled to yield to both forces, we make a compromise and reach neither goal." What Rousseau wants to do is to find a way so to combine these contradictory aspects of human experience — nature and convention — as to be able to reach the goals of both. There is a kind of double salvation — nature saves man from the misery and oppression of actual society, while the society of the *Social Contract* saves man from the ignorance and backwardness of the state of nature.

Rousseau makes it fairly clear that he did not derive any pleasure from eighteenth-century French society, much preferring the delights of rustic solitude. His dislike of the artificiality of society was a personal reaction before it was a philosophical position. In the *Confessions* he describes his intense weariness with the *ennui* of society, the emptiness of the endless need for entertainment on the part of the wealthy and idle. Such people were rendered "insipid by constraint", by social convention, and Rousseau came to find company much more to his interest in "a poor simple hawthorn bush, a hedge, a barn, or a meadow", things which freely and spontaneously are what they are. It is society that has ruined and corrupted the original human nature — it constrains human nature so that "all his life long man is imprisoned by our institutions". At this point Rousseau emphatically disagrees with Hobbes regarding the salvific capabilities of society. Indeed, Rousseau's society corresponds much more to Hobbes' state of nature as the realm of evil and of fallen human nature. "God [*L'auteur des choses*] makes all things good; man meddles with them and they become evil." Social life degenerates man — as he becomes sociable he grows "weak, timid and servile".

And so Rousseau seeks the natural, the original man, not as a way of escaping from society or providing some alternative to it but as a way of providing it with the proper foundation. It is the nature of man that is the real foundation of society, a society that will fulfill rather than corrupt and suppress human nature. Accordingly, in *A Discourse on the Origin of Inequality* he characterizes his purpose as "to distinguish properly between what is original and what is artificial in the present [*actuelle*] nature of man". This does, of course, present some difficulties. As Rousseau himself asks, "What experiments would have to be made, to discover the natural man? And how are those experiments to be made in a state of society?" Rousseau is well aware that such a procedure is impossible. Men in society are too much habituated to the social to be able to provide an example of the natural. In this work Rousseau says only that he will proceed on the basis of two principles prior to reason in the human soul — compassion and the impulse toward self preservation.

Fortunately there is a specimen of the natural man fairly close to home, and in the *Confessions* Rousseau is more candid about the actual identity of the mysterious natural man. "I have entered upon an undertaking which is without precedent, whose accomplishment will have no imitator. I wish to show to my fellows a man in the whole truth of nature; and this man shall be myself. I alone. I know [*Je sens*] my heart and I know [*je connais*] men; I am not made like anyone I have met; I dare to believe that I am made like no one in existence. If I am not better, I am at least different." [8]

It is Rousseau's own unique soteriological personality that is to be the real foundation of a society in which men will be happy rather than miserable, and he is the paradigm for all human happiness. At the beginning of *Emile*, his course of instruction to educate a natural man, he says, "It is enough for me that, wherever men are born into the world, my suggestions with regard to them may be carried out, and when you have made them what I would have them be, you have done what is best for them and best for other people." But what is this all but extinct natural man who must regenerate the true human nature out of his own existence?

We found that Hobbes' philosophical anthropology was marked by anti-cosmy — fundamental contradictory premises that man is in need of salvation and that man is capable of saving himself. In Rousseau we find a similar anticosmic structure, for in his philosophical anthropology man is beset by a similar internal contradiction. As in the case of Hobbes, the contradiction in Rousseau arises from a rejection of a significant aspect of human experience as expressed in the tradition. At the beginning of *A Discourse on the Origin of Inequality* Rousseau announces that he is going to proceed on the basis of hypotheses that will save the appearances rather than on the basis of a concern for truth. "Let us begin then by laying facts aside, as they do not affect the question. The investigations we may enter into, in treating this subject [the state of nature], must not be considered as historical truths, but only as mere conditional and hypothetical reasonings, rather calculated to explain the nature of things than to ascertain their actual origin." The state of nature is a pseudo-mythic presentation of the world of light which exists or has existed nowhere except in Rousseau's mind; its purpose is to explain what man truly is, which is the projection of Rousseau's own pseudo-mythic self-image as *l'homme naturel*. And this myth is designed to present a picture of man somewhat different from that conveyed by religion, according to which "God Himself having taken men out of a state of nature immediately after the creation, they are unequal only because it is His will they should be so." This religion-commanded belief does not, however, prevent us from forming "conjectures based solely on the nature of man, and the beings around him concerning what might have become of the human race, if it had been left to itself."[9] First of all, the state of nature means that all men are created equal by nature and it is only by divine intervention that they become unequal. But secondly, and more importantly, Rousseau's conjectures are concerned with the nature of man quite apart from any divine intervention, with how man would have developed completely on his own. To be so considered man must be stripped of not only all the accretions of society but also of all his "supernatural gifts" so that he will appear "just as he must have come from the hands of nature." Rousseau makes rather a radical distinction between God and nature, the latter being the source of truth and order. By implication, whatever God may have done has contributed only to the misery of the human race, since the search for truth requires ignoring or eliminating all divine intervention and supernatural gifts. God is a threat to human order. It is not going too far to say that there is here a replacement of God with Jean-Jacques Rousseau, as there is in *Emile* a replacement of grace with Rousseau's pedagogical efforts. Therefore, much as Hobbes announces that we must forget about the traditional *summum bonum*, so Rousseau announces that in order to arrive at the truth we must forget about grace and any relationship between man and God.

According to these "hypothetical" reasonings, in the state of nature man's "chief and almost sole concern" is self-preservation, which concern requires that man be completely independent and solitary by nature, and that he love himself first of all. There is, of course, no society in the state of nature since none is needed. All men are self-sufficient and capable of satisfying all their wants and desires. Rousseau differs from Hobbes in excluding ungovernable passions from the state of nature, thereby rendering it quite tolerable. The passions of the savage never exceed his basic physical wants. "The only goods he recognizes in the universe are food, a female, and sleep: the only evils he fears are pain and hunger." Being in such an "animal state" man is ignorant of death. He comes to know death and so to fear it only when he leaves the state of nature. There is no competition for the means of subsistence because Rousseau gratuitously presupposes, if not abundance, at least superfluity, and no man either desires more than he needs or needs more than he can himself supply. Through such solitude and freedom man is happy and naturally virtuous because he is powerful within his own existence. As Rousseau expresses it in another work, "He who does as he likes is happy provided he is self-sufficing; it is so with the man who is living in the state of nature."[10] This happiness of being self-sufficing, which we might call autarky, is the first and perhaps dominant pole of human nature. It is also the *summum bonum*: "There is only one man who gets his own way — he who can get it single-handed; therefore freedom, not power [*autorité*], is the greatest good. That man is truly free who desires what he is able to perform, and does what he desires. . . . Society has enfeebled man, not merely by robbing him of the right to his own strength, but still more by making his strength insufficient for his needs." [11]

For Rousseau, this autarky is the power of self-sufficiency, independence of other men, and sovereignty over one's existence. Men participate in divinity through such an existence — autarky is the outstanding characteristic of Rousseau's idea of divinity, as can be seen in a prayer he composed. "All-powerful God, eternal Father, my heart ascends in your presence to offer you the homage and the adoration which it owes to you; my soul, penetrated by your immense majesty, by your terrible power and your infinite grandeur, humbles itself before you with sentiments of the most profound veneration and the most respectful abasement. O my God, . . . I recognize you as the creator, conservator, master and absolute sovereign of all that exists, as the absolute and independent being who needs only himself in order to exist." [12] Metaphysically, at least, there is nothing in this prayer with which Aquinas or Augustine could not agree: God is necessarily the supreme, absolutely self-sufficient Being. However, Rousseau does not limit this autarky to God, but applies it primarily to man, as we have seen, as a self-sufficiency that is considerably more than merely material independence, according to the Savoyard Vicar who, by Rousseau's later admission, spoke Rousseau's own beliefs. "Supreme happiness consists in self-contentment [*La suprême jouis-sance est dans le contentement de soi-même*]; that we may gain this self-contentment we are placed on this earth and endowed with freedom, we are tempted by our passions and restrained by conscience." [13] Although it is obvious from Rousseau's state of nature that material self-sufficiency is an important part of self-contentment, this alone does not explain why it is *self*-contentment rather than simply contentment, and why it is *la suprême jouissance*.

In Rousseau's view self-contentment is based on *amour de soi*, which is also the foundation of the autarkic preservation of one's own existence. "Self-preservation requires . . . that we shall love ourselves, [and we must love ourselves above everything], and it follows directly from this that we love what contributes to our preservation." [14] This *amour de soi*, as the basis of self-preservation, "is always good, always in accordance with order."

Although Rousseau praises this self-love as the wellspring of all good and virtue, it is, nevertheless, precisely the *amor sui*, or the seeking one's satisfaction in the self, or pride, that Augustine regards as the origin of all sin and human misery. The Savoyard Vicar, speaking for Rousseau, explains this metaphysical self-sufficiency quite explicitly: "I long for the time when, freed from the fetters of the body, I shall be myself, at home with myself, no longer torn in two, when I myself shall suffice for my own happiness [*et n'aurai besoin que de moi pour être heureux*]. . . . all the real good that I can get out of this life depends on myself alone." [15]

There are a few conclusions we can draw here. First, death appears as both an ending of all inner conflicts and, consequently, as a kind of self-divinization. Second, since he has said earlier in *Emile* that man's inner conflicts are essentially those between his wishes and his duties, or between the "man" and the "citizen", we have the implication that the resolution of such conflicts, the making man at one with himself, which Rousseau wants to achieve by re-establishing society on the true foundation of the natural, self-sufficient man, is a kind of apotheosis of man through the re-founding of society on the true man. Augustine's theonomy has been replaced by autonomy.

This *amour de soi* is the primary motive for man's actions and the fundamental constituent of human nature. It is the original passion, coeval with man, and the source of all the rest. This passion is "primitive, instinctive, it precedes all the rest, which are in a sense only modifications of it." Moreover, this *amour de soi* plays the role of *amor dei* in the thought of Augustine for it is the source of all goodness and the "antithesis" of the self-love that caused original sin. "There is no original sin in the human heart, but the how and why of the entrance of every vice can be traced. The only natural impulse is self-love or selfishness taken in a wider sense. This selfishness is good in itself and in relation to ourselves; and as the child has no necessary relations to other people he is naturally indifferent to them". [16] Rousseau describes in some detail the effect of this self-love on human relationships in the state of nature — because every man suffices for his own happiness there are no real ties between parents and child, or between parent and parent, and they do not even recognize each other when they meet. What this says is not that there ever was such a state of affairs, but that, as human nature truly is, each individual is capable of being perfectly happy in the enjoyment of himself. There is no need either for God or for other people.

The skunk in this idyllic garden is the passions, which, developing beyond man's ability to satisfy them, undermine and eventually destroy his self-sufficiency, thereby preventing him from fully realizing himself as God. As

Emile, grown to manhood, says to his tutor, "But for my passions, I should be in my manhood independent as God himself, for I only desire what is and I should never fight against fate." As this statement indicates, autarky means not omnipotence but a superiority of powers over desires, or perhaps an equilibrium of desires and powers. Self-contentment is a kind of limited omnipotence – the individual is all-powerful within the boundaries of his own existence. Having no needs which he cannot himself satisfy he is dependent neither on God nor on other men. The "fall" from such divine autonomy occurred with the awakening of man's passions.

For Rousseau the passions represent the opposite pole of human nature. Even though self-love is a passion and the origin of all the other passions there is no difficulty so long as the passions remain quiescent. It is only when man begins to desire more than he can himself supply that he falls from the paradise of the state of nature by becoming dependent on others. It is the passions that destroy autarky by introducing into human nature weakness, or asthenia, not an absolute but a relative weakness. "What is the cause of man's weakness? It is to be found in the disproportion between his strength and his needs. It is our passions that make us weak, for our natural strength is not enough for their satisfaction." [17] Moreover, in Rousseau's specific sense, it is ungoverned passions, that is, passions which the possessor cannot himself satisfy, that are the source of evil.

Disagreeing with both Augustine's and Hobbes' contention that the wicked man is "a strong child" in that he combines the emotional immaturity of the child with the physical maturity of the adult, Rousseau maintains, rather curiously, that "all wickedness comes from weakness. The child is only naughty because he is weak; make him strong and he will be good; if we could do everything we should never do wrong." [18] The logical conclusion is that God is infinitely good because He is fortunate enough to be omnipotent. This is certainly an unusual point of view, but it follows from the premise of Rousseau's philosophical anthropology that the ideal of happiness is autarky.

In the state of nature the happiness and goodness of the savage are due entirely to the somnolence of his passions. For Rousseau the passions are a form of pleonexy: Rousseau, like Hobbes, regards the passions, once aroused, as insatiable and therefore the source of conflicts. Salvation, then, is effected by restoring the balance between man's desires and powers, in accordance with the design of nature. "True happiness consists in decreasing the difference between our desires and powers, in establishing a perfect equilibrium between the power [*la puissance*] and the will. Then only, when all its forces are employed, will the soul be at rest and man will find himself in his true position."

This pristine harmony is the condition in which nature, "who does everything for the best", placed man in the very beginning. "To begin with, she gives him only such desires as are necessary for self-preservation and such powers [*facultés*] as are sufficient for their satisfaction."[19] If this be true it is not difficult to see that the purpose or end of human life as ordained by nature is simply its continuance, and man is designed by nature as a being that finds complete satisfaction simply in maintaining his own existence. The fall from this idea state occurs when man aspires to something beyond the simple preservation of his life, when he seeks, in a curious reversal, to be less than God. It is closeness to nature and to its design of virtue that is the basis of human happiness and self-contentment.

We have already quoted the statement of the Savoyard Vicar that we are tempted to abandon autarky by the passions and are restrained by conscience. Conscience, the faculty that protects man from asthenia and preserves his autarky is the voice, not of reason, but of the "sentiments of nature". Rousseau makes here a distinction between passions and feelings or sentiments, the latter rather than rational judgments, being the decrees of conscience. Reason, from causes that Rousseau does not explain, is much too unreliable to serve as the guide to our actions. "Too often does reason deceive us; we have only too good a right to doubt her; but conscience never deceives us; she is the true guide of man; it is to the soul what instinct is to the body; he who follows his conscience obeys nature, and he need not fear that he will go astray."[20] In somewhat more traditional terms Rousseau also maintains that "Conscience is the voice of the soul, the passions are the voice of the body." It is the role of conscience to preserve man's autarky by restraining his inclination to give free rein to his passions. This freeing of the passions corrupts human existence by making the individual less self-sufficient. As the Savoyard Vicar rhapsodizes, "Conscience! Conscience! Divine instinct, immortal voice from heaven; sure guide for a creature ignorant and finite indeed, yet intelligent and free; infallible judge of good and evil, making man like to God! In thee consists the excellence of man's nature and the morality of his actions."[21] It is conscience, the voice of autarky, that transforms human nature into divine nature.

Autarky and asthenia are, then, the two contradictory poles of human nature, and the tension between them is the primary source of inner conflicts, as explained by the Savoyard Vicar: "When I felt myself carried away, distracted by these conflicting motives, I said, No, man is not one; I will and I will not; I felt myself at once a slave and a free man." Asthenia constitutes man's need for salvation through the return to autarky, and it is autarky that represents man's ability to save himself. Asthenia is the source of vice, disorder, and evil while autarky is the source of virtue, order, and goodness.

It should be noted that asthenia has a certain ambivalent character – although primarily a mark of man's 'fallen' condition, it is present also in the state of nature in the form of compassion, which provides man with a rudimentary social instinct. "Man's weakness makes him sociable. Our common sufferings draw our hearts to our fellow-creatures; we should have no duties to mankind if we were not men." For Rousseau, every affection [attachement] for another human being is a sign that we need others and are therefore not self-sufficient. If we were self-sufficient we would not think of associating with anyone else. "So our frail happiness has its roots in our weakness. A truly happy being is a solitary being; God only enjoys absolute happiness; but which of us has any idea what that means?"[22]

To some extent compassion here has a role similar to that of the secret corruption which Augustine resorted to in order to explain how Adam and Eve, created perfect, could have sinned. Compassion, with all its kindred affections, constitutes a certain detraction from the perfect self-sufficiency that is the ideal.

It turns out, however, that compassion has also a much more vital role to play. Compassion is "a natural feeling, which, by moderating the violence of love of self in each individual, contributes to the preservation of the whole species." In this respect Rousseau's compassion is analogous to Hobbes' fear as the force that inhibits desire, thereby being ultimately responsible for the preservation of the whole species by functioning essentially as a check to amour-propre or egotism, the destructive aspect of self-love. It prevents man from becoming so absorbed in the desire for self-preservation and self-sufficiency that he will seek to preserve himself at any cost, even the life of another human being. In the state of nature it "supplies the place of laws, morals and virtues" as the basis of order.

The principle of order in the state of nature shows the influence of compassion – "Do good to yourself with as little evil as possible to others." This is natural goodness based on an amour de soi, a self-love or self-preservation which is primary and primordial and which neither unduly encroaches upon nor totally ignores another's efforts to preserve his existence, and which thereby aids in the preservation of the species. It is compassion which prevents Rousseau's tranquil, idyllic state of nature from degenerating into Hobbes' state of the war of all against all with the arousal of the passions, and therefore it is compassion rather than fear which makes social existence possible, society being the equivalent for Hobbes' state of nature as the realm in which men are fallen. So we find that compassion has somewhat the same ambivalent character as fear does for Hobbes — while it is the psychological response to "fallenness", in this case asthenia, it is also the psychological factor necessary for society, which brings us to the meaning of society for Rousseau. It would seem that society represents more an affirmation of man's 'fallen' condition, his weakness, rather than a salvation from it. Obviously, man cannot live as a perfectly happy solitary being in society.

Considering his philosophical anthropology there were available to Rousseau three possibilities for saving man from asthenia: (1) advocating a return to the state of nature; (2) attempting to change society to accord with the true human nature; and (3) attempting to change human nature to accord with society. Since he is only too well aware of the material and cultural advantages of society as well as of the non-existence of the state of nature, Rousseau never gives serious consideration to the first alternative. On the basis of his excoriation of actual society one would expect Rousseau to choose the second, and indeed this does seem to be the direction in which he is headed in *A Discourse on the Origin of Inequality*, when he emphasizes the necessity of removing all the artificial accretions from human nature so as to restore the true and original human nature which should serve as the foundation of society. However, what seems surprising after the *Discourse* is that in *The Social Contract* Rousseau also advocates the third alternative, perhaps even more strongly than the second. "He who dares to undertake the making of a people's institutions ought to feel himself capable, so to speak, of changing human nature, of transforming each individual, who is by himself a complete and solitary whole, into part of a greater whole from which he in a manner receives his life and being." [23] It is in the complexities of effecting such a two-fold alteration of reality that we can discern the structures of Rousseau's salvation.

First of all we must consider in more detail how man came to this fallen estate, how he abandoned the happiness of the state of nature for the misery of society. The distinguishing characteristic of the state of nature is the divine ability to rest in the enjoyment of one's being — Rousseau feels that nothing is greater than "to be free and virtuous, superior to fortune and opinion, and independent of all exterior circumstances". Accordingly, in *Emile* Rousseau advises that the tutor should teach his pupil to cultivate this sense of existence, "to live rather than to avoid death: life is not breath, but action, the use of our senses, our mind, our faculties, every part of ourselves which makes us conscious of our being." This ability to enjoy his being for its own sake is the foundation both of man's divinity and his true human nature.

Therefore for Rousseau man in his original, 'unfallen' nature is much more directly and exclusively concerned with the continuance of his personal existence than is man in society who must devote much of his energy to fulfilling duties. One might go so far as to say that for man in the state of nature essence is the preservation and enjoyment of existence. Compassion is relatively incidental to man in the state of nature: on the whole the primitive man rests in the tranquillity of *amour de soi*, a tranquillity symbolized by the equilibrium or identity of desires and power. Society, then, represents the diremption of man's essence from his existence – man in society is no longer at rest in preserving his existence while owing it to no one but himself; he becomes depraved and loses his self-sufficiency in desiring things that have nothing to do with self-preservation. "So long as only bodily needs are recognized man is self-sufficing; with superfluity comes the need for division and distribution of labor." This superfluity leads to "industry and the mechanical arts which make men useful to one another". In other words, as soon as men begin to desire luxuries, they become dependent on other men, which type of dependence is asthenia; "there are two kinds of dependence: dependence on things, which is the work of nature; and dependence on men, which is the work of society. Dependence on things, being non-moral, does no injury to liberty and begets no vices; dependence on men, being disordered, gives rise to every kind of vice, and through this master and slave become mutually depraved." [24] Dependence on men is Rousseau's equivalent for sin.

According to Rousseau's myth, the concrete act that was the equivalent of the fall was the first claim to possession of property, the first indulgence in luxury. In the state of nature this was committed by the first man who, having claimed ownership of a piece of ground, was then able to convince other people that he really did have a special right to it. The unchallenged acceptance of this was the cause of "crimes, wars and murders, ... horrors and misfortunes". Like Augustine Rousseau does not see this as an evil that suddenly sprang into existence out of nowhere, so to speak. It was the manifest accumulation of prior evils: " ... there is great probability that things had already come to such a pitch, that they could no longer continue as they were; for the idea of property depends on many prior ideas, which could only be acquired successively, and cannot have been formed all at once in the human mind." [25] And here Rousseau becomes ambivalent regarding the state of nature and the moral value of society. "Mankind must have made very considerable progress, and acquired considerable knowledge and industry which they must also have transmitted and increased from age to age, before they arrived at this last point of the state of nature." In other words, human nature must have begun to change even within the state of nature, for it is difficult to see how completely solitary and self-sufficient individuals could have acquired knowledge and industry, much less passed them on to succeeding generations. And, although society has depraved and degenerated man while being the cause of untold misery, it is also the realm of "progress", "knowledge", and "industry". Even man's "fall" into the darkness of society is a manifestation of "progress". Rousseau wanted the best of both worlds, both self-sufficiency and society, and this is in fact what he set out to achieve in his political theory.

Since, as has been already mentioned, Rousseau chooses a twofold, somewhat contradictory salvation — both changing man to suit society and changing society to suit man — it is not surprising that this salvation has two distinct components, one pedagogical and the other social or political. The first is simply to educate men in Rousseau's image, and so restore the natural man. Emile, the archetypal pupil, is to be molded as a natural. self-sufficient man able to live in society insofar as this is necessary. Accordingly, the education he receives is designed to make him virtuous, or controlled by the sentiments of nature, and immune to the evils and luxuries of society. Therefore he cherishes his independence, for he is trained to live for himself.

Although in the true state of nature a man scarcely needs education in order to be natural, conditions are now so deplorable that education is absolutely necessary. "Under existing conditions a man left to himself from birth would be more of a monster than the rest. Prejudice, authority, necessity, example, all the social conditions into which men are plunged, would stifle nature in him and put nothing in her place." [26] Therefore, in order to achieve Rousseau's pedagogical plan of salvation Emile must be educated in isolation from all other human beings save his tutor, who is the voice of self-sufficiency, so that Emile can be protected as much as possible from the debilitating effects of society. "Living in the whirl of social life, it is enough that he should not let himself be carried away by the passions and prejudices of men; let him see with his eyes and feel with his heart, let him own no sway but that of reason", [27] for it is reason that is the basis of self-sufficiency. Thus, the longed-for results of Emile's education — he is to be as immune as possible to asthenia.

The second, social component of salvation, which corresponds to the third alternative mentioned above, is considerably more complex since it involves altering the original human nature so as to make it a suitable foundation for society. In fact, society is to be the realm of reconciliation of wishes and duties, or, as Rousseau states in *The Social Contract*, "the essence of the body politic lies in the reconciliation of obedience and liberty". The natural man must come to find his self-contentment in being a member of the society, and thereby becoming "unnatural". Whereas the natural man lives only for his own sake and depends only on himself, "the citizen is but the numerator of a fraction, whose value depends on its denominator [,] . . . the community. Good social institutions are those best fitted to make a man unnatural, to exchange his independence for dependence, to merge the unity in the group, so that he no longer regards himself as one, but as a part of the whole, and is only conscious of the common life."[28]

If this is the case, then why should men become natural in the first place? Why educate Emile as a natural, independent man only so that he might enter society and become dependent? This is not a question that Rousseau answers directly. What he implies, indirectly, is that such self-love is required so that it can be sublimated into patriotism. The reason why Christians make such poor citizens is that they are sadly lacking in *amour de soi*.

The problem, then, as Rousseau formulates it at the beginning of *The Social Contract* is not the abolition but the legitimation of those social institutions that are built on man's asthenia. "Man is born free; and everywhere he is in chains. One thinks himself the master of others, and still remains a greater slave than they. How did this change come about? I do not know. What can make it legitimate? That question I think I can answer."[29] In the *Discourse* Rousseau actually does provide an answer to the first question, albeit a purely hypothetical answer. What is at first sight surprising, in the light of the *Discourse*, is that Rousseau asks not how the chains can be removed but how they can be made all the more secure. Yet on a closer inspection these turn out to be the same thing — freedom is slavery, and slavery is freedom. The "change" is only in the primary object of one's love and devotion, and it hinges on the concept of right.

" . . . the social order is a sacred right [*un droit sacré*] which is the basis of all other rights. Nevertheless, this right does not come from nature, and must therefore be founded on convention." Rousseau distinguishes between the right of convention and the right of nature. "Let us lay it down as an incontrovertible rule that the first impulses of nature are always right [*sont toujours droits*]."[30] In view of the fact that among the first impulses of nature, or perhaps *the* first impulse of nature, is *amour de soi*, and also that "self-love is always good, always in accordance with order", it seems that whatever is *droit* is what is good and order-producing: in the state of nature it is self-sufficiency based on the balance of desires and powers. Luxury, therefore, as the destroyer of autarky, is the greatest evil.

For Rousseau, the autarkic self is the source of order, since "goodness is the necessary result of boundless power and of that self-love which is innate in all sentient beings",[31] and goodness is the love of order that creates order. The meaning of God for Rousseau is the omnipotent, autarkic, self-loving being, and he is good because he is these things. Man is made good in the image of God by being autarkic and self-loving. "God's goodness consists in the love of order, for it is through order that he maintains what is, and unites each part in the whole",[32] and therefore if men are to be divine and participate in divine goodness they must conserve the existence of what is, uniting each part in the whole. There is, in the state of nature, no whole over which man can exercise control, save his own isolated self. But the foundation of a world, even a small world, such as a society, becomes an exercise of divine power, an essential part of which is uniting parts into a whole. Thus the social order is a sacred right because by this conventional act that separates him from nature man becomes like a god. Through a transvaluation of values, society becomes the mark not of man's fallenness, as in the *Discourse*, but of his divinity, as in *The Social Contract*. This transvaluation can be seen in its early stages in an ambivalence in the Profession of Faith of the Savoyard Vicar. Two pages before announcing that he longs for the time when he will suffice for his own happiness, and that all the real good he can get out of life depends on himself alone, the Vicar refers to his "natural feelings, which spoke of the common weal, and [his] reason, which spoke of self", and goes on to say that "wherever there is feeling and intelligence, there is some sort of moral order. The difference is this: the good man orders his life with regard to all men; the wicked orders it for self alone." This imputation of wickedness to the autarkic man strikes a discordant note with the *Discourse*. This, however, is the beginning of the reconcilation of liberty with obedience, man with citizen. In the transformation of human nature *amour de soi* must be replaced by *amour de la société* as the basis of autarky and therefore divinity. Goodness becomes dependent on a man's love of society even to the contempt of self; he must in fact surrender his will to the will of the whole society, which then becomes the source of his virtue: "If you would have the general will accomplished, bring all the particular wills into conformity with it; in other words, as virtue is nothing more than the conformity of the particular wills with the general will, establish the reign of virtue."[33]

We have said that perhaps the most fundamental evil of society for Rousseau is the separation of man's essence from his existence, which is the basis of the conflict between the citizen and the man. Therefore, his salvation is aimed at restoring this unity on a higher plane by resolving the conflict through, paradoxically, transforming the extreme of freedom into an extreme subjection that will be called freedom, so that the citizens might, in a curious phrase, "bear with docility the yoke of the public happiness". On the other hand, Rousseau seeks the legitimation of chains in terms of freedom. He formulates the fundamental problem solved by *The Social Contract* as that of finding "a form of association which will defend and protect with the whole common force the person and goods of each associate, and in which each, while uniting himself with all, may still obey himself alone, and remain as free as before".[34]

The basic symbol for this salvific association is the general will, *la volonté générale*, the salvific efficacy of which rests on its relation to human existence. We have already quoted Rousseau's statement that "the first impulses of nature are always right [*sont toujours droits*]", and said that the first impulse of nature is *amour de soi*, or a devotion to onself and to preserving one's existence as divinely self-sufficient. We have also said that compassion, by moderating *amour-propre*, the darker side of self-love, mediates between *amour de soi* and the preservation of the species, the preservation of the individual man being the primary reality. Of the general will Rousseau says, "*La volonté générale est toujours droite*". In other words, the general will is always founded on the sacred right of preservation of the society's existence in autarky. It is through the general will that man becomes unnatural in the sense that preservation of the individual ceases to be the primary reality or the central purpose of existence. The situation of society is the reverse of that of the state of nature, for instead of the species being preserved through the individuals through the mediation of compassion, it is the individuals which are preserved through the species, or society, through the mediation of the general will. In the state of nature, the maxim of order emphasizes doing good to oneself with as little evil as possible to others, while in society the maxim, the Golden Rule, emphasizes doing good to others as of first importance. Therefore, in society men become unnatural in the sense that they become conscious of themselves only as part of the whole, for they derive their individual existences from that of the society. Paradoxically, the general will both expresses and conceals the reversal: It expresses it insofar as the general will is a higher 'divine' will to which the wills of the members of the society must conform if they are to be happy, yet it conceals the reversal insofar as Rousseau characterizes the general will as the means by which each citizen can continue to obey only himself. The general will, as an indivisible whole in which each man participates, symbolizes each citizen's concern with and devotion to the existence of the society to which he belongs. The general will is incorruptible – it can be misinformed but never wrong because it springs from the first impulse of nature and is necessarily aimed at the new salvific *summum bonum*, the preservation of the autarky of the society.

This relationship between the individual and the society – that the individual has transferred self-love to the society, thereby transforming self-contentment into patriotism – this relationship is reflected in Rousseau's understanding of the laws. The decrees of the general will are laws, which are also the decrees of the sovereign. It is particularly important for Rousseau that the laws be general. "When the whole people decrees for the whole people, it is considering only itself", that is, the people is concerned only with its own existence; "and if a relation is then formed, it is between two aspects of the entire object, without there being any division of the whole. In that case the matter about which the decree is made is, like the decreeing will, general."³⁵ Law, as an expression of the general will, is concerned with the preservation of the whole people and symbolizes the divine autarky of the society as a whole. The legitimation of man's chains is accomplished by having man find his divinity through participating in the autarky of the society. The laws, representing the general will, insure that the society is governed by reason, or the sentiments of nature, rather than by passion which merely undermines the concern with self-preservation. The independence of the general will has two aspects – the independence of the society as a whole and the independence of each member of the society. Since in the society each citizen manages to continue to obey only himself, within society each citizen purportedly possesses the unrestrained freedom and autarky of the natural man by his participation in the autarky of the society through the general will. For Rousseau the general will resolves the conflict between the man and the citizen, and therefore all of men's inner conflicts, by functioning as the higher will to which man must surrender his own particular self-centered will in order to find happiness and perfection.

However, the fallibility of men also necessitates a legislator to provide enlightened judgment so as to guide the general will. "The public wills the good it does not see..... [It] must be taught to know what it wills. If that is done, public enlightenment leads to the union of understanding and will in the social body: the parts are made to work exactly together, and the whole is raised to its highest power. This makes a legislator necessary."³⁶ The legislator, as Rousseau describes him, must be divine – a mind seeing and understanding all human passions without being susceptible to them, a mind alien to human nature yet well-acquainted with it, a mind above human happiness and able to enjoy the distant advantages of present actions, in other words, a mind that surveys human experience without being subject to it. As Rousseau puts it succinctly, "it would take gods to give men laws".

The legislator should be a divine being, of "great soul", enjoying absolute autarky, as indicated by his freedom from the passions. It is possible to see the legislator as Rousseau delivered from the burden of his passions. The legislator lacks executive power, for he has the power only to draft the laws, not to impose them on the people, because that would detract from their freedom. According to Rousseau, "only the general will can bind the individuals". Therefore, we must ask how the legislator persuades the general will to adopt his scheme of changing human nature so that man can enjoy autarky while simultaneously enjoying the benefits of society. Rousseau's answer to this is essentially Livy's view of Numa — the legislator puts his own decrees into the mouth of the gods.

Since merely human authority lacks a certain persuasiveness, especially to human beings concerned with their independence, founders of nations have always found it expedient "to have recourse to divine intervention and credit the gods with their own wisdom", so that the people might thereby be persuaded that the author of the city is also the author of men, and so, finally, "bear with docility the yoke of the public happiness". Man must be duped into happiness. In fact, compared with the legislator, all other human beings are merely "the common herd". Actually, the mere fact that the people believe the legislator when he attributes his own ideas to the gods is an indication of the legislator's superiority to ordinary mortals. Rousseau's conclusion is that at the beginning of a nation's history religion is used as an instrument for politics. Although this type of reflection does not encompass Rousseau's view of civil theology, it does serve to indicate that it is prudent, if one wishes a society to endure, to found it on some kind of divine authority to persuade the citizens that the voice of the government is the voice of God. More specifically, the legislator claims to speak with the voice of God so that the general will accepts his decrees, believing then that it speaks with the voice of God.

Much as Hobbes used fear as both the psychic force that impelled men to leave the state of nature and the necessary foundation of society, so Rousseau uses the passions, asthenia, as both the factor that undermines man's idyllic, autarkic happiness and as the basis of society. For, inasmuch as "a man without passions would certainly be a bad citizen", the society requires le zèle patriotique, a passion, as devotion to its order. Nevertheless, upon close inspection, the passion necessary for good citizenship turns out to be the basic natural passion, amour de soi. "If, for example, [men] were early accustomed to regard their individuality only in its relation to the body of the State, and to be aware, so to speak, of their own existence merely as a pàrt of that of the State, they might at length come to identify themselves in some degree with this greater whole, to feel themselves members of their country, and to love it with that exquisite feeling which no isolated person has save for himself; to lift up their spirits perpetually to this good object, and thus to transform into a sublime virtue that dangerous disposition which gives rise to all our vices."[37] We see here the reversal both of the value of *amour de soi* and of the relation between individual and species, or society, that was mentioned earlier. No longer is *amour de soi* the source of all human goodness but instead it is the "dangerous disposition" that is the source of all human vices. And salvation comes through a complex sublimation of *amour de soi* and the other passions into *amour de la société*, that is, love of the autarky of the society. Rousseau transforms society from the earthly city, realm of all human misery, to the City of God, or realm of all human perfection and fulfillment, in which the citizens participate in the divine autarky by adhering to the divine general will. The passions are 're-educated' to be supportive rather than destructive of society and the State, and the divine will "invest [s] the sovereign authority with a sacred and inviolable character" in order to insure the endurance of the social order in autarky.

The "purely civil profession of faith" which Rousseau proposes as reinforcement for the social order is exceedingly simple. It is the responsibility of the Sovereign in each civil society to determine certain "social sentiments", rather than explicitly religious dogmas, which are indispensable for being a good citizen or a faithful subject, that is, a participant in the divinity of the society. These social sentiments or dogmas of civil religion ought to be few, simple, and exactly worded, without explanation or commentary. The existence of a mighty, intelligent and beneficent Divinity, possessed of foresight and providence, the life to come, the happiness of the just, the punishment of the wicked, the sanctity of the social contract and the laws – these are its positive dogmas. Its negative dogmas I confine to one, intolerance, which is a part of the cults we have rejected."[38] This "purely civil profession of faith" is essentially the natural religion of the Savoyard Vicar. We should note that Rousseau specifically rejects a civil theology such as that of Varro on the grounds that "being founded on lies and error, it deceives men, makes them credulous and superstitious, and drowns the true cult of the Divinity in empty ceremonial". Since the purpose of Rousseau's civil religion, as will be seen, is to legitimate the authority of his salvific society which is founded on his philosophy of human nature, the civil religion he proposes can be unique to a particular society only in the "dogmas" fixed by the sovereign, apparently rather arbitrarily. In fact he does not want a religion that is too specific, for it is apt to distract men from the concern with *amour de soi* in its social form as *amour de la société*. Patriotism is not a matter of worshipping particular gods, but rather a devotion to worshipping oneself, or the human species, as embodied in the society.

Rousseau corrects Hobbes' error by using natural, and therefore universal religion rather than revealed religion as the foundation of society. According to the dogmas of this natural religion those who share in the autarky of the society can expect to be rewarded in the life to come, while those who do not love the society more than themselves can expect the opposite. Rousseau left the contents of the civil religion deliberately vague — what is important is not what is to be believed but the fact that all the citizens will unite in believing it. Rousseau does agree with Hobbes that political order is virtually impossible unless the citizens are united by the "proper" religion. "Now it matters very much to the community that each citizen should have a religion. That will make him love his duty; but the dogmas of that religion concern the State and its members only so far as they have reference to morality and to the duties which he who professes them is bound to do to others."[39] Although Rousseau does not say so explicitly here, perhaps the major effect of the civil religion is to maintain the freedom of the citizens through making them love their duty. He who loves his duty loves promoting and supporting the autarky of the society, and it is only by participating in autarky that human beings can be free.

Christianity is not suitable for making men love their duty, for it has no particular relation to the body politic nor inclination to be subordinate to the needs of politics, and its orientation toward another world produces the difficulty "that a society of true Christians would not be a society of men", by which Rousseau means that a society of Christians would resolve the inner conflict by renouncing all earthly desires that are necessary to keep a civil state in operation. Rousseau prefers to resolve the conflict by renouncing Christianity, or all concern with transcendence.

We have seen that for Hobbes the civil theology and the Commonwealth to which it belonged functioned as a displacement-substitute for the City of God or community of saints after Hobbes rejected the highest good that was the *raison d'être* of the City of God. Rousseau achieves much the same effect by eliminating grace, as he indicates at the beginning of *A Discourse on the Origin of Inequality*: although religion commands the belief that God took men out of the state of nature immediately after creating them, this "does not forbid us to form conjectures based solely on the nature of man, and the beings around him, concerning what might have become of the human race, if it had been left to itself". In short, man is to be taken as having no relationship with God whatsoever, as being entirely "natural". And "if we strip this being, thus [physically] constituted, of all the supernatural gifts he may have received . . . ; if we consider him, in a word, just as he must have come from the hands of nature, we behold an animal weaker than some, and less agile than others; but, taking him all round, the most advantageously organized of any."[40] (We shall meet yet again in Saint-Simon and Comte with this virtual reduction of man to an animal through the elimination of grace.) But grace is immediately replaced with autarky, which men lose by whatever increases their desires beyond their power to satisfy them.

Here again we find anticosmy — the contradiction between man as "fallen", as subjected to self-aggrandizing passions, and man as "divine", as divinely resting in the enjoyment of his own existence. Through society man regains in a sublimated form the divinity which he possessed originally. There is almost a dialectic here — autarky as the thesis, asthenia arising as antithesis, with social autarky, or the *amour de la société* as the synthesis, a kind of *Aufhebung* resolving all contradictions. The rudiments of this dialectic are present in Hobbes but he lacks the nascent dynamism present in Rousseau. For Hobbes divinity and corporeality exist in the state of nature in static contradiction — there is no sense of temporal or historical development. But with Rousseau we find the beginnings of a dialectic, for man is first divine, then fallen, and then, through establishment of the salvific society the divinity and the passions are reconciled in a higher synthesis in which love of self and all the weaknesses that put man in society in the first place become the basis of the autarky of society. Rousseau is not, of course, speaking of factual history; but his mythic, constructed history does involve a temporal sequence largely lacking in Hobbes.

What this means for Rousseau is that in society man achieves a reconciliation of divinity with its opposite — fallen, self-centered humanity. This was, of course, the reconciliation that Augustine posited as occurring through conversion and the graced participation in the divine existence through the City of God, and it is a transformation and perfection of human existence that depends entirely on God — unaided human efforts cannot achieve it. But Rousseau claims to have achieved an entirely immanent version of it by stripping man of grace so that man can then be the supreme being for man. When human flaws make their presence felt and man finds himself miserable in society, exiled from his divinity, Rousseau, the natural man, appears as redeemer, reconciling humanity and divinity in his own person and establishing the salvific society to transform human nature through restoration of divinity, which is, however, realized on a higher level, encompassing all the good that flows from man's desires that can be satisfied only in society. In Augustinian terms, what we have is analogous to a member of the earthly city becoming a member of the City of God, which is a higher City of God for man's having passed through the earthly city. One might of course, refer to the *felix culpa*, but in Rousseau's thought the outpouring of divine grace is replaced by the superior wisdom of Rousseau himself, *l'homme naturel*.

At this point we may well inquire more specifically about the meaning of Rousseau's civil religion. It seems strange, to say the least, when regarded as the capstone of Rousseau's philosophical anthropology and political philosophy. In fact, in mandating the belief in a "Divinity" the civil religion, it would seem, is denying the implicit divinity of man. There are, however, two points to be considered regarding this civil religion which should throw some light on its significance in Rousseau's thought. First of all, the civil profession of faith is deliberately couched in vague terms (and with the prohibition of explanation or commentary they will remain vague), a vagueness that reveals an important ambiguity — is the "Divinity" a transcendent God or the Legislator? Indeed, Rousseau's terminology is quite compatible with the description of the Legislator: the Divinity is "mighty", not almighty, "intelligent", not omniscient, and merely "beneficent", not perfectly good. And the Legislator is necessarily possessed of foresight and providence, by the requirements of his office. And the Savoyard Vicar, another of Rousseau's alter egos, believes in the life to come when, freed from the fetters of the body, he shall suffice for his own happiness. In fact, the profession of faith is made deliberately ambiguous, serving as both a natural religion enjoining "the true cult of the Divinity" and also as a cult of the Legislator, the divine ordering force in human affairs. When made so vague the civil profession of faith is not incompatible with the divine self-sufficiency of man.

The second point to be considered in understanding this civil religion is that, strictly speaking, there is no public philosophy visible in Rousseau's political theory. There are no commonly accepted philosophical principles, save perhaps for the idea that the general will should rule, nor is there an accepted, traditional view of the order of the cosmos that serves implicitly or explicitly as the basis of society. Rousseau does not begin with an analysis of the world or human nature as they are ordinarily and commonly experienced. Instead he begins with a myth, a myth that re-orders the cosmos in his own image, a myth that involves a rejection of the traditional, Western, Christian view that man was not left on his own after leaving the Garden of Eden, or, in other words, that man cannot be understood apart from his relationship with God. Essentially, then, all of Rousseau's "philosophy" is civil theology, or to use an equivalent and more accurate term, it is an egophany. The cosmos and human nature are, through the myth, remade in the image of Rousseau's own ego, very much as they were remade in the image of Hobbes' own ego through his myth of the state of nature.

And, just as in Hobbes, the rejected tradition does not simply disappear at Rousseau's bidding, but emerges in his egophanic philosophy in the form of displacement-substitutes, such as the salvific society, the divinity of *l'homme naturel*, the remaking of man as unnatural as conversion, the general will as replacement for the will of God — these are all somewhat distorted aspects of the man-God relationship that is rejected. And it is because this part of reality is rejected that the dichocosmy degenerates into anticosmy — when the transcendent God of the public philosophy, as in America, is eliminated, the still present need for salvation requires that man take over the job of redeemer. In the case of the American civil religion we found that there was tension but not contradiction between the public philosophy and the civil theology — the sense of salvific mission and national glory was never entirely divorced from the sense that salvation was granted by God and depended upon the people's righteousness before God. This tension becomes contradiction when man must be both savior and saved, even in a purely immanent form of salvation, mainly because the immanent salvation assumes the aura of ultimate salvation.

Therefore, underneath Rousseau's civil religion, which resembles a paradigmatic civil theology, we find that his philosophy as a whole is really an eschatological civil theology, or egophany, divorced from the balancing force of a public philosophy. It is, therefore, quite susceptible to hypertrophy, and we shall see in the development of ideologies to what this susceptibility leads.

REFERENCES

[1] George H. Sabine, *A History of Political Theory*, Hinsdale, Ill., Dryden Press, 1973, pp. 529–530.
[2] Jean-Jacques Rousseau, *The Social Contract*, Vol. XXXVIII of *The Great Books of the Western World*, ed. by Robert Maynard Hutchins, 54 vols.: Chicago, 1952, IV, 8, p. 436. In a number of places the translation of Rousseau's works has been amended so as to render them more literal. The French text used was *Oeuvres Complètes*, published

under the direction of Bernard Gagnelin and Marcel Raymond, Bibliotheque de la Pleiade, 1969.

[3] *Ibid.* IV, 8, p. 436.
[4] *Ibid.* IV, 8, p. 437.
[5] *Ibid.* IV, 8, p. 437. Italics added.
[6] *The Confessions of Jean Jacques Rousseau*, New York, Walter J. Black Company, p. 268–9.
[7] Jean Jacques Rousseau, *Emile*, tr. by Barbara Foxley, M. A., London, J. M. Dent & Sons, 1911, p. 8.
[8] *Confessions*, p. 1.
[9] Rousseau, *A Discourse on the Origin of Inequality*, Vol. XXXVIII of *The Great Books of the Western World*, p. 334.
[10] *Emile*, p. 49.
[11] *Ibid.* p. 48.
[12] Jean-Jacques Rousseau, *Religious Writings*, ed. by Ronald Grinsley, Oxford, Clarendon Press, 1970, p. 4.
[13] *Emile*, p. 244.
[14] *Ibid.* p. 174. The clause in brackets is not found in the text of the *Oeuvres Complètes*.
[15] *Ibid.* p. 257.
[16] *Ibid.* p. 56.
[17] *Ibid.* p. 128.
[18] *Ibid.* p. 33.
[19] *Ibid.* p. 44.
[20] *Ibid.* pp. 249–50.
[21] *Ibid.* p. 254.
[22] *Ibid.* p. 182.
[23] *The Social Contract*, II, 7, p. 400.
[24] *Emile*, p. 49.
[25] *Inequality*, p. 348.
[26] *Emile*, p. 5.
[27] *Ibid.* p. 217.
[28] *Ibid.* p. 7.
[29] *Social Contract*, I, 1, p. 387.
[30] *Emile*, p. 56.
[31] *Ibid.* p. 245.
[32] *Ibid.* p. 248.
[33] Jean-Jacques Rousseau, *A Discourse on Political Economy*, Vol. XXXVIII of *The Great Books of the Western World*, p. 372.
[34] *Social Contract*, I, 6, p. 391.
[35] *Ibid.* II, 6, p. 399.
[36] *Ibid.* II, 6, p. 400.
[37] *Political Economy*, p. 376.
[38] *Social Contract*, IV, 8, p. 439.
[39] *Ibid.* IV, 8, p. 438.
[40] *Inequality*, p. 334.

CHAPTER X

SAINT-SIMON AND COMTE: THE RELIGION OF PROGRESS

In Saint-Simon we encounter the beginning of another phase in the development of modern European civil religion, a phase in which many of the problems and contradictions in Hobbes and Rousseau are translated into new terms. Saint-Simon does not approach the problem of civil religion so directly and specifically as do Hobbes and Rousseau. Nowhere does he use terms such as "civil religion" or "civil theology" or "Christian Commonwealth", nor does he speak of assuaging such difficulties as the conflict between the Christian and the man, or between wishes and duties. He was interested not in the inner conflicts of the soul but with the external disorders of society, which he thought were historically conditioned and could be historically corrected. Between Rousseau and Saint-Simon lies the great abyss of the French Revolution which abolished so many institutions and had a momentous impact on the development of European thought. For Saint-Simon the Revolution left in its wake an almost continent-wide disorder which he sought to remedy by a reinterpretation of Christianity.

The experience that induced Saint-Simon to reflect upon the meaning and order of human existence has two aspects. The primary is on the level of politics – the French Revolution, the rise of Napoleon and the ensuing disorder not only within France, but in all of Western Europe, since nothing has yet filled the vacuum. The new system has not yet been formed. Europe is in a state of transition, without a *système*, without a secure structure of order. The "true question" which Saint-Simon has undertaken to study is prophylactic: "How can the European body politic be cured? How can calm be re-established on the continent, how can a stable order of political affairs be constituted there?"[1]

This condition of continental disorder resulting from the overthrow of the *ancien régime* is the basic political reality. The second aspect of the disorder, which flows from the political, is intellectual disorder, which consists first of all in ignorance. In *Du Système Industriel* Saint-Simon quotes "un mot de Franklin" in this regard: "Political quarrels (or others) are only misunderstandings, wickednesses are only acts of ignorance." According to Saint-Simon, "it is from the effect of our ignorance that we are in conflict with each other, instead of combining our forces to act upon nature, in such a way as to

175

obtain from it most abundantly the means to satisfy our needs."[2] Therefore, man's existence is disordered because he is ignorant, a conclusion similar to that at which Hobbes had arrived, with similar conflict and inadequate satisfaction of needs resulting. Like Hobbes, Saint-Simon speaks of "the inextricable confusion of political ideas", implying that men are ignorant of the truths of the political and moral order. And it is ignorance and intellectual disorder that allow the greatest force for disorder to develop and so hinder the progress of humanity. "The decadence of the former general doctrines has allowed egoism to develop, which invades society day by day, and which eminently opposes the formation of new doctrines." Egoism prevents the development of positive ideas, by which society lives — because of egoism society is in "extreme moral disorder" with men isolated from each other in their own self-interests. All this prevents the development of the new doctrines needed to restore order to Europe. "It is to this egoism that it is necessary to attribute the political illness [la maladie politique] of our epoch, an illness which puts in abeyance all the labors useful to society."[3] This disordered condition of society in which the truth of political order has not yet come into existence Saint-Simon characterizes as "the world turned upside down [le monde renversé] " — that is, society is plunged into immorality, disorder, and ignorance, and it is this condition of human existence which has impelled Saint-Simon to seek a remedy.

This, then, is essentially man's contemporary, "fallen", disordered condition for Saint-Simon. Humanity is temporarily halted in the march of civilization by the political disorder of Europe and the ignorance and egoism of the men living in Europe. Saint-Simon locates the source of this disorder primarily in the environment, rather than in man himself — even egoism is not truly innate in man but is conditioned by his social milieu. As Saint-Simon sees it, disorder is relative, a function of time: Man's existence becomes disordered either when a condition which at a certain time ought to cease to exist, for some reason does not disappear, or when the new order which should replace it fails to arrive. There must be constant progress from one thing to another, much as in Hobbes' definition of felicity. Therefore, the existence of such disorder has impelled Saint-Simon to seek a means of ameliorating the disorder and satisfying man's needs.

In undertaking this cure Saint-Simon deliberately surrounded himself with a certain aura of divinity. "If the conclusions which I have presented are just, if the doctrine which I have set forth is good, it is in the name of God that I have spoken."[4] "Listen to the voice of God, which speaks to you through my mouth."[5] However, such claims to "prophetic" authority are somewhat undermined by the fact that Saint-Simon was an atheist and regarded God as at times a progressive and at other times a retrograde idea. Saint-Simon's strongest atheistic statement is in *On the Unity of Causation* in *Introduction aux Travaux Scientifiques du XIXe Siècle*, published in 1808.

According to Saint-Simon it is simple to demonstrate that the idea of God as the single cause of the world "lags behind the present stage of enlightenment". In fact, man has made such impressive progress in the mathematical and physical sciences precisely because the belief in God has declined. This idea is "sterile" without the idea of revelation and every scientific discovery has disproved revelation. Therefore, "the idea of God is nothing but the idea of human intelligence universalized". Even more, the idea of God is self-contradictory, which Saint-Simon reduces to a proof of the non-existence of God, a proof as philosophically rigorous as Hobbes' proof of the non-existence of the highest good. "If God is a purely spiritual being, His existence is thought: but if God is completely foreseeing, He can only think once; in a single thought He foresees everything that will happen. Therefore His existence can only last for the duration of a single act of thought; and so he no longer exists." God's omniscience has the consequence of making His existence altogether supererogatory to the world once it is created – since God is omniscient He must have created the world perfect and so in no need of His guidance.

God's non-existence demotes man from his central station in the universe, since man was regarded as having such a position only in relation to God. "Man, having invented [*inventé*] God, considers himself to be an important being: he believes that the Universe was created for his benefit, and that the planet he inhabits is the centre of the Universe, the stars revolving around it for the whole purpose of illuminating it. All these ideas are now known to be false." The downgrading of God as creator of the world to an obsolete idea is also the downgrading of man to an accidental being. Nevertheless, it should be mentioned that Saint-Simon finds God an idea worth inventing in the political realm, "since it is the best means that has been discovered of managing the fundamental political relations".[6] Such superstitions have their uses.

There is, unfortunately, little consistency in Saint-Simon's thought – he bent ideas to suit his own purposes at any given moment. For example, even though Saint-Simon found his own world overflowing with chaos he did not hesitate to affirm that after its creation the world was so perfectly ordered that the Creator could do nothing but retire into oblivion. In fact, Saint-Simon makes a distinction between the outmoded God of the physical world and the still occasionally useful God of the political and moral world. In practice, Saint-Simon is the author of the new system that will restore the world to its pristine order, and he is the god of this new system. "The conception of the new system ought to be unitary, that is to say this conception ought to be formed by a single mind." [7] Saint-Simon presents himself as the one semi-divine founder of the new system, that truth of order which will be man's fulfillment and greatest happiness. Saint-Simon then becomes the source of order for mankind. This conclusion is strengthened by his statement, "The opinion which I am going to present to you has no need whatever of demonstration, it does not admit of discussion, because common sense suffices to judge it, and because it is a direct consequence of the great principle of morality which serves as the foundation of the Christian religion [i.e. the Golden Rule] ". [8] In his explicit atheism Saint-Simon is more direct than either Hobbes or Rousseau, who both chose indirect means of building a philosophy involving either God's non-existence or his non-relevance to the world of human affairs. There is little practical difference between the two. However, the metaphysical structures of Saint-Simon's thought are much the same as those of Hobbes and Rousseau.

Saint-Simon begins from the elimination of the public philosophy, involving the necessity of understanding man in relationship with God. Since God does not exist man must be seen purely as a natural being, which means, as it does in Rousseau, that man is very much like the "other animals", for the general effect of regarding man simply as a natural being is *aplanissement*, a smoothing or levelling down of all metaphysical differences. Man differs from the other animals not essentially but only in having a superior intelligence that resulted from a superior organization. "Man, at the beginning of his existence, enjoyed, over the other animals, only the superiority of his intelligence, which resulted directly from his superiority or organization, and this superiority was very little." [9] Superior intelligence is a merely qualitative difference. "Man ... was not at all of a nature different from that of the other animals." [10]

Concomitant with this *aplanissement* of humanity to animality is the reduction of politics to political economy, for as a natural being man has only natural, economic needs, and society then exists only to satisfy such and not to fulfill any moral or spiritual needs, as in Aristotle's view of the good life. Saint-Simon was not alone among modern thinkers in maintaining that "the preservation of property is the great object of politics", but he does go farther than most in his assertion that "political science consists today, therefore, essentially in making a good budget. Now, the ability necessary to make a good budget is the administrative ability, from which it follows that the administrative ability is the first political ability."[11] Elsewhere Saint-Simon chracterizes politics as the "science of production". According to Saint-Simon, the role of government is simply to protect industry by insuring that "useful work", *les travaux utiles*, is not hindered or troubled. To this end, society is founded on the right to private property, particularly "industrial" property. "The establishment of the right of property and the arrangements to make it respected are incontestably the only foundation which it would be possible to give to a political society."[12] However, since man is not *essentially* different from the other animals, the observed differences can be explained only in terms of his superior social organization.

Unlike Rousseau, Saint-Simon does not have a kind of dialectic in which the perfect, original, natural man falls away from his pristine perfection, and then is restored to it on a higher level. What Saint-Simon does have is a view of history as human progress from darkness into light, the old and obsolete ceaselessly giving way to the new, and a view of human existence as capable of endless perfectability. Further human progress toward perfection requires (1) termination of the Revolution so as to provide Europe with a stable political order, and (2) establishing the ordered, salvific society for the natural man, which society he calls *le régime industriel*.

Related to this view of man as a purely natural being is a rejection of all theological or metaphysical concerns as obsolete. Just as man the individual progresses from a life according to the imagination in childhood to a life according to reason in adulthood, so the rise of natural science has completely discredited metaphysics and theology and replaced them with certain, empirical knowledge. For, "the great force is the force of intelligence", and Saint-Simon finds it far more rational to submit to a demonstration than to believe in metaphysical and theological conjectures. Theology did, of course, have value at one time, and even its own internal state of progress from idolatry to polytheism to theism (by which he presumably means monotheism). However, this theism itself is now *usé*, and will soon be superseded by the new *système* based on positive science and the principle of universal gravitation (which, in the absence of God, holds everything together). Religion, for Saint-Simon, as for Epicurus, consists primarily of conjectures that conceal ignorance of causes. Man has "progressed" beyond a need for religion as he has realized that all phenomena are ultimately caused by the one immutable law of universal gravitation. The rapid advances in science have rendered theism, or the belief in God as the First Cause, unnecessary and obsolete. Once man is seen as a purely natural being in a universe that is a perfectly functioning system the childish need for belief in God will wither away. "The whole theological system is founded on the supposition that the whole earth was made for man, and the entire universe for the earth; remove this supposition and all the religious doctrines collapse."[13] Saint-Simon regards modern astronomical theory and theology as "absolutely incompatible", as indeed, in his understanding of them they are. God as the supreme being for man and man as the supreme being for man are completely incompatible premises.

So, with this display of eliminating contradictions Saint-Simon goes on to base his entire *système* on the contradiction between man as purely natural being and man as supreme being for man. The rejected City of God emerges in the displacement-substitute form of the *régime industriel*, the society devoted primarily to maintaining man as a species-being in existence. In this context individual life is of equal importance with the individual life of any of the other animals — with regard to the general life the lives of individuals are only the cogwheels (*rouages*). The secondary purpose of the *régime industriel* is to provide all of its members with the greatest possible happiness by satisfying all of their needs. It achieves this worthy purpose by acting continually upon the environment, upon nature rather than upon men.

This leads to Saint-Simon's concept of *utilité*, a central idea in Saint-Simon's view of human existence. First of all, "nations, the same as individuals, are able to live in only two ways, in plundering or in producing".[14] Obviously, plundering is not a very orderly means of livelihood — production is by far the better means. "The object of the political association of the French is to prosper by peaceful labor of a positive utility."[15] *Utilité* is the criterion for distinguishing order-producing human endeavors from those that produce disorder, which are *inutile*, or *usé*. As Saint-Simon explains, "the object of my enterprise is to free the men who are occupied with labors of the most positive and direct utility from the domination exercised over them until now by the clergy, the nobility, the judicial order, just as by the proprietors who are not manufacturers."[16] A society in which everyone works is spontaneously ordered — it is idleness that is the root of all disorder and all vices. Industry, in fact, is the source of all order and all virtues. "Finally, we observe that the progress of industry, of the sciences, and the fine arts, in multiplying the means of subsistence, in diminishing the number of the idle, in enlightening the minds and in refining morality, tends more and more to make disappear the three greatest causes of disorder: poverty, idleness, and ignorance."[17] Industry is really an analogue of grace as the source of all human happiness and fulfillment, and idleness is Saint-Simon's version of sin.

Not surprisingly, as the class devoted completely to work or industry, the source of life, "the industrial class is the fundamental class, the life-giving [*nourricière*] class of the whole society, that without which no other could subsist".[18] And as a consequence, "the other classes ought to work for [the industrial class], because they are its creatures, and because it maintains their existence".[19] As the source of natural grace for the natural man the industrial class should be served by all those other classes which it maintains in existence.

So we find that Saint-Simon's salvific society, *lé régime industriel*, is single-mindedly devoted to *les travaux utiles* by which it creates order and maintains its existence through acting upon nature to produce the means for satisfying human needs and sustaining life. Idleness creates disorder because insistent needs not satisfied by industry must be satisfied by plunder. This salvific industrial society is the end toward which mankind has been tending throughout history — "This system will be the final system; all the other political systems which have existed ought to be considered as preparatory systems."[20] This final system will be a *régime* in which all authority will be given to the leaders of industry and science, a *régime* in which the primary aim will be the satisfaction of physical needs so as to insure *"une grande prospérité à l'espèce humaine"*, a prosperity that will also be *"le plus grand bonheur possible de l'espèce humaine"*.[21] This greatest possible happiness of the human species which is also the "greatest happiness of each in particular", is the redemption of man from all physical wants, from all poverty and disorder. The industrial régime then provides men with the highest good through a kind of fraternal love called *amélioration*: "Mankind has always worked for the amelioration of its condition" through the satisfaction of man's physical and moral needs. History, it seems, has tended always, and particularly through the developments of science and industry, toward *l'amélioration du sort de l'espèce humaine*.

Saint-Simon is more like Hobbes than Rousseau in that the ground of man's happiness lies in economic activity and the chief function of government is to repress any actions that might hinder the orderly processes of science, technology, and industry. Therefore, neither government nor politics is the locus of man's salvation. In fact, in one of his letters Saint-Simon refers to government as *"un mal nécessaire"*. It is in economic society that men are united in the happiness of having their physical needs satisfied. This is the earthly paradise, transmogrified from the celestial paradise and relocated in the future.

This leaves us with one important question in Saint-Simon's social philosophy, that of what it is that will make men love their duty. What will persuade men to devote their energies to production and order rather than plunder and disorder? What will convince men that they should turn away from their egoism?

For Saint-Simon this persuasive force is Christianity, or, more accurately, "New Christianity". Like Rousseau, Saint-Simon finds religion and the idea of God useful in persuading the members of society to maintain the social order. This must, however, be a religion adjusted to the level of enlightenment attained by man — otherwise to promote it or defend it is to hinder human progress. For example, in his *Mémoire sur la Science de l'Homme* he quotes the passage from Cicero's *De Natura Deorum* in which Cotta says that in matters of religion he submits not to philosophers but to such as C. Laelius, a wise man and an augur. Saint-Simon comments that "Cicero should have perceived that polytheism was worn out; that this belief, which was very much behind the state of enlightenment, was so ridiculous, that he himself often said that he could not conceive how two augurs could have looked at each other without laughing; that one could not return vigor to this religion, and that it would inevitably be replaced by another more in proportion with the state of enlightenment." [22] In an earlier work, *Introduction aux Travaux Scientifiques du XIXe Siècle*, he had also quoted the same passage and there had accused Cicero of the same intellectual tergiversation. "Cicero wished to check the progress of enlightenment. He did not stop the progress of the human mind, and he has left to posterity a proof that his own mind was unable to rise to the highest level of thought." [23] Like Augustine, but for different reasons, Saint-Simon rejects Cicero's understanding of the importance of the Roman civil religion. Saint-Simon finds this state religion not contemptible but simply worn out, that is, his judgment is not moral as was Augustine's but "moral" on the basis of his own view of human existence and happiness as being little more than an animal's.

Accordingly, Saint-Simon proposes a religion that is well attuned to the level of enlightenment attained by an industrial society, a religion that is not arbitrarily selected but is in fact the one true religion finally realized in its perfection. This makes Saint-Simon's epoch "Messianic", "an epoch in which the religious doctrine would be presented with all the generality of which it is susceptible; that it would regulate equally the action of the temporal power and that of the spiritual power, and that then all of mankind would have only one religion, even one organization." [24] This Messianic epoch is the full realization of the one, true, universal Christian religion which will not, as Rousseau thought, distract men from this world, but will instead turn all their attention toward the perfecting of conditions in this world. "Certainly all Christians aspire to eternal life, but the only way to obtain it consists in working in this life for the increase of the well-being of mankind."[25] This new Christianity, as compared with the old, is the passage from heavenly to earthly morality, or, in another phrase, from *"morale théologique à la morale industrielle"*.[26] Furthermore, since Saint-Simon finds it "discouraging" to think that *"le bien a précédé le mal"*, that man enjoyed a perfect existence before he fell, the terrestrial paradise is to be located in the future rather than the past and the celestial paradise, now completely worn out, will simply fade away. Saint-Simon thus effects a complete immanentization of human experience.

The new Christianity is the "social doctrine that men should treat each other as brothers". Christianity is thus reduced to ethics, the "sublime principle [that] comprises all that is divine in the Christian religion".[27] Although Saint-Simon begins his work on new Christianity with a statement that he believes in God and the divine origin of Christianity, this amounts to nothing more than pretending to speak with divine authority so as to convince the credulous people. He uses another of his rhetorical theological arguments to prove that brotherly love is necessarily the only principle of Christianity, ignoring the fact that love of neighbor is only the second commandment. "Naturally God has related everything to a single principle, and deduced everything from a single principle – otherwise His will towards men would not have had coherence. It would be blasphemy to assert that the Almighty has founded His religion on a number of principles."[28] The Old Christianity, i.e., the institutional Church, did have its uses in promoting human progress, but having fulfilled its function, it has now become a burden on society. It is time it is replaced with true Christianity which abandons dogma and spiritual authority for ameliorating the condition of the poorest classes.

There are suggestions in Saint-Simon's writings that there should be some public cult aspects to this religion. This cult, however, has nothing to do with expressing the identity of any particular society but rather with educating the members of the society to regard *le régime industriel* as the pinnacle of human happiness. Saint-Simon directs that the governing body of the industrial society should establish throughout the country *"fêtes publiques"* of two types: festivals of hope in which orators will exhort the people to work harder to ameliorate their condition, and festivals of remembrance in which orators will point out to the people how much their condition has improved over that of their ancestors. Both festivals are simply propaganda designed to convince the people that they are happy.

While Saint-Simon as a thinker is inferior to both Hobbes and Rousseau he does follow their example in rejecting an essential aspect of man's traditional understanding of the basis of an ordered existence, namely God. All of Saint-Simon's philosophy, then, is a projected cosmos in which the rejected public philosophy appears as much the same displacement-substitutes as in Hobbes and Rousseau: *le régime industriel* as the salvific society in which man will realize the fullness of human happiness, industry as the equivalent of grace, man as a purely natural being achieving a purely natural happiness, new Christianity as the "civil religion" that will direct men's attention to this world and away from any other world. There is in all these hypertrophied civil theologies a desire to take control of reality, to change it in accordance with a cherished myth, a comfortable myth, a desire that experience will conform to expectation. Underlying civil theology, in America, as well as in Europe, is the desire to live in a dream world, a world in which either man or the social order, or both, are perfect, a world without conflict, without metaphysical tensions or unsatisfied desires. The crucial difference is that America retained a voice of reality to counteract its dreams, but European philosophers have silenced reality from the very start. But reality makes its presence felt even in the midst of dreams, for the dreams invariably emerge as parodies of the rejected world of real experience.

Comte, originally a disciple of Saint-Simon, was a far more thorough and complex thinker than the latter, expanding and developing Saint-Simon's ideas into something more closely resembling a *système*. From Saint-Simon Comte took an emphasis on positive science and the modelling of philosophy on the methods of the sciences, as well as the general view of history as the progress of mankind toward perfection, which, like Hobbes, Rousseau, and Saint-Simon before him Comte sees as deriving from a rejection of all of man's supernatural gifts: "Since the adequate extension of Rome's dominion, the more advanced populations are vainly seeking for an universal religion. The experience gained in this search has made it quite clear that no supernatural belief can satisfy this, the ultimate longing of humanity."[29] The desire for union with the transcendent God is replaced with the longing for a universal religion, the basis of the unification of all humanity. This religion will be the full realization of truth, so much so that no other religious or philosophical beliefs will be possible or even conceivable.

Like Saint-Simon, Comte regarded the French Revolution as the cause of widespread disorder that required remedy. Yet he saw the Revolution in an ambiguous light. Besides wreaking havoc, the Revolution also gave rise to "a real sense of human development . . . in minds of the most ordinary cast".[30] It was the Revolution that first clearly revealed the fact of human progress, and it was the crisis created by the Revolution that both proved the urgent necessity for social regeneration and "gave birth to the only philosophy capable of effecting it". So the Revolution both revealed the problem and provided the solution.

However, again following Saint-Simon, Comte sees the most serious disorder not on the social but on the moral and intellectual level, a disorder so severe that Comte refers to it as "anarchy". In the dialogue of the *Catechism of Positivism* Comte has the woman interlocutor say, "Above all, at the present day, we women are struck with terror at the moral ravages attributable to the intellectual anarchy. It threatens, at no distant period, to dissolve all the bonds that bind men together, unless some irresistible convictions step in to prevent the further growth that seems naturally to await it."[31] Prevention of disorder requires that *all* men accept some irrefutable truth. In this sense Hobbes' Commonwealth has been expanded to Humanity. Comte elsewhere characterizes this "anarchy of the Western world" as "the revolt of the intellect against all legitimate control". Comte attributed intellectual anarchy to a clinging to old, worn-out beliefs and ideas, ideas which admit of no demonstration and are "radically illusory". Comte sees the Intellect as the major cause of social disorder and feels that the only solution is to chain the Intellect with some irresistible convictions, some new kind of belief, so that humanity can fulfill its longing for order.

And then there is the disorder caused simply by the imperfections of human nature. What Comte refers to as *l'égoisme fondamental*, essential egoism, has discordant tendencies that are in themselves much stronger than the *dispositions sympathiques de la sociabilité*. The remedy that Comte supplies for political disorder and intellectual anarchy will first of all have to include an antidote to human pride.

Hence along with the first component of Comte's proposed cure which is scientific demonstration to save man from intellectual anarchy, there is an emphasis on feeling, specifically social feelings, as a means of overcoming the moral anarchy caused by egoism. "It is feeling along which preserves Western society from a complete and irreparable dissolution",[32] and Comte certainly regarded his task as that of the "spiritual reorganization of the civilized world", which is also a regeneration of man and society. He comments on "how impossible it is to effect any permanent reconstruction of the institutions of society, without a previous reorganization of opinion and of life. The spiritual basis is necessary not merely to determine the character of the temporal reconstruction, but to supply the principal motive force by which the work is to be carried out."[33] Comte's remedy for disorder is to bring man to the "perfect unity" of his existence by spiritually reorganizing and reconstructing society.

This condition of perfect unity which Comte refers to as *Religion*, is "the distinctive mark of man's existence, both as an individual and in society, when all the constituent parts of nature, moral as well as physical, are made habitually to converge towards a common purpose". For Comte, religion is concerned not with man's relationship with a transcendent God, but simply with man's union with himself, as a collective being. "Religion . . . consists in regulating each one's individual nature, and forms the rallying point for all the separate individuals."[34] Comte's religion, Positivism, achieves this perfect unity by affecting "the gradual predominance of sociability over personality", that is, of social sympathy over egoism.

Comte's positivistic religion is, of course, atheistic, and Comte's proof for the non-existence of God is reminiscent of Saint-Simon's proofs, in that it is obviously contrived and proves only the undesirability of God's existence from a certain point of view. For Comte the impossibility of God's existence is indicated simply by the "necessary incompatibility of Theology and Positivism. It is a consequence of the irreconcilable opposition between laws and supernatural will." God cannot exist because he would threaten the order that Comte wants to exist. "What becomes of the wonderful order we have traced, which, by a graduated series, connects our noblest moral attributes with the lowest natural phenomena, if we introduce an infinite power? The capricious action of such a power would allow of no prevision. It would threaten our order at any moment with an entire subversion."[35] Comte's justification for his assumption that God is, or would be "capricious", or that he would be likely to subvert the wonderful order that connects man's noblest moral attributes with the lowest natural phenomena, is that God is a solitary, not a social being, and therefore can be only *un immense égoïsme*. Only the preponderance of social feeling in a collective being can prevent egoism and its capricious, anarchic effects. In fact, Comte's argument is as specious as is Hobbes' "proof" of the non-existence of the highest good – both misrepresent the undesirable aspect of reality so that the reader will also find it undesirable and therefore incapable of existing. Only what is desired is to be allowed to exist in the projected cosmos.

Having removed God from the world, Comte proceeds to develop "a systematic conception of the whole order of the world", or "one comprehensive system" embracing every aspect of human life, the social as well as the individual. It is a complete synthesis of man's outer world and his inner world, and includes the three kinds of human phenomena: Thoughts, Feelings, and

Actions. This perfectly unified conception is sought not for its own sake but for its ability to guide human action. In this respect Positivism assumes the position vacated by one of the superannuated ideas. "For the principal field of Positive thought will in future be that known to the old theologians under the title of Grace; a subject henceforth reducible to definite laws enabling us to base action upon sense knowledge."[36] The result of the elimination of grace is not only certainty regarding actions but, as Comte explicitly admits, that man must draw from himself the resources against all the surrounding evils.

Man is, for Comte, as for Hobbes, Rousseau, and Saint-Simon, a purely natural being. St. Paul's "imaginary conflict between nature and grace" is now abandoned. "And we replace it by the real opposition between the posterior part of the brain, the seat of our personal instincts, and its anterior region, the seat both of our sympathetic impulses and our intellectual faculties, which, however, have distinct positions."[37] The reconciliation of pride and the love of God is now shown to be no more metaphysically demanding than the overcoming of egoism by social sympathy, which, significantly, resides in the forward part of the brain.

And as a purely natural being man is not essentially different from the animals. "Man's existence is really but the highest step in animal life", and therefore sociology is merely a development of biology. The implication of this reduction of man to the purely natural is the elevation of the natural to the divine. "It becomes easier for us to grasp our sublimest theoretic conception, if we learn to look on each species of animals as potentially a Great Being."[38] Man has won the contest, but every other animal species was an effort to achieve a collective being. As a purely natural being man has importance only in the collective — the individual has no value and the human person is abandoned along with grace. "The only real life is the collective life of the race: ... Individual life has no existence except as an abstraction."[39] Since only the Whole is real, the individuals composing it are not distinct beings but merely organs of the Great Being. Anything less than complete subordination to the whole is egoism.

Along with the displacement of grace and the human person is the replacement of the absolute with the relative, and spontaneous growth with systematic progress, while altruism is the force that restrains egoism. "In a word, Humanity definitely occupies the place of God, but she does not forget the services which the idea of God provisionally rendered."[40] The idea of God associated with the capricious absolutism of egoism has become worn out and a cause of disorder through its ability to hinder progress, although it was at one time useful.

In some ways Comte's system reveals more clearly the disguised presence of the public philosophy within the civil theology, or equivalents thereof. For example, take Comte's characterization of sociology as comprising two essential parts: "the one statical, or the theory of order; the other dynamical, or the theory of progress".[41] On the face of it this looks very much like a rough statement of the difference between public philosophy and civil theology, for, at the risk of oversimplification, the public philosophy does tend to be a philosophy of order, and the civil theology, within the Christian tradition, a theory of progress. Nevertheless, in Comte these are explicitly anticosmic rather than dichocosmic theories, as we shall see.

First, the theory of progress, Since God has been dethroned, the way is now clear for man to usurp the title of Supreme Being, or *le Grand Etre*, a position progressively achieved through history. "We are now able to condense the whole of our Positive conceptions in the one single idea of an immense and eternal Being, Humanity, destined by sociological laws to constant development under the preponderating influence of biological and cosmological necessities."[42] This is, of course, an ambivalent passage – man is both Supreme Being and subject to necessity. The full ambivalence will become clearer as we proceed.

This "immense and eternal Being, Humanity", is "the Being who manifests to the fullest extent all the highest attributes of life". Humanity is the culmination of life itself and therefore "the constant end of human life . . . is to preserve the Great Being, whom we must at once know, love, and serve".[43] Besides being Omega the Great Being is also Alpha – "Everything we have belongs to humanity. For everything we have comes from her – life, fortune, talents, information, tenderness, energy, etc."[44] On closer inspection this supremacy of Humanity involves some serious limitations, however, for Humanity is supreme not absolutely but only for man, that is, only with reference to human powers and wants. In a sense, just as Rousseau's *l'homme naturel* was essentially his own god in the equilibrium of his powers and desires, so Comte's *Grand Etre* is the supreme being for man in its ability to satisfy human desires and wants. However, the Great Being is also rather severely limited by the non-human world. In the cosmos not Humanity but Nature is supreme and Humanity is "subordinate to a universal Order, which has evident objective existence, and which by its necessary preponderance forms the principal instrument in controlling human life".[45] Although man depends on the world, the world in no way depends on man, who is naturally subordinate to the world.

Essentially, this emphasis on man's subordination to the world derives from Comte's reduction of the human to the biological and the necessary subordination of the organism to the milieu, or so Comte regarded it. "In order to rule or rally [*rallier*] us, religion ought, then, before everything to subordinate us to an exterior power, of which the irresistible supremacy allows us no certitude [*dont l'irresistible suprematie ne nous laisse aucune certitude*]. This great sociological dogma is, at bottom, only the full development of the fundamental notion elaborated by the true biology or the necessary subordination of the organism to the milieu."[46] As Comte sees it this necessary subordination or submission or subjection is an essential condition for human divinity.

So, as Comte himself presents this ambivalence, "the highest of all beings, Humanity, is that which is most dependent on the World, but also that by which the World is most largely modified. Thus we find the idea of Submission and Power, rightly understood, to be united even in their source."[47] Submission and Power are, of course, analogous to Hobbes' subjection and sovereignty and Rousseau's asthenia and autarky, and in general with beastliness and divinity, respectively, which represent the contradictory premises of anticosmy. In Comte there coexist a human cosmos in which man is the supreme being, and a natural cosmos in which man is merely an accidental event, subject to an "irresistible Fatality". Dichocosmy degenerates to anticosmy because an essential part of reality and human experience, namely God, has been eliminated, and the remaining beings, to compensate, are required to do more than they are metaphysically capable of doing. With the firing of God, the metaphysical cosmos is understaffed, so to speak, and in order to keep the cosmos functioning in its accustomed manner man finds himself constrained to bilocate, being both supreme being, object of reverence and worship, and very ordinary human being, little more than the animals, in need of salvation from the disorders of his existence. And so somehow we must think of man as progressing in supremacy and power by subjecting himself to natural necessity.

Not surprisingly the reduction of man to Supreme Collective Animal Species implies the shrinking of the universe to man's private domain, that is, man's perspective of the universe is limited to himself. "The Universe is to be studied not for its own sake, but for the sake of Man or rather Humanity."[48] Astronomy, for example, must abandon the study of the Heavens and turn to the study of the Earth, for only in this more limited realm is true unity possible. There is in fact no unity or order in the cosmos, so there is no point in studying any of the other heavenly bodies, which have nothing to do with Humanity and provide Humanity with no useful knowledge.

Man is the center of the small part of the cosmos in which he is the supreme being.

As we have said, man the supreme being is a collective being. What is needed, then, is a religion that will make the members of the society love duty, love their being mere abstractions of the great whole, love promoting their social feelings over their egoism. This religion is Positivism, which replaces theology and metaphysics, previous and outmoded views of order. Positivists regard life as "a continual act of worship; worship which will ennoble and invigorate our actions". Positivism subordinates politics to morals in requiring that social sympathy, the force that holds the whole together, should preponderate over self-love. "The true religion must be concerned with the physical, intellectual, and moral improvement of man."

Therefore, the full realization of human perfection requires the victory of social feeling, which, for Comte, rests on the separation in society of the moral power of counsel and the political power of command. Because the repression of the "coarser" egocentric desires requires a strong coercive power, the political power of command should be preponderant. "In the absence of all compulsory authority, our actions even as individuals would be feeble and purposeless, and social life still more certainly would lose its character and its energy. Moral force, therefore, by which is meant the force of conviction and persuasion, is to be regarded simply as a modifying influence, not as a means of authoritative direction."[49] So the purpose of political authority is rather Hobbesian — to repress the egoistic passions of men so that they can live together in society. All the meaning of existence is to be found in the positive religion, not in politics.

The meaning of social sympathy is that men live for the preservation of the race rather than for their own preservation, a sublimation quite similar to Rousseau's sublimation of *amour de soi* to *amour de la société*. The society, or Humanity, is the macroanthropos. "Consider Humanity as being like yourself only in a more marked degree, impelled by feeling, guided by intelligence, and supported by action." The precise name for the force that holds this Comtean Leviathan together is Love. "For this direct and universal tie nothing can be substituted. But its influence is powerfully aided by the sense of a common Fatality in the world without and in that of our own nature: and in the demonstration of this Fatality the religious value of Science lies."[50]

In order to place Love in its proper place in the structure of Comte's thought we shall have to backtrack a bit. Comte rejects the existence of God because a transcendent God would destroy the world and human knowledge as the system which Comte would like them to be. However, the elimination of God leaves man responsible for maintaining his existence and saving himself from evil. This dirempts man into two self-contradictory roles: the Great Being, comprising the totality of human beings living, dead, and yet to be born, and individual men, the "organs" of Humanity. It is Humanity that enjoys divine autarky, while individual men are sunk in the asthenia of egoism from which they require salvation by absorption in Humanity. Salvation consists in the *metanoia* of the organs of Humanity, their conversion from egoism, the force of chaos, to Love, the force of cohesion and order. This is quite analogous to the *metanoia* in Augustine, man's conversion from the metaphysical nothingness of sin to participation in God's divine, absolute existence through grace, now replaced by "definite laws". And Comtean Love leads, if not to participation in eternal life, at least to some kind of immortality. "The main object of education is to lead us to live for others, in order to live again in others by others, whereas we are naturally inclined to live for ourselves." [51] Living for others in order to maintain the existence of Humanity and thereby to maintain one's own existence through participation in the Great Being is Comte's displacement-substitute for living in the City of God through divine grace and through union with the will of God. The moral ravages caused by egoism are the equivalent of the earthly city.

The details of the Positive religion, the cults, such as the Worship of Woman, designed to instill social sympathy, are not important here. What is important is that the Positive religion is a civil theology, or egophany, of which the principal structures are displacement-substitutes for the rejected public philosophy. This is a hypertrophied eschatological civil theology that creates a cosmos in the image of Comte's dream of a complete, immanent realization of human happiness. He does not consider the loss of the human person and the meaninglessness of individual life to be too high a price to pay for such divine happiness.

What Comte wants is a universal religion that effectively denies meaning to any particular society, just as meaning is denied to the individual members of society. He has gone beyond his predecessors in proposing a unity of all men and all societies in the Great Being of Humanity, that is, it is not participation in a particular society, or society *per se* that is salvific, but participation in Humanity, the totality of all human beings from the beginning to the end of the world. At this point the eschatological civil theology becomes ideology, a re-making of the cosmos according to desire without any public philosophy or equivalent of public philosophy. It is a complete replacing of the traditional order with a new order which is however closely modelled on the rejected order. By way of comparison, there are latent tendencies toward this sort of ideological transformation in the American civil theology, such as in the nineteenth-century rapturous worship of Democracy as the salvation of all mankind. For our purposes an ideology can be seen simply as the translation of Christianity into purely immanent terms. That much is lost in the translation is the reason for the internal contradictions, the anticosmy, of ideology.

REFERENCES

[1] *Oeuvres de Claude-Henri de Saint-Simon*, ed. by E. Dentu, Tome III, Vol. 6, Paris, Editions Anthropos, 1966, p. 101. Unless otherwise indicated all quotations from Saint-Simon are from this edition of his works. Only tome, volume, and page numbers will be given.
[2] III, vii, 30.
[3] III, vii, 184.
[4] III, vii, 115–116.
[5] III, vii, 192.
[6] Henri de Saint-Simon, *Social Organization, The Science of Man and Other Writings*. ed. & tr. by Felix Markham, New York, Harper Torchbooks, 1964, pp. 19–20.
[7] III, vi, 249.
[8] III, vi, 84.
[9] V, xi, 42.
[10] V, xi, 176.
[11] II, iii, 201.
[12] II, iii, 89.
[13] II, iv, 100.
[14] III, vii, 81.
[15] III, vi, 96.
[16] III, v, 158.
[17] II, iv, 152.
[18] IV, viii, 4.
[19] IV, viii, 4.
[20] III, v, 166.
[21] II, iii, 71.
[22] V, xi, 167.
[23] *Social Organization*, p. 14.
[24] III, vii, 114.
[25] III, vii, 154.
[26] II, iii, 39.
[27] *Social Organization*, p. 83.
[28] *Ibid*. p. 83.
[29] Auguste Comte, *The Catechism of Positivism*, tr. by Richard Congreve, London, 1858, p. 8.
[30] Auguste Comte, *A General View of Positivism*, tr. by John Henry Bridges, New York, Robert Speller & Sons, 1957, pp. 68–69.

[31] *Catechism*, p. 191.
[32] *Catechism*, p. 28. Also, "In the life of the individual, and still more in the life of the race, the basis of unity, . . . must always be feeling." *General View*, p. 13.
[33] *General View*, p. 155.
[34] *Catechism*, p. 46.
[35] *Ibid*. p. 218.
[36] Auguste Comte, *System of Positive Polity or Treatise on Sociology*, tr. by John Henry Bridges, Paris, 1851, Vol. I, p. 366.
[37] *Catechism*, p. 253.
[38] *Ibid*. p. 223.
[39] *General View*, p. 404.
[40] *Catechism*, pp. 427–28.
[41] *Ibid*. p. 231.
[42] *Ibid*. pp. 63–64. This passage reveals the ambivalent metaphysical status of laws in Comte. Strictly speaking, positive laws cannot destine anything, for they are merely phenomenally descriptive.
[43] *Ibid*. pp. 181–82.
[44] *Ibid*. p. 307.
[45] *System*, p. 337.
[46] Auguste Comte, *Système de Politique Positive ou Traité de Sociologie*, Paris, 1853, Vol. II, pp. 12–13.
[47] *System*, p. 356.
[48] *General View*, p. 39.
[49] *Ibid*. p. 358.
[50] *System*, p. 330.
[51] *Catechism*, p. 283.

CHAPTER XI

HEGEL AND MARXISM-LENINISM: THE RESOLUTION
OF THE CONFLICT

In Hegel's philosophy of history as the Absolute Spirit's coming to self-realization we have the culmination of the rejection of public philosophy and its replacement with civil theology, or, more specifically, egophany. In a sense we find in Hegel the ultimate reconciliation of contradictories in an atheistic philosophy. Whereas Hegel's predecessors attempted relatively half-heartedly to set man upon the vacant divine throne, Hegel goes about this enthronement with much fanfare while disguising man as the manifestation of God. In fact, his justification of God in history is actually a recreation of history and the cosmos in the image of Hegel's will to power. Our concern here is simply with outlining those aspects of Hegel's thought which have to do with his resolution of anticosmy.

Stripped of all its baroque detail, Hegel's system, his philosophy of history, of man and the state, is designed as an impressive and irrefutable resolution of anticosmy by stating first that the tensions of anticosmy are the force that drives history toward the formal realization of man as God (or God as man, an equivalent expression). This reconciliation and realization is the fullness of freedom, which man achieves through his participation in the state.

"The true State is the ethical whole and the realization of freedom", the realm in which the individual has his substantial freedom", but "on the condition of his recognizing, believing in, and willing that which is common to the whole".[1] The state is the realm of true freedom because it is the "unity of the unversal, essential will, with that of the individual; and this is 'morality' ".[2] Furthermore, a human being can possess worth and apiritual reality only through the state. This is, of course, essentially Rousseau's view that man the citizen derives all his value from the community, through which he also realizes his freedom. In Rousseau this requires a remaking of human nature so that the individual will be content to enjoy autarky only through the autarky of the state. Hegel's equivalent is "the cunning of reason", which uses the individuals with all their personal desires, passions, and ambitions, to further the realization of the universal.

This type of salvific world-view which Comte entitled Religion, Hegel calls more deceptively "philosophy" — the esoteric knowledge of how all contradictions are resolved. "The insight to which . . . philosophy is to lead us, is that the real world is as it ought to be, that the truly good, the universal divine reason, is not a mere abstraction, but a vital principle capable of realizing itself. This *good*, this *reason*, in its most concrete form, is God. God governs the world; the actual working of His government, the carrying out of His plan, is the history of the world."[3] Hegel's "philosophy" shows the union of Kant's noumenal world of divine reason and phenomenal world of nature and appearances by explaining how the phenomenal world reveals the underlying noumenal world.

The crux of Hegel's resolution of anticosmy is in his *Philosophy of History*, in which he combines Kantian reason with Rousseau's view of man in his autarky and asthenia, and the reconciliation of the two, and creates history as the process by which spirit (or reason) realizes itself as God in man. "The history of the world is none other than the progress of the consciousness of freedom",[4] that is, divine autarky, which is the essence of spirit. Spirit comes to know himself as God only by emptying himself, alienating himself into the world, his creatures, and when he is completely so alienated he will at last know himself as God in man through man's self-consciousness. In other words it is only by "falling" completely away from himself that Spirit truly becomes God through the creation and reconciliation of all contradictions.

Hegel takes a somewhat different approach to anticosmy from that of his predecessors. He does not begin by eliminating God, or grace, or the highest good in order to replace God with a purely natural man. Instead he eliminates man by 'elevating' him to a mere externalization of the divine absolute spirit. Spirit, with its self-manifestation, its self-externalization and its hunger for self-knowledge, is all there is. Man becoming man is for Hegel man realizing himself as God, which is at the same time God realizing himself as God. The result is much the same as for Hobbes, Rousseau, Saint-Simon, and Comte, with the difference that, ostensibly, Hegel creates the anticosmy in the divine spirit itself, thereby seeking to legitimate it as an intrinsic element of the foundation of the universe.

Hegel states that it is the Christian religion which reveals to man the nature of God as pure spirit. And when he asks what spirit is, he answers that "it is the one immutably homogeneous infinite – pure identity – which in its second phase separates itself from itself and makes this second aspect its own polar opposite, *viz.*, as existence for and in self as contrasted with the universal."[5] The second phase is the "fall" of spirit, and it is in this phase that man becomes "a constituent element in the divine being". Hegel achieves this divinization of man through a process of legerdemain in which he asserts that in ideality, the polar opposite of spirit is "the Son of God", but "reduced to limited and particular conceptions, it is the world-nature and finite spirit". So, besides manifesting the nature of God as pure spirit, the Christian religion also posits the unity of man with God, not because of divine grace but because man is "comprehended in the idea of God". But man is not simply and immediately God, but God "only in so far as he annuls the merely natural and limited in his spirit and *elevates himself* to God".[6] No grace, no assistance from God is required — man divinizes himself through realizing that he is the externalization of Spirit. In the next sentence Hegel indicates the realization of the truth and man's duty which he himself reached: " . . . it is obligatory on him who is a partaker of the truth, and knows that he himself is a constituent of the divine idea, to give up his merely natural being: for the natural is the unspiritual."[7] Hegel, knowing himself to be a constituent of the divine idea, dutifully surrenders his unspiritual being. It is this idea of God as necessarily including man in "the *reconciliation* that heals the pain and inward suffering of man", that reconciles all man's inner conflicts by deifying him. This unity of man with himself through self-elevation to God exists first "only for the thinking speculative consciousness", that is, Hegel, but it must appear and in fact has appeared in Christ, who, in his own person, reconciled God and man. It is the thinking speculative consciousness that, reflecting on Christ, first comprehended the "subjective freedom of the ego itself". Consequently the Christian God can manifest Himself as human (the sensuous form appropriate to spirit) only once, for "God is realized as subject, and as manifested subjectivity is exclusively one individual." But who is this God who manifests himself in the redeemer?

Some of Hegel's comments on the Fall shed light on his understanding of man. The Fall was not really an act of disobedience or rebellion or pride on the part of man as in Augustine, or even Hobbes — an attempt by man to transform himself into his own god. In Hegel, the Fall is "the eternal history of spirit", arising through knowledge which is the total annulment of the unity of "mere nature". Nevertheless, as the "eternal mythus of man", the Fall is the transition by which spirit alienates itself and man becomes man. The Fall is, then, the source of human misery, for man is prey to sorrow and inner discord so long as he is only man, and yet the Fall also contains a kind of reconciliation in God's remark, in the Biblical account, after Adam has eaten of the tree of knowledge: "Behold Adam is become as one of us, knowing good and evil." Hegel takes this to mean that through knowledge of the universal and the particular, the particular being the locus of evil, man comprehends God Himself. What this means is that man realizes himself to be the alienated form of God, and the knowledge of this is the source of infinite reconciliation. What Hegel has done is to effect a radical transvaluation of values by substituting identification with God for the more traditional notion of union with God. Among other things Hegel has eliminated humility as a necessary precondition for the ending of all human inner conflicts. On the basis of this Hegel builds a cosmos in which God and man have always been consubstantial, although Hegel is the first to realize this. Therefore, by a subtle transformation Hegel avoids the difficulties of attempting to turn the natural man into the Supreme Being. It is, in fact, precisely by becoming the natural man, alienated from spirit, that man reaches the point of development at which he is able to be completely reconciled with God, or the spirit. What Hegel has done in conjunction with this is to shrink the cosmos so as to eliminate transcendence and all the ways in which it affects immanence. Transcendence means simply all those things that man in his soul perceives as existing outside the world of his ordinary experience, without being able to comprehend these events in his soul by his own efforts. Immanence, and transcendence in its immanent aspect, are accessible to some kind of human experience, but transcendence *per se* is the unknown ground and limit of all experience. Hegel has replaced this with a somewhat different perspective according to which transcendence is not what man cannot know (at least not in this world) or cannot know merely by the application of his own mind, but simply what man does not yet know. When this knowledge is attained man understands himself to *be* God, and all conflicts are resolved.

The catch is that God is only one subjectivity, and human beings can be God only by surrendering themselves to the universal, somewhat in the manner in which Rousseau's men rediscover their autarky by surrendering their particular wills to the general will. Hegel is confronted with the problem of how the multitude of men can really be united. How can all human beings come to see themselves as God? How is this realization to become reality for them?

In fact, Hegel himself is God, for his is the consciousness in the vanguard of mankind, the thinking speculative consciousness that first grasps the unity of man with God. In itself this is not much different from Rousseau's self-appointment as *l'homme naturel*, or Saint-Simon's announcement that he speaks with the voice of God. Hegel seeks to resolve the problem by creating a world in which all men can realize the fullness of freedom. His philosophy of history has, seemingly, two points of culmination, one being Hegel's divine mind, the other being the state, but it is through participation in the state that all men are to be made in the image of Hegel.

Strictly speaking, of course, Hegel's divine knowledge has not developed through history any more than Rousseau's natural man was a sudden re-emergence of the truth of human existence that had existed in the long lost state of nature. Like Rousseau, Hegel sets aside facts and creates a myth of a cosmos centered around himself, a cosmos in which he is the Messiah who sets up, or designates a salvific society, in this case the State, through which men are to share in divinity. The State is the Hegelian City of God, the realm of true morality and freedom, the perfect reconciliation of the universal with the particular. It is, of course, a displacement-substitute City of God, since the public philosophy, or its equivalent, has again been rejected and forced into the philosophical unconscious. The rejection consists in the identification of man and God. The result here is essentially a combination of the para-digmatic and the eschatological civil theologies, according to which the ultimate design of the world has not been realized but projected onto the cosmos. The artificiality of this projection can be seen in the distortions of history and previous cultures as well as in such obvious distortions as the inclusion of Islam in the "Germanic" world, all in the interest of "creating the appearances" of an orderly progression from China Westward to the fullness of knowledge and being in Hegel.

The state is the realization of freedom, which is the essence of spirit. Somewhat in the manner of Spinoza Hegel maintains that "all the qualities of spirit exist only through freedom; that all are but means for attaining freedom; that all seek and produce this and this alone".[8] Unlike matter which seeks a kind of perfect unity that would destroy it, spirit has its center in itself. It is autarkic, self-sufficient, for it exists in and with itself; it is "self-contained existence". And it is precisely this self-sufficiency that is freedom. 'For if I am dependent, my being is referred to something else which I am not; I cannot exist independently of something external. I am free, on the contrary, when my existence depends upon myself. This self-contained existence of spirit is none other than self-consciousness, consciousness of one's own being."[9] True and perfect autarky arises from complete self-consciousness. The self knows all there is to know about itself and depends on no being outside itself for either knowledge or existence. So, history is the process of spirit's discovery of its own freedom, or, in other words, history reaches its culmination when man realizes that he is God and therefore self-contained existence, when, as Hegel puts it, the German nation reached the "consciousness that man, as man, is free", that all are free. The destiny or final cause of the spiritual, substantial world is the realization of its own freedom or self-contained existence. This idea is a combination of Rousseau's autarkic *amour de soi* with Kant's autonomy of the will of the morally legislating rational being, reason being for Hegel divine wisdom. The common basis is man's metaphysical self-sufficiency.

In this realization religion plays a certain essential part. The state is, as has been said, the unity of absolute freedom and subjective will. Religion is the highest of the forms of the conscious union of freedom and subjectivity, or objectivity and individual personality. "In [religion], spirit — rising above the limitations of temporal and secular existence — becomes conscious of the absolute spirit, and in the consciousness of the self-existent Being, renounces its individual interest."[10] This is analogous to Rousseau's *le zèle patriotique*, the feeling through which the individual's feeling for himself is elevated, transformed, through an *Aufhebung*, into a devotion to the whole. Religion is the consciousness which the mind gives to itself of the "identity of the *subjective* or *personal* with the *universal* will".

Hegel's understanding of religion in its relation to the state oscillates between a pseudo-public philosophy and civil theology. On one hand, he says that "the form of religion . . . decides that of the state and its constitution". The state is, in fact, based on religion, a religion that pre-exists and creates the state, which, then, rests on religion. On the other hand, "religion is the sphere in which a nation gives itself the definition of that which it regards as the true", somewhat more a civil theology than a public philosophy, which antedates the state. There are two basic ways in which religion can present the truth to the state: one is by recognizing the "idea" in separation from the world, that is God as transcendent, "Highest Being, Lord of heaven and earth, living in a remote region far from human actualities"; the other is by considering the idea in its unity — "God as unity of the universal and individual; the individual itself assuming the aspect of positive and real existence in the idea of the incarnation". The difference is that between a transcendent God who is envisioned before man realizes that he himself is God, and the immanent God thus realized as identical with man. Accordingly, religion is the sphere in which a nation decides for itself whether it will regard the truth in its separation or its unity. "The conception of God, therefore, constitutes the general basis of a people's character." Those people with the more primitive characters are those who have not yet realized the idea in its unity, and therefore do not yet realize that "freedom can exist only where individuality is recognized as having its positive and real existence in the Divine Being".[11]

There is, then, for Hegel, no civil religion in Rousseau's sense of "a purely civil profession of faith" which is added to the society by the sovereign. Everything flows from the immanent spirit, and it is the form of religion which decides that of the state and its constitution. The ability of the state to choose its religion seems to be a function of its geographical and temporal location.

The identification of man with God is to be the final resolution of the anticosmy, achieved not by rejecting God and transcendence but by absorbing them into immanence. Or, one could just as easily say that immanence is absorbed into transcendence, which thereby ceases to be transcendence. The difference between Hegel's approach and that of his predecessors is that instead of being reduced to a purely natural being who must also assume the role of supernatural being, man elevates himself to the supernatural, which is, in fact, completely dependent on man for self-realization. The same distortion has occurred — it has merely been shifted to the other end of the spectrum of being: it is divine being that is reduced to immanence, rather than human being that is reduced to the animal. There is, however, still the same result of the elimination of all metaphysical tensions between immanence and transcendence, between this world of everyday experience and the equally real sense that there is a higher realm experienced in the depths of the soul.

The details of Hegel's philosophy of history are not important for our purposes. What is important is his concept of alienation. Robert Tucker traces this back to Kant's split of the human psyche into noumenal and phenomenal parts and, just as for Kant the true man in the noumenal world was a being of god-like perfection while his phenomenal self was the locus of all human imperfections, so for Hegel the spirit splits into a divine noumenon and a phenomenal alien world into which the spirit empties itself. But as we have seen this diremption of man into a schizophrenic combination of the divine and the "human" is rather common in modern philosophy, and alienation is the psychic term for anticosmy. The rough dialectic in Rousseau in which godlike man falls away from perfection and loses himself in conventional society to be restored by Rousseau to knowing his perfection, freedom and self-sufficiency through the general will becomes in Hegel a rather refined dialectic in which spirit falls away from and empties itself into a phenomenal world in which it realizes itself through the human mind, thus resolving the anticosmy, for in its self-realization and self-knowledge spirit will be at one with itself, as men will resolve all inner conflicts in realizing themselves as God. Hegel has simply transposed the entire drama into a slightly higher key. Rather than being a fall and deification of man it is the fall and deification of man disguised as spirit.

Actually, Hegel's entire philosophy is built on a displacement-substitute for the public philosophy. The rejected transcendent God is replaced by the spirit which is simply the Hegelian ego. Hegel speaks the language of theology to destroy it and replace it with the imperial ego. Freedom as Hegel describes it is enslavement to the State, the City of God on earth; Hegel's God is really "*un immense égoisme*" to borrow a phrase from Comte, because it empties itself into the world not out of love but out of the egocentric desire for self-knowledge, and thereafter simply uses all beings, man first of all, for its self-realization. Marxism-Leninism uses essentially the same structures except that the divine is so completely absorbed in the natural material world that the concept of Being is lost and man realizes himself as God, or the supreme being for man, in his own right, and not as the alienated form of spirit.[12]

With Marxism-Leninism we enter yet another new phase in the search for purely immanent meaning, a phase in which anticosmy has become so extreme that only one possible resolution can be seriously imagined — violence. The dialectic, the resolution of the contradictories, is no longer carried forward by any essentially preservative process, for it is no longer possible to resolve the contradiction by reconciling the extremes. Matters have become simpler — one of the extremes must be destroyed. For Marx, perhaps even more than for Hegel, the concept that refers to anticosmy is alienation, for it is through alienation that the two contradictory extremes are fully realized and the stronger violently annihilates the weaker. The revolution is a physical version of what Ludwig Feuerbach regarded as necessary for man to reabsorb God into himself.

Feuerbach, the major figure in the transition from Hegel to Marx, published in 1841 *The Essence of Christianity*, a work which had a tremendous impact on the philosophical life of Germany. The book is a description of a Hegelianized Christianity, with a rather significant reversal of Hegel. Whereas for Hegel God realizes himself as God in man, Feuerbach proclaims the verbal reverse: the overcoming of alienation is man's realizing of himself as God, period. Man is alienated from himself because he has projected his true nature as a divine being external and alien to him, and man will be fully himself only when he realizes that there is no absolute, perfect, divine being standing above him and impoverishing him by its existence. "The true statement is this: man's knowledge of God is man's knowledge of himself, of his own nature. . . . Where the consciousness of God is, there is the being of God — in man . . . "[13] Thus the reversal of Hegel, for in Feuerbach's view history is man's self-realization as God, without the necessity for positing any Absolute Spirit, or any other kind of God, and this idea is the principle of Marxism, although its development in Marx is considerably more complex than it is in Feuerbach. What Feuerbach took from Hegel as esoteric psychology

(Tucker), Marx transforms into esoteric economics, for Marxian man is a purely natural, economic being.

First of all, the central idea of Marx's thought in this context is alienation. Marx took Hegel's thought as the outline of the course of history in material reality, and not simply in thought, and sought a way of conforming world history to this materialized Hegelianism. Like Feuerbach, Marx chose to begin to philosophize on the basis of the real man in his real, concrete, material existence, and "following Feuerbach, Marx conceives the whole of history as a single great episode of self-externalization, alienation and transcendence of alienation".[14] Marxian alienation is actually an economic parallel of Feuerbach's religious alienation. Just as for Feuerbach man is alienated from himself because he empties himself into a divine being that stands over and against him, so for Marx man is alienated from himself because he empties his being into a material, economic god that rules his life. This economic alienation is common to men at all times; it is under capitalism, however, that alienation as the *summum malum* becomes intolerable and so is ripe for destruction by revolution.

In an early work, *On the Jewish Question*, Marx identifies this economic god of practical need and self-interest as money, which "is the alienated essence of man's work and existence; this essence dominates him and he worships it. . . . Just as man, so long as he is engrossed in religion, can only objectify his essence by an *alien* and fantastic being; so under the sway of egoistic need, he can only affirm himself and produce objects in practice by subordinating his products and his own activity to the domination of an alien entity, and by attributing to them the significance of an alien entity, namely money."[15] This egoistic need, an economic parallel of religion, Marx elsewhere calls greed or avarice and identifies this love of money with the worldly religion of the Jew, announcing that man cannot be free until the world is cleansed of economic Judaism, for money is man lost to himself. It is not simply man's need to labor for his living that is the source of alienation. Rather it is an egoistic desire to accumulate labor, to gain more than is needed for life. As the excess of desires over needs and powers of the individual it is very close to Rousseau's asthenia, the desire for more than the individual truly needs to maintain life. In the case of Marx, however, this leads not precisely to the dependence of the individual on other men but to the exploitation of other men by the one who is able to control the means of production. Alienation is roughly equivalent to asthenia as self-sufficient man lost to himself.

The most important discussion of alienation in Marx's early writings occurs in *The Economic and Philosophical Manuscripts* of 1844, and what is perhaps the most famous passage translates Feuerbach's theological alienation into production or economic alienation. In this case the god is the accumulation of objects produced by labor. This results in the de-humanization of man, who transfers his life to the objects he produces. "For it is clear on this presupposition that the more the worker expends himself in work the more powerful becomes the world of objects which he creates in face of himself, the poorer he becomes in his inner life, and the less he belongs to himself." [16] Man is a closed, limited system — in the present state of affairs whatever he creates represents a loss of his own substance. In an ideal order whatever a man produces in his life activity belongs to him and will serve to augment his own life. He himself is the master, for he can choose what to produce and when — he dominates the object. However, the meaning of alienation is that men are enslaved by greed — they bow down and worship the object, and the money that enables them to hoard objects. This labor process causes a split in the existence of the worker, which Marx consistently characterizes as paradox: "the more the worker produces the less he has to consume; the more value he creates the more worthless he becomes; the more refined his product the more crude and misshapen the worker". The worker is simply alienating himself as the Hegelian God alienated himself in his creatures.

Marx always maintains that he begins with facts, with concrete material reality, with "the existence of living human individuals" who differentiate themselves from the animals by producing the means of their own subsistence. The significance of this is that it is characteristic of man that he maintain his own existence by his life activity, not simply by seizing or gathering whatever nature may grant him, not by conforming himself to his environment, like the animals, but by mastering nature and creating a human world through controlling and developing the means of producing the goods necessary for his existence. Always the focus is on man, the human world; nature and objects should serve to enhance human existence.

However, the contemporary state of affairs Marx perceives is quite different. "We shall begin from a *contemporary* economic fact. The worker becomes poorer the more wealth he produces and the more his production increases in power and extent. . . . The *devaluation* of the human world increases in direct relation with the *increase in value* of the world of things." [17] The more the worker empties himself into the material god the more he sinks below the level of humanity. Here as in Hegel we can see anticosmy presented not as simply a particular philosophy, but as *the* process of history — history *is* the creation and resolution of the contradiction. As central to the process of history, the increasing alienation of industrial workers onlv indicates that history is nearing its culmination.

Much of the meaning of alienation lies in the compulsoriness of labor. "[The worker's] work is not voluntary but imposed, *forced labour*. It is not the satisfaction of a need, but only a *means* for satisfying other needs . . . so that activity of the worker is not his own spontaneous activity. It is another's activity and a loss of his own spontaneity."[18] But this spontaneity is really meant to be exercised not for the good of the individual, but rather for the good of the species. One of Marx's major premises is that man is a species-being or a universal being because he is related to and capable of mastering all of nature, all the forces of production. "The universality of man appears in practice in the universality which makes the whole of nature into his inorganic body: (1) as a direct means of life; and equally (2) as the material object and instrument of his life activity. . . . To say that man *lives* from nature means that nature is his *body* with which he must remain in a continuous interchange in order not to die. . . . [M]an is a part of nature."[19] Therefore man is universal only because of the potentiality of universal cooperation in mastering nature. Nature itself is all that is, the complete universal, and because man is part of nature and is required to maintain and express his life through interaction with nature he is a species-being, rather than a mere aggregate of individuals. There is no human nature that can be found in an individual mortal such as Socrates; there is only the species man, which requires that all men exist in active, creative interaction with nature. Any individual who does not so exist prevents man from realizing himself as a universal species-being and as the supreme being for man. Universality is here the rough equivalent of the general will as the means by which man realizes his divinity.

Thus far man has never yet realized himself as a species-being because he has been burdened with alienated labor. The evil of alienated labor is that it disrupts man's species life, fragmenting humanity into separate, egoistic individuals. "For labour, *life activity, productive life*, now appears to man only as *means* for the satisfaction of a need, the need to maintain his physical existence. Productive life is, however, species life. It is life creating life. In the type of life-activity resides the whole character of a species . . . ; and free, conscious activity is the species-character of human beings."[20] As a species-being man reproduces the world in his own image. That is, the meaning of work, or labor, is not the mere satisfaction of individual needs but the constuction of a human world, what Marx calls "the objectification of man's species-life". In this way man is at one with his inorganic body, nature. Alienated labor, however, prostitutes man's labor to the satisfaction of individual egoistic needs, and species-life then becomes a means for individual existence. Men do not cooperate with each other in the mastery of nature for the good of all, but instead compete with one another in controlling the forces of production for the private good of a few.

Here Marx breaks somewhat with his position in *On the Jewish Question* that money is the economic god. In the *Manuscripts* the alien being is not money but man himself. "The alien being to whom labour and the product of labour belong, to whose service labour is devoted, and to whose enjoyment the product of labour goes, can only be *man* himself. If the product of labour does not belong to the worker, but confronts him as an alien power, this can only be because it belongs to *a man other than the worker*."[21] The anticosmic cleavage is not within the soul of the individual, in his inner conflicts, but rather within man as an aggregation of individuals.

It must be pointed out that alienated labor is not the result of the activity of a man other than the worker. Rather it is alienated labor that created "the domination of the non-producer over production and its product". In Feuerbach it is not God who alienates man from himself – God does not exist as an independent being. It is rather man who alienates himself from his own being in his own creation of God. So in Marx it is not the non-producer who alienates man, but the producer, the worker, the representative of man, who, by his mode of labor, alienates himself and all mankind with him. The alienation is rooted in the structure of human labor, when the worker consents to labor for another who owns or controls the sources of the means of subsistence. Thus alienated labor creates private property.

Therefore history is the process of man's increasing alienation through a kind of labor that has the positive effect of developing the forces of production and the negative effect of creating private control of these forces. Because man works to create private property that serves private, egoistic interests, he loses himself to alien objects. Labor is not an end in itself, a life-activity of man, but simply the means for sustaining his life. It is this condition of alienation from which humanity must be emancipated. "From the relation of alienated labour to private property it also follows that the emancipation of society from private property, from servitude, takes the political form of the *emancipation of the workers*; not in the sense that only the latter's emancipation is involved, but because this emancipation includes the emancipation of humanity as a whole. For all human servitude is involved in the relation of the worker to production, and all the types of servitude are only modifications or consequences of this relation."[22] In a famous passage in an earlier work, *Introduction to the Critique of Hegel's Philosophy of Right*, Marx had already designated the proletariat as the class representative of humanity as a whole, the class responsible for emancipating humanity. The reason for this is simply that the proletariat best fits Marx's scheme of alienation and emancipation, for it is that part of mankind which has been reduced to animality, and therefore stands at the opposite pole from divinity. This is, then, the class ultimately responsible for establishing man as god.

The seeds of what is considered mature Marxism are to be found in the *Manuscripts*, particularly, according to Tucker, in Marx's decision, mentioned previously, that "man's self-alienation could and should be grasped as a social relation of 'man to man'", that is, the worker and the capitalist. From this point Marxism became a matter of class conflict, to the point that it could proclaim that "the history of all hitherto existing society is the history of class struggles". All of history has been a process of increasing alienation of workers from owners. And both classes suffer from the same alienation, which is why the proletarians represent the humanity of the bourgeoisie as well as its own. As Marx described it in *The Holy Family*, "The possessing class and the proletarian class represent one and the same human self-aliena-tion. But the former feels satisfied and affirmed in this self-alienation, apprehends the alienation *as its own power*, and possesses in it the appearance of a human existence; the latter feels annihilated in this alienation, sees in it its own impotence and the reality of a non-human existence." [23]

Marx continues this concern with alienation in *The German Ideology*, written in collaboration with Engels. In the first part of the book he outlines the course of history in terms of the development of production and increas-ing alienation. Men begin by producing their means of subsistence as a way of expressing their life, as a "definite *mode* of life. As individuals express their life, so they are." Gradually productive forces are developed through increasing population and cooperation. And as the productive forces are developed, so is the division of labor. "The various stages of development in the division of labour are just so many different forms of ownership; i.e., the existing stage in the division of labour determines also the relation of individuals to one another with reference to the material, instrument, and product of labour." [24] Marx then discusses the various stages of ownership from the tribal to the feudal, and goes on to state the premises of his analysis. He separates himself from German philosophy which moves from thought to material reality. Instead Marx chooses to "ascend from earth to heaven". "We set out from real, active men, and on the basis of their real-life process we demonstrate the development of the ideological reflexes and echoes of this life-process." [25]

All forms of human thought derive from the mode of material production. However, because of alienation intellectual and material activity fall to different individuals, to different classes. The men who produce objects are not the men who produce ideas, nor even the men who consume the objects. In *The German Ideology* Marx has transformed alienation into the division of labour. The basic meaning is the same — both imply a break, a differentiation within humanity based on the relative development of productive forces. This division of humanity prevents man from being god, the supreme being for man. "Further, the division of labour implies the contradiction between the interest of the separate individual or the individual family and the communal interest of all individuals who have intercourse with one another."[26]

There is "a cleavage . . . between the particular and the common interest", a lack of harmony. Why? It is because "activity is not voluntarily, but naturally divided". The division is imposed upon individuals, not chosen by them. Marx is not suggesting that in the ideal society all men will do everything, for if each man does everything there is only the isolation of Rousseau's state of nature. He is instead suggesting that each man should choose his own sphere or spheres of activity without becoming identified with them. In this way he remains master of his own activities rather than being controlled by them. And the invisible hand of the Communist society "regulates the general production", and thus makes it possible for a man to do one thing today and another thing tomorrow, or even several things within the same day. Division of labor and private property are the same evil, for both imply the power of one man to dispose of the labor activity of another man. In a society free of alienation, all men have free and equal access to the means of production, and each man determines the disposition of his own labor. When this is the case, when each man reaps the rewards of his own labor, he will no longer look upon it as an onerous burden. It will become life's prime want, the free expression of his humanity for the benefit of himself and all other men. Men, as part of the divine species-being, will spontaneously work according to their abilities, not in order to enrich themselves, for there will be no money and no accumulation of wealth, but simply because they choose to, because to work will be their primary desire. And consumption will be limited to the satisfaction of needs rather than the accumulation of wealth. Marx simply assumes that this nebulous, idyllic Communist society will be able to achieve the balance of production and consumption. It seems likely that the ultimate control rests with nature, that even though man is master of nature he is still part of it. It is arguable that, on the Hegelian model, Communist society is nature come to full consciousness of itself through man.

The cleavage between the individual and the common interest is abolished in the transcendence of alienation, because each person spontaneously labors for the good of all. There will be no division of labor in any sense, not even between mental and physical labor — not that labor will revert to a primitive undividness, but each worker will determine his own labor. Therefore, in the ideal society, every man will voluntarily work according to his abilities and will voluntarily consume according to his needs.

It is because of this increasing alienation that history is so characteristically violent. It is the violence of contradiction without reconciliation, for there is no common ground between the extremes. Marx, of course, dogmatically reduces man to a purely natural being who is, moreover, to owe his existence to no one but himself. To be fully human man must be autarkic, dependent on no other being. Therefore, the idea of the creation of the world, and of human beings, must be eliminated — nature and man exist on their own account. Marx goes on to explain that since all human beings originate through acts of coitus "even in a physical sense man owes his existence to man". Anyone inquisitive enough to wonder who or what engendered the first human being Marx accuses of maintaining a "perverted" point of view. Such questions are meaningless because they threaten to expose the falseness of Marxism-Leninism's claim to absolute truth. And Marx follows the custom of misrepresenting the position he is rejecting. "If you ask a question about the creation of nature and man you abstract from nature and man. You suppose them *non*-existent and you want me to demonstrate that they *exist*. I reply: give up your abstraction and at the same time you abandon your question."[27] This is a distortion of the meaning of creation, according to which one does not prove existence but rather takes existence as the given and seeks to explain how all that is came to be, or, in other words, how the abyss between non-existence and existence was leaped. Marx further conflates contingency with meaninglessness in that the consideration of the possibility of the non-existence of man and nature is absurd — they are necessary, absolute beings. Man creates himself through labor, much as Hegel's spirit realizes itself through phenomenal beings in history.

Alienation, then, or anticosmy, is the central characteristic of Marx's thought. Increasingly, through labor, man alienates himself, empties himself into objects which are appropriated by the capitalist. Since the proletariat is the class most intensely alienated it is the only class eligible for divinization. When the process reaches extremes, when the proletariat is so alienated and emptied of humanity as to be barely human, then the contradiction is resolved by the violent destruction of the capitalist class. There is no common ground between capitalists and proletariat to mediate a resolution of alienation — their interests are not reconcilable — nor is there any kind of ground of being, even the most rudimentary, to mediate a synthesis of the antithetical anti-cosmic extremes. There can be only destruction of one by the other.

It is because Marx's thought is built squarely upon anticosmic alienation that violence pervades all levels of this thought. As an example, let us turn to the construction of history in *The Communist Manifesto*, which opens with the sweeping pronouncement that "the history of all hitherto existing society is the history of class struggles", that is, history is created by the struggle between social classes. Marx and Engels then distill all the complexity of historical events, actions, persons, and motivations into a short paragraph. "Freeman and slave, patrician and plebeian, lord and serf, guild-master and journeyman, in a word, oppressor and oppressed, stood in constant opposition to one another, carried on an uninterrupted, now hidden, now open fight, a fight that each time ended, either in a revolutionary reconstitution of society at large, or in the common ruin of the contending classes." History is simply the alternation of covert with manifest violence, a contest between oppressor and oppressed — a struggle for power. That such struggles are all too common in human existence is beyond dispute; the radical ideological transformation of Marx and Engels is to define human existence simply as violence, and to precipitate out of the course of human events everything that does not contribute to the struggle between irreconcilable class interests, which is the exacerbation of the contradiction. Moreover, the bourgeois class has so intensified the level of violence in human existence as to destroy even the vestiges of order in human life, because "for exploitation, veiled by religious and political illusions, it has substituted naked, shameless, direct, brutal exploitation". In the Marx-Engels interpretation, the bourgeoisie pitilessly reveals the violence that, in more concealed and tolerable forms, has always governed human existence. The bourgeoisie has brutally and cynically collapsed this existence to its true characteristics — naked self-interest and exploitation. Furthermore, the bourgeoisie is an insatiable catabolic force, for "it cannot exist without constantly revolutionizing the instruments of production", without constantly metabolizing order into chaos: "All that is solid melts into air, all that is holy is profaned, and man is at last compelled to face with sober senses, his real conditions of life, and his relations with his kind."[28] Through this revolutionary prestidigitation, the too too solid illusions of the human condition are melted into the dismaying truth. From constantly having the rug pulled out from under his feet man loses the ability to ignore the nakedness of self-interest and exploitation, the forms of violence that determine human existence. And Lenin, more Marxian than Marx, regards th bourgeoisie as a veritable scourge of mankind. "Naturally, to be successful, such an undertaking as the systematic suppression of the exploited majority by the exploiting minority calls for the utmost ferocity and savagery in the matter of suppressing, it calls for seas of blood, through which mankind is actually wading its way in slavery, serfdom and wage-labor." [29] If bourgeois violence is so ferocious one can imagine the sort of diabolical fury that will be required to overcome it.

Lenin's polemic, *The State and Revolution*, is the work in which this process of destruction of anticosmy is most fully and explicitly discussed. For the moment let us consider first this problem of anticosmy, according to which man must be both savior and saved. If we study *The State and Revolution* carefully we find that it is a complex and subtle interplay between two contradictory concepts of force, each of which embodies one of the anticosmic premises. The state embodies the dead, mechanical, material, unnatural, enslaving unconscious force. It is significant in this regard that Lenin constantly describes the state and his opponents in terms of death and corruption. The state power, once necessary for maintaining life, has now become obsolete, a hindrance to life. Because of the developments in human consciousness, the former ordering force has become a disordering force and now represents man's "fallen" condition, his subjection to evil and his need for salvation.

Socialism, on the other hand, embodies the living, immanent, natural, spiritual, conscious force, the Aristotelian *physis*. It is this force which, directing the proletariat, will save man from the evils of capitalism, exploitation, and alienation. These forces constitute a dualism within the natural world, and their struggle to resolve the conflict drives history. We can characterize them further: The coercive force, the state, symbolizes mortality, the past, bondage, lack of direction, lack of consciousness, violence, evil; the natural force, socialism, symbolizes immortality, the future, freedom direction, knowledge, progress, good — in short, redemption.

In order to understand the process in which these two forces conflict it is necessary to refer to an earlier work of Lenin, *Materialism and Empirio-Criticism*, written in 1908. According to Lenin's materialism, matter is primary, the substratum, and there is nothing in the world but matter in motion through space and time. Sensation is the direct connection between consciousness and the external world; it is the transformation of the energy of external excitation into the fact of consciousness, which is an internal state of matter. Consciousness is matter in motion as an immanent, natural force, and therefore sensation is the transformation of an external force into an immanent force, a change of quantity into quality, a theory of sensation and consciousness that is rather reminiscent of Hobbes. Thus, the dialectic: an increasing external force produces a correspondingly increasing internal force until the latter reaches a level of intensity at which it explodes or erupts back into the world as an external force. Consciousness, which grows entirely through being acted upon by the external forces of sensation and coercion is capable of itself becoming an external force, which takes the form of an overpowering will. Consciousness reaches this level through the complete transformation of external force into internal force, and at this level consciousness is capable of maintaining itself in existence. For Lenin, nature is transformed, through this process, from a thing-in-itself to a thing-for-us. Once coercion and sensation have increased the level of consciousness sufficiently, consciousness exerts its own force on nature, which is not a coercive force because nature cannot be coerced, but basically a life-force, of which man is the carrier. This consciousness leads to the exercise of will according to necessary laws.

Will is at first a coercive, oppressive force, which emanates from those who have power but lack the consciousness of necessity and its laws, and which increases the inner forces of the oppressed, or their consciousness of necessity, until this consciousness erupts as an overwhelming will-power. The will that must be destroyed is the will that is rooted in the individual self and is directed towards, and coerces, society to follow the egoistic desires of the individual. This is based on a false consciousness, the lie that the individual is superior to society. It will be replaced by a will rooted in society, coercing the self to abandon all egoism. The first will alienates part of society from itself, it "specializes" part of society, while the second will unites society. True consciousness expresses itself initially through violence, lashing out at a world which does not conform to the true consciousness of the laws of necessity. The world then becomes a manifestation, or reflection, of true consciousness.

This analysis is an oversimplification of Lenin's thought, for it reduces the process to merely a rather crude mechanism of forces. Actually, the process is made more complex by the fact that consciousness is dispersed through the entire population and concentrated in only a few persons. The mass of the population is inert and sluggish, and the task of the privileged few is to do their utmost to increase the consciousness of the others by judicious application of such external stimuli as agitation and propaganda, agitation for those who need the most stimulation, propaganda for those who need less.

Agitation and propaganda work by increasing the external force of sensation, which in turn increases the internal force of consciousness, which then erupts in violence. Thus, the irruption into history of the transcendent power is replaced by the eruption of an immanent human power. The few with the high degree of consciousness possess the most profound knowledge of the laws of necessity, and according to this knowledge they are able to lead the others and to direct the violence when it erupts.

This is a basic outline of the process of the interaction of the contradictory forces in *The State and Revolution*. But properly to understand these forces we must investigate their origins in modern Western philosophy, for just as Lenin did not originate anticosmy, neither did he originate the idea of the conflict of forces. We can trace this conflict of forces back at least as far as Mesmerism, which was begun in Paris by Anton Mesmer in 1778 and was concerned with achieving "harmony" or the physical and moral accord between man and the laws of nature. This "harmony", or the recovery from sickness to health, was effected by convulsions or crises. Mesmer's ideas were not new, having descended from those of predecessors such as Paracelsus in the sixteenth century. Mesmer was primarily concerned with "animal magnetism", and magnetism or the harmony of opposing forces became paradigmatic.[30] The major importance of Mesmerism in this context is the influence it had on German Romanticism.

Romanticism was concerned with a living process, an evolution, and expressed an attempt to conquer infinity. The romantic endeavor was primarily to achieve a complete integration of man into the natural order of things, to make man completely at home in the world. Man's place in this natural order had become problematic with the beginning of modern science, when there arose the dual problem of bridging the gap between man and the "other animals" and yet of assuring man a privileged position in the hierarchy of nature. Since nature was conceived as dynamic, the temporal dimension of human existence became pre-eminent, as it had been in the progressive philosophies of Saint-Simon and Comte. In the romantic poets there is a longing for emancipation from time, for he who can escape from time becomes as a god. This temporal and evolutionary aspect led to a dynamic conception of the hierarchy of beings, according to which God is evolving from the hierarchy of nature.

In Herder, who was extremely influential with the Romantic movement and a major influence on Hegel, there is almost an apotheosis of force: "The two great theses of the *Conversations* are the interrelated conceptions of divine immanence and the dynamism of nature. God is found revealed in every point of nature. The universe is conceived as a unified complex of forces, arranged in a hierarchy and operating according to immutable laws which are at one and the same time the evidence of the divine power, and the activity of God himself realized in the world order." [31]

In Fichte we find an extreme dualism of reason and nature, bridged only by the will. For Fichte the will is "divine" and an indication of man's extreme autarky. "I stand in the center of two entirely opposite worlds: a visible world, in which action is the only moving power, and an invisible and absolutely incomprehensible world, in which will is the ruling principle. I am one of the primitive forces of both these worlds. My will embraces both." [32] The Fichtean will becomes a creative, non-coercive force by acting according to necessity, to the laws of nature, for nature is the unquestionable ground both of its own and of man's existence. We find also in Fichte an emphatic insistence on the same point stressed by Marx, and also Hegel, the importance of man's responsibility for his own existence. "There is within me an impulse to an absolute, independent self-activity. Nothing is more unendurable to me than to be merely by another, for another, and through another; I must be something for myself and by myself alone." [33]

This will give a rough idea of the development of the notion of the conflict of forces in European philosophy. There is another aspect of the background of Lenin's thought which we must consider, namely, the development of Russian revolutionary thought, specifically with respect to violence. A brief examination of three major revolutionaries will shed some light on Lenin's thought.

First is Bakunin, who was an anarchist, and whose perhaps most famous statement is "The passion for destruction is at the same time a creative passion." [34] Like Fichte, Bakunin also glorified the will: "Concentration of energy in the will is the only way. When we are able to say: '*ce que je veux, Dieu le veut*,' then at last we shall be happy and our suffering over." [35] "There's only one real misfortune that can afflict a man, one real disaster – that is to lose the will, the desire, the energy for activity, and to have no purpose in life." [36] He expected a future, a new world, which would be free. And, like Saint-Simon and Comte, he regarded God's existence as undesirable; in *God and the State* he presents a "proof" for the non-existence of God. "If God is, he is necessarily the eternal, supreme, absolute master, and if such a master exists, man is a slave; now, if he is a slave, neither justice, nor equality, nor fraternity, nor prosperity are possible for him. . . . God's existence necessarily implies the slavery of all that is beneath him. Therefore, if God existed, only in one way could he serve human liberty – by ceasing to exist." [37]

If we inquire what constitutes this precious human liberty, we find that it is merely submission to necessity. "The liberty of man consists solely in this: that he obeys natural laws because he has *himself* recognized them as such, and not because they have been externally imposed upon him by any extrinsic will whatever, divine or human, collective or individual."[38] The non-existence of God creates the autarky of the human will; as will it is self-sufficient. It surrenders itself to no other will, but only to the laws of nature.

Sergei Nechaev continues the development of metaphysical, and also physical violence. In his book *Roots of Revolution* Franco Venturi describes Nechaev as being "the very embodiment of violence" and as possessed by an "overwhelming passion for immediate action". In collaboration with Tkachev, Nechaev wrote *A Programme of Revolutionary Action* that begins with "a series of observations on the spiritual impossibility of living in the existing world". Paragraph 23 of the *Revolutionary Catechism*, written by Bakunin and Nechaev, states, "The only revolution that can save the people is one that destroys every established object root and branch, that annihilates all State traditions, orders and classes in Russia."[39] Another work written by Bakunin and Nechaev, *The Principles of Revolution*, ends with an appeal "to all young Russians to unite in brotherhood with those who will act in the same way throughout Europe, and to start work at once on the sacred cause of *eradicating evil* and cleansing the soil of Russia with sword and fire".[40] Nechaev was described as being a man of iron will who demanded complete submission from his followers. This aspect of his character and his conviction that speed was essential for bringing on the revolution seem to lie at the basis of his emphasis on violence. In a manifesto addressed to the "students of Russia", Nechaev said, "From now on, every step we take must be marked by rigid calculation and inflexible logic; every feeling must be stifled in the breast: one single passion alone must live in us: the will to create a collective force. Comrades . . . Do not test yourselves any longer to arouse with the words of truth a dying world which has now had its day. Its end is inevitable, we must act to hasten that end!"[41]

According to Venturi's interpretation of Tkachev, "In history there are no laws, but only ends or, perhaps, one end, according to which everything can and must be judged." Tkachev envisioned the revolution as consisting of two stages, the first destructive and the second constructive. "The essence of the first stage is the fight, and therefore violence; the fight can be carried out successfully only on the following conditions: centralization, severe discipline, speed, decision, and unity in action. . . . Constructive revolutionary activity, on the other hand, though it must proceed at the same time as the destructive activity, must by its very nature rely on exactly opposite principles. The first is based mainly on material force, the second is based on spiritual force; the first relies mainly on speed and unity, the second on the solidity and vitality of the changes it has brought about. The first must be carried out with violence, the second with conviction."[42] The violence is necessary to leap the abyss between the past and the future, which is also the abyss between the anticosmic contradictories. "One must not conceal the fact that there is an abyss between them, that however much one tries to bring them together, the abyss remains and it is difficult to bridge it."[43] The revolution requires the transformation of the spiritual power of the revolutionaries and of the people into the coercive material power of violence.

The relevant characteristics of the thought of these three revolutionaries are the following: (1) a feeling of spiritual alienation from the world. They find it impossible to live with the metaphysical order of reality; (2) the passion for violence as a means of accelerating events and also as a manifestation of the power and autarky of the human will, for it is the human will that is to determine the metaphysical structure of being; (3) an emphasis on the salvific power of the will; (4) the concept of a force impelling man toward life, freedom, a new world. This is the immanent, spiritual force; (5) the idea of revolution as a crusade to purge the world of evil with violence. To use Eric Voegelin's concept, the revolution is *metastasis* because it will completely change the structure of reality; (6) the idea of history as progress towards a state of perfection; and (7) the ambivalent notion that human happiness consists in man's metaphysical dominion over reality while he yet remains subject to the laws of nature. Ultimately the physical violence is merely a manifestation of the metaphysical violence which must be perpetrated if the structure of reality is to be remade according to man's desire to be God. Reality must be forcibly changed so that man will find it easy to maintain himself in existence: everything that threatens or casts doubt upon his ability to maintain his own existence must be eliminated.

With this in mind, let us return to *The State and Revolution*. At the basis of this work we find the attempt to resolve the conflict between the contradictory premises regarding man's "fallen" nature, his asthenia, and his autonomy, his autarky. Although Socialism, which is the force of autarky, symbolizes freedom it is relatively impotent practically *vis-à-vis* the perpetrators of slavery, at least for Lenin. Violence can be overcome only by violence, for power is manifest only in strength. Hence, socialism must acquire and must unite itself with coercive force. This it does by means of the human will, and the power of the acquired coercive force is dependent upon the strength of the will. The salvific revolutionary will is also the autarkic, self-sustaining will, the will that has replaced the divine will as the cause of man's continued existence. Those who have such will and such consciousness are not sufficiently numerous to support a revolution of savage violence, while the mass who are capable of such violence do not have the consciousness themselves, but must be led.

For Lenin the will thus leaps over the abyss between past and future, man and God, because the tension between the two forces creates the space for political and revolutionary action, which is the manifestation of will. The annihilation of the dualism requires a political action capable of exerting a force stronger than the forces maintaining the repressive state in existence. Since the will of the Socialist, of the true Marxian thinker, gains its power and authority from its rootedness in the knowledge of necessity, it is grounded and therefore capable of greater forcefulness than the will of those without such knowledge or such consciousness. In other words, the state can be destroyed because it is supported by a will which is no longer in accordance with the structure of reality.

The revolution is the supreme exertion of the metaphysically "true" will that overcomes the dualism and anticosmy and destroys the dead, unnatural, imposed order of the state to allow the natural order to emerge freely. It is the *aplanissement* of all metaphysical tensions, the reconciliation of spirit and matter, history and nature, and the leap into a new life. It is the fulfillment of consciousness and its complete manifestation. The revolution is war, the struggle of the proletariat to impose its will on the bourgeoisie, for man can be saved only by becoming God. The revolution is also a climax, a catharsis of history viewed as a dramatic struggle, and the catharsis is followed by the denouement in which the last conflicts and tensions are resolved and history comes to its end. The revolution is a purging of evil from the world in order to allow the good fully to come into being. As Lenin writes, "This 'factory' discipline, which the proletariat, after defeating the capitalists, after overthrowing the exploiters, will extend to the whole of society, is by no means our idea or our ultimate goal. It is only a necessary *step*, for thoroughly cleansing society of all the infamies and abominations of capitalist exploitation, and for further progress."[44]

In the new life, the anticosmy is resolved in that the coercive, mechanical forces that subjected man to asthenia by maintaining the state in existence are united with the natural forces that are an expression of man's autarky. Ultimately, with the withering away of the state the coercive force also atrophies along with the repressive politics of the State, which has long since come to serve no useful purpose. With the reconciliation of forces history and politics will cease to exist because they are both phenomena of a "fallen" contradictory world, not a redeemed world. Eventually man's only activity will be production, labor, the maintenance of his existence in a perfect society. In the new society, the tensions that produce forces will be reduced to an absolute minimum, if not altogether annihilated. The complexity of the present society will be reduced to the utmost simplicity. Since history will be done away with, as there will be no conflicting forces, the new society will not be able to fall away from the pristine perfection of its beginning when the last conflict is overcome, when the last vestiges of subjective will are eradicated. Man's "spirit" will find expression, not in the state, but in production, since maintaining and enjoying his own divine existence will be the highest activity to which he can aspire.

The main thesis of this work, therefore, is that a violent revolution is absolutely essential for achieving the Communist paradise. Lenin insists adamantly and vehemently upon the necessity for violence, for smashing the state. To some extent, this dogmatic, even fanatic insistence on the absolute necessity of violence can be traced to the Russian revolutionary tradition, as has been pointed out, as the notion of the conflict of forces can be traced back through European philosophy, but neither the Russian revolutionary tradition nor Lenin's emulation of the revolutionary Rakhmetov in Cherny-shevsky's novel *What Is To Be Done*? seems sufficient to account for Lenin's. inflexible refusal even to consider the possibility of a non-violent revolution. Such a revolution is simply not forceful enough to effect the radical changes required by the advent of Communism. Like Bakunin, Marxism-Leninism also has its passion for destruction.

Here we can see the radical development of the problem in Marxist-Leninist analysis as compared with that of Hobbes, for example. Hobbes dirempted human nature into the same anticosmic contradictory poles, but he saw no need for violent revolution or for the annihilation of one extreme by the other. The reason is that Hobbes located the conflict within each person, in the conflict between the the Christian and the man, and since they were found to coexist *within* the individual there was necessarily a common ground on which the resolution or reconciliation could be effected — the individual's desire for self-preservation. Total destruction of either autarky or asthenia would require destruction of the individual which would certainly be counter-productive. In this respect Hobbes, and Rousseau, elected not to root the wheat out with the weeds. Hegel transfers the conflict from the individual psyche to the psyche of spirit, which also does not contemplate its own annihilation. But Marx has completely removed the conflict from the realm of the psychic, and has removed all common ground and common interests from the opposing sides. The conflict now exists between classes with no community of interest – all are seeking their own preservation or enrichment, and the mediating force of fear or compassion has been replaced by naked physical force, destruction. Therefore, the psychic ambivalence which had always somewhat concealed the true nature of the conflict is completely missing in Marx and anticosmy emerges in its true colors. The physical violence of the revolution is the external manifestation of the replacement of humility with the will to power. Just as there can be no reconciliation of class interests so there can be no reconciliation of man's desire for autarky with anything that might diminish it.

However, if we look more closely we can find a certain similarity between Marxism-Leninism and Hobbes. In *The State and Revolution* Lenin quotes Engels' characterization of the state as "a power seemingly standing above society, that ... alleviate[s] the conflict [between classes] and keep[s] it within the bounds of 'order'". This view of political authority is not new, for we saw it in the chapter on Hobbes where these words were applied to Hobbes' sovereign. In fact, for Hobbes the sovereign is the force that prevents the *libido dominandi* pole, man's desire to be a god, from destroying everything, man included – through the mediation of terror. Should the sovereign be removed, the immediate result is a return to the state of nature where all men are governed by their greedy passions. The unfortunate result of universal war derives from the fact that Hobbes relates the *libido dominandi* and the desire for self-preservation to the corporeal passions rather than to the divine office of judging good and evil. And of course for Hobbes every man is pitted against every other man – there are not even any class interests. Nevertheless, we can see in Hobbes an adumbration of the significance of the loss of all common ground, for the sovereign does not create order but only the appearance of order, and if all men were not afflicted with the same inner conflict they would prefer to annihilate each other. Marx, on the other hand, simply locates the *libido dominandi* in the class which has the power to enforce its will, and since it has nothing to lose, it exploits or annihilates the opposing class.

To continue our comparison with Hobbes – if, in the state of nature one man were to succeed in annihilating all other men, or if the divine, autarkic side of man were to acquire an absolute rule over the corporeal part, the sovereignty would no longer be necessary. So for Marx it is the need to repress certain classes that constitutes the *raison d'être* of the state. "As soon as there is no longer any social class to be held in subjection, as soon as class rule, and the individual struggle for existence based upon the present anarchy in production, with the collisions and excesses arising from this struggle, are removed, nothing more remains to be held in subjection – nothing necessitating a special coercive force, a state."[45] The removal of psyche from the ground of the cosmos, as is done by both Hobbes and Marxism-Leninism, allows no basis for any kind of unification other than the coercive, which Marxism-Leninism prefers to regard as the instrument of the true life-force.

We find that ultimately the Communist paradise is a displacement-substitute for the City of God in which each person, as the "new man" is asked to give according to the talents he has received and is given "grace" according to his needs, as expressed for the ideology in the slogan "From each according to his ability, to each according to his needs." They are both societies based on gratuity, the only difference being that the Communist paradise does not require God. In this society labor will be "not only a livelihood but life's prime want"; in other words, the *summum bonum* will be man's desire to enjoy his autarky, his self-sufficiency, for man as a species-being will be entirely self-sufficient.

The revolution is the analogue of the Last Judgment in Augustine's City of God, after which all politics become superfluous, even impossible, and all of the 'elect', that is, the proletariat live in the holy community, the City of God, which in this case is the society of the Communist paradise. The proletariat is united in labor rather than in *amor dei*, and maintains itself in existence through labor, analogous to the union of the saints in the will of God which maintains them in existence. In other words, the proletariat represents the conflation of God and the Saints. The damned, or the bourgeoisie, are annihilated in the flames of the holocaust of the revolution. In this respect, all of Marxism-Leninism is either eschatological civil theology or egophany, depending on whether it is seen as emanating from a solitary thinker or a Communist society.

In a sense Marxism-Leninism can be seen as the ultimate consequence of Hobbes' statement that there is no *summum bonum*, human felicity consisting only in the continual satisfaction of desires. The elimination of the supernatural, or transcendent, from human nature and existence dirempted man into beast and god. So long as the conflict between them was kept within the psyche they had a common interest in self-preservation – Hobbes' Commonwealth chains the beast but does not destroy it. In Marxism-Leninism the conflict is no longer psychic but economic. The proletariat, as reduced to the sub-human, is the beast, which, having nothing to lose but its chains, falls upon and destroys the 'god' – the non-laboring bourgeoisie – and thereby becomes itself the god by taking back into itself everything which the former god had expropriated. This is meant to be the complete and definitive resolution of the conflict, requiring the mediation of neither absolute sovereignty nor general will nor religion of Humanity. The new man, who is supposedly now gestating in Soviet society, will be divine, his own god, as a species-being, purely on his own, spontaneously. The Communist paradise is actually a Rousseauian society in which the members, no longer plagued by the asthenia of the self-centered passions, can dispense with the general will, the laws, the sovereign, and the legislator. Labor and social unity will be spontaneous, and no man will desire more than he truly needs. Thus, as a species-being man will enjoy autarky without the need to put up with any of the disadvantages of asthenia.

So, unlike the American society which exists in the tension between the responsibilities of the public philosophy and the aspirations of the civil theology, the Communist society, as the vanguard of history, has no responsibility to any higher law, or standard of righteousness – it is a law unto itself, regarding itself as the moral ideal of mankind and the highest good, and the Party is the source of all truth and wisdom.

It is most likely Communism's claim to abolish completely all conflicts that has been the source of its appeal – theories promising a less complete resolution, such as those of Hobbes, Rousseau, Saint-Simon, and Comte after all never had actual historical societies based on them. Communism was, however, achieved this, and as such it now serves in the Soviet Union as a civil theology of the eschatological variety, for it is now the expression of the sense of identity of the Soviet Union (for the sake of simplicity, consideration of Communism is here restricted to the Soviet Union). This certainly appears to be a contradiction of the very meaning of Marxism-Leninism as the universal order of all mankind. However, we should keep in mind the fact that the American civil theology, particularly in its eschatological version, is a form of the Christian myth of redemption, which is also a universal truth, and in this form it serves to define America as the source of world-order. Similarly, this is the meaning of Communism as the civil theology of the Soviet Union, for the Soviet Union also sees itself as a shining example of the truth of order, a kind of Factory Upon a Hill. The important difference is that the Soviet Union is not hampered by any considerations of righteousness but has only self-interest and the interest of spreading the revolution to consider. To put in a nutshell the difference between the possession of a public philosophy and metaphysical tensions and the lack of them, the American civil religion (in its balanced form) promises the freedom to pursue happiness, while the Communist civil theology promises happiness itself, which is the difference between being God's People and being God.

REFERENCES

[1] Hegel, *The Philosophy of Law*, in *Hegel Selections*, ed. by J. Loewenberg, New York, Charles Scribner's Sons, 1957, p. 443.
[2] Hegel, *The Philosophy of History*, [1837], in Vol. XLVI of *The Great Books of the Western World*, p. 170.
[3] *Ibid.* p. 169.
[4] *Ibid.* p. 161.
[5] *Ibid.* p. 306.
[6] *Ibid.* p. 306. Italics added.
[7] *Ibid.* p. 306.
[8] *Ibid.* p. 160.
[9] *Ibid.* pp. 160–161.
[10] *Ibid.* p. 176.
[11] *Ibid.* pp. 176–77.
[12] See Gerhart Niemeyer, *Between Nothingness and Paradise*, Baton Rouge, Louisiana State University Press, 1971, pp. 86–87.
[13] Quoted in *Philosophy and Myth in Karl Marx* by Robert Tucker, Cambridge, At the University Press, 1972, p. 86. Much of the discussion of alienation is based on Tucker's analysis.
[14] Tucker, p. 151.
[15] Karl Marx, 'On the Jewish Question', [1844], in *Karl Marx, Early Writings*, ed. by T. B. Bottomore, New York, McGraw-Hill, 1963, pp. 37–39.
[16] Karl Marx, 'Economic and Philosophical Manuscripts', [1932], in Bottomore, pp. 122–23.
[17] *Ibid.* p. 121.
[18] *Ibid.* p. 125.
[19] *Ibid.* pp. 126–27.
[20] *Ibid.* p. 127.
[21] *Ibid.* p. 130.
[22] *Ibid.* pp. 132–33.
[23] Quoted in Tucker, 175.
[24] Karl Marx and Friedrich Engels, *The German Ideology*, [1846], ed. by R. Pascal, New York, International Publishers, 1947, p. 9.
[25] *Ibid.* p. 14.
[26] *Ibid.* p. 22.
[27] Bottomore, p. 166.
[28] Karl Marx and Friedrich Engels, *The Communist Manifesto*, [1848], in *Essential Works of Marxism*, New York, Bantam Books, 1965, p. 16.
[29] V. I. Lenin, *The State and Revolution*, Moscow, Progress Publishers, pp. 81–82.

[30] This paradigmatic harmonizing of conflicting forces also plays a major role in alchemy, which antedates Mesmerism, and which has much in common with modern philosophy. "Alchemy ... is based on the view that man, as a result of the loss of his original 'Adamic' state, is divided within himself. He regains his integral nature only when the two powers whose discord has rendered him impotent, are again reconciled with one another. This inward, and now 'congenital' quality in human nature is moreover a consequence of its fall from God, just as Adam and Eve only became aware of their opposition after the Fall and were expelled into the current of generation and death. Inversely, the regaining of the integral nature of man (which alchemy expresses by the symbol of the masculine–feminine androgyne) is the prerequisite – or, from another point of view, the fruit – of union with God." Titus Burckhardt, *Alchemy*, tr. by William Stoddart, Baltimore, Penguin Books, 1971, p. 149. In some ways modern philosophy is an alchemy which has replaced union with God with creation of man as God.

[31] Frederick H. Burkhardt, Introduction to *God, Some Conversations*, [1787], by Johann Gottfried Herder, Indianapolis, Bobbs-Merrill, 1941, pp. 39–40.

[32] Johann Gottlieb Fichte, *The Vocation of Man*, [1800], in *The European Philosophers From Descartes to Nietzsche*, ed. by Monroe C. Beardsley, New York., Modern Library, 1960, p. 516.

[33] *Ibid*. p. 419.

[34] Quoted in Franco Venturi, *Roots of Revolution*, tr. by Francis Haskell, New York, Grosset & Dunlap, 1966, p. 44.

[35] *Ibid*. p. 37.

[36] *Ibid*. pp. 37–38.

[37] Michael Bakunin, *God and the State*, [1882], New York, Dover Publications, Inc., 1970, pp. 27–28.

[38] *Ibid*. p. 30.

[39] Venturi, p. 367.

[40] *Ibid*. p. 370. Italics added.

[41] *Ibid*. p. 383.

[42] *Ibid*. p. 419.

[43] *Ibid*. p. 402.

[44] Lenin. p. 92.

[45] *Ibid*. p. 17.

CHAPTER XII

POSTSCRIPT

> *If what is good, what is right, what is*
> *true, is only what the individual 'chooses'*
> *to 'invent', then we are outside the tradi-*
> *tions of civility. We are back in the war*
> *of all men against all men.*
> *... [Philosophers who cease] to believe*
> *that behind the metaphors and the*
> *sacred images there is any kind of in-*
> *dependent reality that can be known*
> *and must be recognized ... reject 'the*
> *concept of "truth" as something depen-*
> *dent upon facts largely outside human*
> *control,' which, as Bertrand Russell says,*
> *'has been one of the ways in which*
> *philosophy hitherto has inculcated the*
> *necessary element of humility. When this*
> *check upon pride is removed, a further*
> *step is taken on the road towards a*
> *certain kind of madness – the intoxica-*
> *tion of power which invaded philosophy*
> *with Fichte ... and to which modern*
> *men, whether philosophers or not, are*
> *prone. I am persuaded that this intoxica-*
> *tion is the greatest danger of our time,*
> *and that any philosophy which, however*
> *unintentionally, contributes to it is*
> *increasing the danger of vast social*
> *disaster.* [1]

It should be apparent from this study that, although the invasion of the
intoxication of power may have become obvious with Fichte, it had been
making subtle inroads into philosophy since at least Hobbes, who, in his
rejection of the *summum bonum*, replaced humility with pride and transformed philosophy from a dialogue with the tradition into a monologue. The
general assumption of the thinkers we have surveyed that a transcendent God
would interfere with the desired order is an indication that what was sought
in reality was not truth but power, a kind of divine control over reality:

And this has been the most decisive difference between the American and the modern philosophic civil theologies — the former is grounded in a reality beyond all human control, while the latter seeks, increasingly, to establish a reality of its own choosing.

This is not to say that America has been completely immune to this kind of intoxication of power, for the nationalism to which it has at times succumbed is the equivalent in an historical society for the egophany of the imagined society. We must keep in mind that the myth is *after* or created by the historical society but the "myth" of the isolated thinker is *prior* to the imagined society, which is the reason why the imagined societies never have any particular identity. Their identity actually lies in the rejection of reality that constitutes their foundation.

It should also be apparent that as the intellectual problem for the patriotic Roman was philosophy, the intellectual problem for modern philosophy has been Christianity, which most simply promises salvation in another world and thereby seems to deny meaning to this world. If one concentrates on interior personal salvation the often miserable conditions of this world can be ignored or simply endured, rather than corrected. And of course much evil has been done in the name of furthering religion. Put most simply the question is how much influence is exerted on this world by a transcendent world, and what meaning this transcendence has for immanence, and, in short, what meaning immanence has. Augustine had profound experience of the presence of transcendence in this life, in the depths of his own soul and spoke of the world as composed of "tottering and falling affairs", decidedly inferior to eternity.

In fact, however, the effect of Christianity on this world is not quite the simple draining away of meaning. It does undermine the claims of bodies politic to cosmic significance on their own terms, but it compensates for this by vastly increasing the importance of this life for the individual through its ability to determine his eternal destiny. The American civil religion is built upon but not limited to this sense of the immanent meaning of Christianity. It was, in fact, founded as the faith of a society of Saints — residing in God's Plantation should have been sufficient qualification for admission to Heaven. Inevitably America came to see itself as the earthly paradise, or redeemer, as giving men the opportunity for the best of both worlds — happiness in this life and the next. But the sense of tension between these two worlds was never lost; neither was the sense that salvation required personal and national righteousness. The civil theology, in its eschatological form promising America as the Kingdom of God on earth, has always existed in tension with the more traditional, non-eschatological forms of the Judaeo-Christian tradition that do not see the parousia as arriving in any earthly society.

Modern European philosophy, on the other hand, has consistently started from a denial of the relationship between the individual and God. Philosophers have proceeded on the assumption that man is best considered and understood in isolation from God. In other words philosophers begin by creating a cosmos according to their own desires, and they often openly admit that since an infinite God would threaten this artificial order he cannot exist. It is the human mind that is the ground of being in this case.

Like the American civil theology, all of the thinkers considered here have used some form of the immanentization of the Christian myth of redemption, *myth* used here in its technical sense as a story that communicates a truth. The fact is that the Christian myth speaks of and to what is perhaps the most profound human experience — the sense of unfulfillment, of dissatisfaction, of searching, of the need for salvation. Probably more blatantly than the American civil theology modern European philosophy as civil theology promises that such fulfillment will be realized in this world, in this life, but in order to realize it everything beyond this life must be forgotten, particularly one of the most important differences between Christianity and the pagan religions, the former's emphasis on an intense interior relationship between God and the individual soul. This is, of course, beyond the control of all governments and societies and so must be denied in the interest of the precarious public order.

The ultimate question is not, then, the meaning of civil society or a particular society, but the meaning of this world. Is it a matter only of patient endurance of suffering, of waiting for death, or is there something more important and enduring to be found here? The "civil theologies" of modern philosophy have sought to provide a meaning for this world entirely on its own terms, and they have sought this by first of all denying the traditional "public philosophy" and by transforming the Christian myth of eternal salvation into their own myth of earthly salvation. In the process they have also sought to be the god of the new, meaningful world. So, in Europe, in one way or another, the cosmos is re-structured so as to increase the importance of this world, whether this involves diminishing the importance of transcendence or abolishing it altogether. This world is elevated by draining it of all connection with transcendence, and eventually of every suggestion that there even is such a thing. And so this world grows in importance in the cosmos created by denying the highest good, or grace, or God, or eternal life.

But this is to destroy the tradition, not to enhance it. Anything intended to increase the importance of this world must be built upon an acceptance of the depths of the human soul, and everything related thereto. There is no lasting truth in a denial of this. The American civil religion is implicitly built upon this – early state constitutions exhorted, almost commanded the citizens to worship God according to their own consciences. The early Americans understood that the man who is in harmony with God will be a good citizen of a state that recognizes and respects the value of the individual. This type of tolerance did not in its fullness come with the Puritans but with later founders, such as William Penn, who believed that the importance of America was not to be the perfection of any "true religion" but a land where men could live according to their inmost needs for God and salvation, as well as more worldly endeavors, and that this is the most secure basis for a political order. This gives the American society an identity as realizing the intentions of transcendence within immanence, which, underneath all the language of millennial glory, is all the identity America has ever claimed.

Modern European civil religion, on the whole, bases itself on precisely the opposite assumption – that transcendence threatens this world with meaninglessness, and does not allow the individual the god-like power he craves, and the only way to restore any meaning here is to deny transcendence. This leaves the experience of transcendence to be accounted for in immanent terms, a venture that merely reveals the inadequacy of seeking to confine the infinite within the finite and to give this world not simply meaning but ultimate meaning. Communism is the ultimate form of the rejection of transcendence, for every less than perfect part of the human being, everything in man that bespeaks dissatisfaction or a need for a salvation or a fulfillment greater than this life can provide is to be eliminated in the transition from Socialism to Communism, for the simple reason that all such human imperfections are an admission that man is not his own god. The "new man" is, in a sense, the perfect hypostatic union of god and natural man – they are in complete and spontaneous harmony within each individual who has, of course, paid for this happiness by the loss of all significance to his own unique personal identity.

On the whole, the American civil religion seems to have found the best solution to the problem, for it has succeeded in giving meaning to its existence in this world for the protection of the individual, not in his selfishness but in his righteousness. This is, of course, an oversimplification of American political existence, and it is true that America's actions have often failed to measure up to America's aspirations, but the fact remains that this is the heart of the American civil religion, for America has chosen to exist in this world according to the mind of the God who transcends this world. Communism, on the other hand, in its attempt to locate ultimate meaning in this world, has provided only a salvation in which the individual is a means rather than an end. As the poet Osip Mandelštam described it, it is a society that builds with man rather than for him, that seeks its power and grandeur at the expense of man's debasement. Ultimately, Communism, as an ideology, is an unrestrained pursuit of power, civil theology without public philosophy; in Augustinian terms it is a desire to have divine knowledge of all there is to know of man, and so to remake him as a being whose existence has neither source nor meaning beyond his grasp.

REFERENCE

1 Walter Lippmann, *The Public Philosophy*, New York, New American Library, 1955, pp. 134–135.

INDEX

228

SOVIETICA

Publications and Monographs of the Institute of East-European Studies
at the University of Fribourg/Switzerland
and the Center for East Europe, Russia and Asia
at Boston College and the Seminar for Political Theory and Philosophy
at the University of Munich

1. BOCHEŃSKI, J. M. and BLAKELEY, TH. J. (eds.): *Bibliographie der sowjetischen Philosophie*. I: *Die 'Voprosy filosofii' 1947–1956*. 1959, VIII + 75 pp.
2. BOCHEŃSKI, J. M. and BLAKELEY, TH. J. (eds.): *Bibliographie der sowjetischen Philosophie*. II: *Bücher 1947–1956; Bücher und Aufsätze 1957–1958; Namenverzeichnis 1947–1958*. 1959, VIII + 109 pp.
3. BOCHEŃSKI, J. M.: *Die dogmatischen Grundlagen der sowjetischen Philosophie (Stand 1958)*. *Zusammenfassung der 'Osnovy Marksistskoj Filosofii' mit Register*. 1959, XII + 84 pp.
4. LOBKOWICZ, NICOLAS (ed.): *Das Widerspruchsprinzip in der neueren sowjetischen Philosophie*. 1960, VI + 89 pp.
5. MÜLLER-MARKUS, SIEGFRIED: *Einstein und die Sowjetphilosophie. Krisis einer Lehre*. I: *Die Grundlagen. Die spezielle Relativitätstheorie*. 1960. (Out of print.)
6. BLAKELEY, TH. J.: *Soviet Scholasticism*. 1961, XIII + 176 pp.
7. BOCHEŃSKI, J. M. and BLAKELEY, TH. J. (eds.): *Studies in Soviet Thought*, I. 1961, IX + 141 pp.
8. LOBKOWICZ, NICOLAS: *Marxismus-Leninismus in der ČSR. Die tschechoslowakische Philosophie seit 1945*. 1962, XVI + 268 pp.
9. BOCHEŃSKI, J. M. and BLAKELFY, TH. J. (eds.): *Bibliographie der sowjetischen Philosophie*. III: *Bücher und Aufsätze 1959–1960*. 1962, X + 73 pp.
10. BOCHEŃSKI, J. M. and BLAKELEY, TH. J. (eds.): *Bibliographie der sowjetischen Philosophie*. IV: *Ergänzungen 1947–1960*. 1963, XII + 158 pp.
11. FLEISCHER, HELMUT: *Kleines Textbuch der kommunistischen Ideologie. Auszüge aus dem Lehrbuch 'Osnovy marksizma-leninizma', mit Register*. 1963, XIII + 116 pp.
12. JORDAN, ZBIGNIEW, A.: *Philosophy and Ideology. The Development of Philosophy and Marxism-Leninism in Poland since the Second World War*. 1963, XII + 600 pp.
13. VRTAČIČ, LUDVIK: *Einführung in den jugoslawischen Marxismus-Leninismus Organisation. Bibliographie*. 1963, X + 208 pp.
14. BOCHEŃSKI, J. M.: *The Dogmatic Principles of Soviet Philosophy (as of 1958)*. *Synopsis of the 'Osnovy Marksistkoj Filosofii' with complete index*. 1963, XII + 78 pp.
15. BIRKUJOV, B. V.: *Two Soviet Studies on Frege*. Translated from the Russian and edited by Ignacio Angelelli. 1964, XXII + 101 pp.

16. BLAKELEY, T. J.: *Soviet Theory of Knowledge.* 1964, VII + 203 pp.
17. BOCHEŃSKI, J. M. and BLAKELEY, TH. J. (eds.): *Bibliographie der sowjetischen Philosophie.* V: *Register 1947–1960.* 1964, VI + 143 pp.
18. BLAKELEY, THOMAS J.: *Soviet Philosophy. A General Introduction to Contemporary Soviet Thought.* 1964, VI + 81 pp.
19. BALLESTREM, KAREL G.: *Russian Philosophical Terminology* (in Russian, English, German, and French). 1964, VIII + 116 pp.
20. FLEISCHER, HELMUT: *Short Handbook of Communist Ideology. Synopsis of the 'Osnovy marksizma-leninizma' with complete index.* 1965, XIII + 97 pp.
21. PLANTY-BONJOUR, G.: *Les catégories du matérialisme dialectique. L'ontologie soviétique contemporaine.* 1965, VI + 206 pp.
22. MÜLLER-MARKUS, SIEGFRIED: *Einstein und die Sowjetphilosophie. Krisis einer Lehre.* II: *Die allgemeine Relativitätstheorie.* 1966, X + 509 pp.
23. LASZLO, ERVIN: *The Communist Ideology in Hungary. Handbook for Basic Research.* 1966, VIII + 351 pp.
24. PLANTY-BONJOUR, G.: *The Categories of Dialectical Materialism. Contemporary Soviet Ontology.* 1967, VI + 182 pp.
25. LASZLO, ERVIN: *Philosophy in the Soviet Union. A Survey of the Mid-Sixties.* 1967, VIII + 208 pp.
26. RAPP, FRIEDRICH: *Gesetz und Determination in der Sowjetphilosophie. Zur Gesetzeskonzeption des dialektischen Materialismus unter besonderer Berücksichtigung der Diskussion über dynamische und statische Gesetzmässigkeit in der zeitgenössischen Sowjetphilosophie.* 1968, XI + 474 pp.
27. BALLESTREM, KARL G.: *Die sowjetische Erkenntnismetaphysik und ihr Verhältnis zu Hegel.* 1968, IX + 189 pp.
28. BOCHEŃSKI, J. M. and BLAKELEY, TH. J. (eds.): *Bibliographie der sowjetischen Philosophie.* VI: *Bücher und Aufsätze 1961–1963.* 1968, XI + 195 pp.
29. BOCHEŃSKI, J. M. and BLAKELEY, TH. J. (eds.): *Bibliographie der sowjetischen Philosophie.* VII: *Bücher und Aufsätze 1964–1966. Register.* 1968, X + 311 pp.
30. PAYNE, T. R.: *S. L. Rubinštejn and the Philosophical Foundations of Soviet Psychology.* 1968, X + 184 pp.
31. KIRSCHENMANN, PETER PAUL: *Information and Reflection. On Some Problems of Cybernetics and How Contemporary Dialectical Materialism Copes with Them.* 1970, XV + 225 pp.
32. O'ROURKE, JAMES J.: *The Problem of Freedom in Marxist Thought.* 1974, XII + 231 pp.
33. SARLEMIJN, ANDRIES: *Hegel's Dialectic.* 1975, XIII + 189 pp.
34. DAHM, HELMUT: *Vladimir Solovyev and Max Scheler: Attempt at a Comparative Interpretation A Contribution to the History of Phenomenology.* 1975, XI + 324 pp.
35. BOESELAGER, WOLFHARD F.: *The Soviet Critique of Neopositivism. The History and Structure of the Critique of Logical Positivism and Related Doctrines by Soviet Philosophers in the Years 1947–1967.* 1965, VII + 157 pp.
36. DEGEORGE, RICHARD T. and SCANLAN, JAMES P. (eds.): *Marxism and Religion in Eastern Europe. Papers Presented at the Banff International Slavic Conference, September 4–7, 1974.* 1976, XVI + 182 pp.
37. BLAKELEY, T. J. (ed.): *Themes in Soviet Marxist Philosophy. Selected Articles from the 'Filosofskaja Enciklopedija'.* 1975, XII + 224 pp.

38. GAVIN, W. J. and BLAKELEY, T. J.: *Russia and America: A Philosophical Comparison. Development and Change of Outlook from the 19th to the 20th Century.* 1976, x + 114 pp.
39. LIEBICH, A.: *Between Ideology and Utopia. The Politics and Philosophy of August Cieszkowski.* 1978, viii + 390 pp.
40. GRIER, P. T.: *Marxist Ethical Theory in the Soviet Union.* 1978, xviii + 271 pp.
41. JENSEN, K. M.: *Beyond Marx and Mach. Aleksandr Bogdanov's* Philosophy of Living Experience. 1978, ix + 189 pp.
42. SWIDERSKI, EDWARD M.: *The Philosophical Foundations of Soviet Aesthetics.* 1979, xviii + 225 pp.